W9-CJM-511

KNOWING CHILDREN

Knowing Children:
Experiments in Conversation and Cognition

Second Edition

Michael Siegal
University of Queensland, Australia

WITHDRAW

Psychology Press
a member of the Taylor & Francis group

Copyright © 1997 by Psychology Press Ltd.,
a member of the Taylor & Francis group
  All rights reserved. No part of this book may be reproduced in any form,
  by photostat, microform, retrieval system, or any other means without the
  prior written permission of the publisher.

Psychology Press Ltd., Publishers
27 Church Road
Hove
East Sussex, BN3 2FA
UK

British Library Cataloguing in Publication Data

A catalogue record for this book is available from the British Library

  ISBN 0-86377-767-8
  ISSN 0959-3977

Typeset by GCS, Leighton Buzzard
Printed and bound in the UK by T. J. International Ltd.

Contents

Preface

Anyone who knows children realises that they have an understanding that is often not reflected in what they say and do. A concerned adult tries to draw out their knowledge patiently. However, this may not be easy. It remains common to attribute children's difficulties in answering questions on the many tasks that have traditionally been used to determine their understanding to a basic limitation in their stage of intellectual or cognitive development.

In this essay, I propose that children's apparently poor performance can frequently be explained in terms of a clash between the conversational worlds of adults and children. Perhaps one of the best examples comes from that provided by Margaret Donaldson (1978, p. 17; see Lee, 1963, p. 50) in which a teacher tells a small boy, "You just sit here for the present." Once home, he tells his mother that he is not going back to school again because, "They said they'd give me a present. I sat there all day but I never got one!" Such difficulties in conversation are so pervasive that these affect not only the attempts of parents and teachers at communication with children but particularly those of developmental psychologists whose aim is to design experimental tasks in order to establish what children know. In specialised experimental situations, young children may not share the assumption that the purpose is the scientific one of establishing their understanding of concepts. They may inadvertently perceive an adult's well-meaning questions to be ambiguous, irrelevant, insincere, or uninformative. In addition, an experimenter may unjustifiably assume that children will share the use of certain words that are prerequisites for understanding questions. Unlike adults who are experienced in conversation and can recognise the implications that flow from different forms of questioning, young children are liable to misinterpret an experimenter's purpose or use of language. They may respond incorrectly, not because they do not know the answer, but because the conversational worlds of adults and children diverge.

Nevertheless, despite difficulties in interpreting the purpose and relevance of conversations, even preschoolers can be astute observers of communication between children and adults. If given the opportunity, they often shrewdly attribute incorrect answers to adults' questions to features of the conversational environment. Once this environment is given support, children themselves are more likely to disclose what they remember and know. I do not propose that they have a full-blown understanding, only an implicit one that constrains their learning and that may be used to enhance their knowledge.

The point that adult forms of communication may obscure an authentic understanding is hardly new (Bruner, 1991; Donaldson, 1978, 1982; Flavell & Wohlwill, 1969; Gelman, Meck, & Merkin, 1986; Hughes & Grieve, 1983; Light, Buckingham, & Robins, 1979; Light & Perret-Clermont, 1989; McGarrigle, Grieve, & Hughes, 1978; Rommetveit, 1979; Siegel, 1978; Sigel, 1974) and has been noted by Vygotsky (1962) and in related accounts of early development (e.g. Rogoff & Wertsch, 1984). All the same, to give due regard to communication difficulties requires systematic tests of how children interpret conversation. There are now experiments where efforts have been made to investigate how children understand the nature of adults' questions. The second edition of this book provides further evidence that children's stage-like performance can frequently be reinterpreted in terms of a clash between the conversational worlds of adults and children. The consequences for children's responses in experiments are serious as, under these conditions, they often do not disclose the depth of their memory and understanding.

In this light, a different model of development emerges. This model attributes more competence to young children than is frequently recognised (e.g., Piaget, 1970; Sugarman, 1987), and reflects in particular the position that development in domains such as number, biology, and psychology is guided by implicit constraints on learning. It proposes that attention to young children's conversational experience is a powerful means to illustrate what they can and do know in health, legal, and educational setting. The implications for instructions in subjects such as mathematics and science are significant.

Acknowledgements

The work reported here spans three sabbatical leaves: at McGill University in the fall of 1986; the University of California, Los Angeles, in early 1990; and the University of Padua, Italy, in 1996. The ideas were developed further in discussions and seminars at Arizona State University, Dokkyo University, Queen's University, Canada, University of Neuchâtel, University of Otago, University of Pennsylvania, and University of Pittsburgh. I am particularly grateful to the staff of the Dipartimento di Psicologia dello Sviluppo at Padua for the use of a Power PC in an office next to a cappuccino machine. It was in that wonderful environment where the manuscript for the second edition was completed.

I am very grateful to those in Australia and overseas who have given suggestions and advice, and to my colleagues and students: Candi Peterson, Mary Barclay, Jan Cowen, Simon Dinwiddy, Yoshi Kashima, Peter Newcombe, Robyn Nugent, Stefano Occhipinti, Jenny Sanderson, David Share, and Lorraine Waters. The shortcomings are of course mine alone. Some of the research described in this book was supported by grants from the Australian Research Council and the National Health and Medical Research Council.

Parts of Chapters 4 and 5 have been adapted from my chapter, "Conversation and cognition" in the *Handbook of perception and cognition, Second edition: Perceptual and cognitive development* (1996) edited by R. Gelman and T. Au (published by Academic Press Inc.). Tables 3.1 and 3.2 originally appeared in *Child Development* and are reproduced by permission of the Society for Research in Child Development. Figure 1.1, Table 3.3, and Figure 5.2

originally appeared in *Developmental Psychology* and are reproduced by permission of the authors (copyright by the American Psychological Association). Figure 2.1 is adapted from the *Journal of Experimental Child Psychology* (published by Academic Press Inc.). Figure 4.1 from *The Child's Conception of Space* by Jean Piaget and Barbel Inhelder is reproduced by permission of Routledge & Kegan Paul.

This book is dedicated to the memory of my father.

M.S.
December 1996

1 What Children Know Before Talking

The answer to the question, "To what extent can young children understand abstract concepts?" is central to research on child development. One view, expressed forcefully by the Swiss psychologist, Jean Piaget (1970), is that young children's knowledge of the world is largely limited to perceptual appearances and that they are incapable of insight into the minds of others. At their own pace, the vast majority will eventually move out of a stage of development marked by severe limitations on the ability to understand concepts.

Over a period of more than 40 years, Piaget set an agenda for research on children's knowledge and came up with a wide variety of evidence from observations and interviews. On this basis, he argued that preschool children are generally not capable of operating logically in their thinking and that their stage of development can be best described as "preoperational". Piaget and his followers maintained that education should have the modest goal of matching the child's stage level. These ideas have had a major impact on educational programmes. Many people have either accepted the view that young children are not ready for instruction—especially in subjects like mathematics and science— or have claimed that programmes should be designed basically to extend children's awareness of the world beyond that of thinking about perceptual appearances.

My aim in this book is to demonstrate that young children actually know a good deal about abstract concepts, for example, of causality, and the identity of persons and objects. The apparent contradiction in the evidence is resolved by a very different explanation that focuses on language. My idea is that children are both sophisticated and limited users of the rules of conversation that promote effective communication: sophisticated when it comes to the use of conversational rules in everyday, natural talk; limited in specialised settings that require knowledge of the purpose intended by speakers who have set aside the rules that characterise the conventional use of language. Such situations may often involve children in experiments where they inadvertently perceive adults' well-meaning questions as redundant, insincere, irrelevant, uninformative, or ambiguous.

There are now experiments where efforts have been made to follow conversational rules in order to ensure that children understand the nature and purpose of adults' questions. The results demonstrate that children do have a substantially greater knowledge of abstract concepts than Piaget estimated and illustrate what they can achieve with assistance from others upon whom they depend for caregiving and instructions. Such results demand a significant shift in educational implications; for example, if preschoolers are able to understand how effects can be caused by factors that are not visible, they should know that food with an apparently fresh appearance may, in reality, be contaminated. This would warrant placing a greater emphasis on early preventive health education. Similarly, if young children are able to understand relations between parts and wholes as expressed by ratios and proportions, a more intensive instruction in the use of symbolic principles of mathematics would be in order.

MODELS OF DEVELOPMENT AND DEVELOPMENTAL COGNITIVE SCIENCE

Since the young have little experience in communication, those such as Piaget who at times claim that they are limited in the ability to understand concepts must ensure that failure can be attributed to a "deep" lack of ability rather than to some misreading of the experimenter's intent in asking well-meaning questions. Moreover, children can have a grasp of a concept and properly interpret the experimenter's intent, yet they may still fail owing to memory difficulties, a lack of familiarity with words or linguistic forms, or a lack of sophisticated motor behaviour. To provide a more accurate characterisation, a model of development is required that proposes a "conceptual competence" implicit within the mind of the child.

This type of model building goes beyond traditional disciplinary boundaries and has been increasingly studied in the field of cognitive science, an amalgam of many disciplines including anthropology, computer science, linguistics, neuroscience, philosophy, and psychology. Linguistics in particular would dictate that any comprehensive study of children's abilities must take into account their interpretation of conversational rules to ensure that their lack of success on tasks that involve knowledge of abstract concepts cannot be attributed to infringements of these rules.

The tasks designed to test children's understanding almost invariably require a degree of language comprehension. In this respect, adult experimenters may seek to determine that children have a particular concept through direct questioning or through prolonged questioning on numerous similar tasks. However, ordinarily we do not repeat requests when an answer has already been given. This is a convention or rule of conversation that promotes communication through non-redundant messages. A gap may emerge between the intent of the experimenter (which is to make a certain judgement about what children know) and children's experience with methods of repeated or other forms of unconventional questioning. In such cases, they may misinterpret these requests as conveying the necessity to respond inconsistently or in an "appropriate" way to satisfy what they perceive as expected. In addition, experimenters may use words which can have different meanings for children than for adults. Because children's responses on many tasks critically hinge on the interpretation of the use of language, any failures cannot be easily attributed to a deep lack of conceptual ability. A lack of performance may instead be due to children's "interpretative theory" of the purpose and meanings of linguistic forms used in the experiment.

No doubt a large part of development can be viewed in terms of children's understanding of language and communication. With increasing experience, an implicit conceptual ability may be expressed more explicitly in words regardless of whether experimenters follow conversational rules.

In my opinion, part of what distinguishes developmental psychology from research with adults in perception, cognition, and social psychology is a methodology specifically directed towards examining children's understanding of abstract concepts as distinct from their comprehension of language. To demonstrate this understanding requires novel methodologies and clever experimentation.

The matter is further complicated in efforts to establish that the rudiments of abstract concepts may be within the grasp of preverbal infants. Not only do infants lack speech (indeed, the word "infant" itself is derived from the Latin *infans*, or the unspeaking one) but, given their restricted motor development, we cannot even rely on their searching or crawling to shed light on their understanding. Even so, the use in testing situations of innovative methods of communicating with infants has increasingly revealed their implicit knowledge. As a guiding model, child development is better characterised by development towards the conscious accessibility of implicit knowledge rather than a simple lack of conceptual ability or coherence.

In the 19th century, two prominent theorists found a place for this type of developmental model. Yet in each case, it was not until recently that the more important of their two major propositions has been accorded recognition. First, the German physicist and physiologist, Hermann von Helmholtz (see Warren & Warren, 1968) advocated the empiricist position that, for the most part, children's perception of the world is not innate but is determined by an unconscious association of ideas in memory that depends on past experience. This is the most enduring legacy of Helmholtz's writings. It has predominated at the expense of his second proposition that the mechanism for making inferences about these ideas is itself innate. According to Helmholtz, "the law of causation, by virtue of which we infer the cause from the effect, has to be considered also as being a law of our thinking which is prior to all experience. Generally, we can get no experience from natural objects unless the law of causation is already active in us. Therefore, it cannot be deduced first from experiences which we have had with natural objects" (Warren & Warren, 1968, p. 201). On this basis, it has been recognised that young children may be equipped with the ability to make "perceptual" inferences which can be developed through instruction (Bryant, 1974).

The other 19th-century developmental theorist is Charles Darwin (1859). His contribution to experimental psychology cannot be underrated and consists of two major legacies. The first was the emphasis on similarities in the evolution and structure of animal and human behaviour. Accordingly, certain principles of animal psychology have been seen to apply as well to humans (Passingham, 1982). Darwin's second proposition concerned the diversity of organisms and their adaptive fit with the environment, and has only recently been acknowledged as meriting the more fundamental recognition (Rozin & Schull, 1988). On this basis, biological species may be viewed as constrained to learn adaptive behaviours. In particular, although the idea has yet to be fully exploited, human children may be constrained to learn behaviour such as parenting, predator avoidance, sheltering, and the procurement of nutrients through developing the accessibility of their innate or early abilities (Rozin, 1976b; Rozin & Schull, 1988).

The findings of modern research on preschoolers and children in the early primary school years are foreshadowed in the writings of Helmholtz and Darwin. However, the astonishing performance of infants in experiments provides some of the most graphic illustrations of early implicit knowledge. This research illustrates the degree to which preverbal infants display an abstract knowledge of the world. It sets the stage to examine the understanding of young children who have become conversationalists.

OBJECT PERMANENCE

One of Piaget's (1954) major claims was that infants are at a "sensorimotor" stage in development. By way of foreshadowing the limitations of preoperational young children, he maintained that infants do not understand objects as permanent entities which continue to exist while out of sight. For Piaget, this basic "object concept" is not achieved until they can reach out to uncover hidden objects. Yet even at 9 months, infants sometimes do not search for an object seen hidden in a new location if they have been used to finding an object in a familiar one. The inability to recover an object in a new place suggests that infants lack object permanence.

Two interpretations of this result are that infants expect that an object does have a permanent existence at the location where it has been previously found or that a formerly successful response will produce the object regardless of where it has been hidden. Alternatively, infants' searching may be based on their knowledge of the function of a location in which objects can be contained (Freeman, Lloyd, & Sinha, 1980) or on their knowledge that there are many similar objects and these are often duplicated (Bremner & Knowles, 1984). Still another straightforward alternative is that infants possess object permanence but lack the ability to perform co-ordinated actions by shifting the focus of their attention to a new location. If so, their searching behaviour may not be a fully adequate measure of their understanding.

An ingenious study carried out by Renée Baillargeon and her co-workers (Baillargeon, Spelke, & Wasserman, 1985) has shown that infants as young as 5 months of age appear to understand that objects exist when hidden. Babies were "habituated" to a screen that moved back and forth through a 180-degree arc in the manner of a drawbridge until they were used to viewing the action of the screen and became clearly inattentive. Then they were shown a solid block in the form of a box centred behind the screen, and viewed two types of events: one that was possible and one that was not. In the possible event, the screen stopped when the box was hidden. In the impossible event, the screen went right through the space that the box had occupied. The attentive reaction of the infants to the impossible event was taken to illustrate their knowledge that objects continue to exist when concealed. This result is compatible with a proposal made by Kellman, Spelke, and Short (1986): Infants anticipate that the movements of objects are constrained by rigid structures and expect that the unity and nature of objects depends on coherent movement.

In later experiments, Baillargeon and Graber (1988) examined 8-month-olds' memory for the location of objects. The infants first viewed an object (an inverted white styrofoam cup decorated with stars, dots, and pushpins) standing on one of two placemats. A screen was then pushed in front of each placemat shielding the object from sight. After a 15-second interval, a hand wearing a silver glove and a bracelet of jingle bells reached behind one of the screens and emerged with the object. The infants were tested under two conditions. In the "possible event" condition, the object was retrieved from behind a screen that shielded the location where it had been seen hidden. In the "impossible event" condition, the object was retrieved from behind a screen that shielded a different location (see Fig. 1.1). Infants looked at the object longer in the impossible event condition.

Apparently, they were surprised to see that it had been retrieved from behind the screen that did not shield the original hiding place. Although many infants

Possible Event   Impossible Event

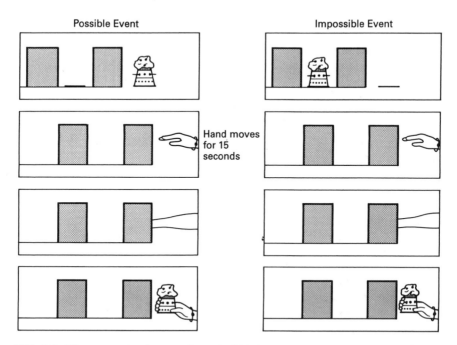

FIG. 1.1 The test events shown to 8-month-old infants (from Baillargeon & Graber, 1988).

may not accurately search for an object, they can still remember where it was before it had been concealed. Their responses undermine Piaget's position on object permanence—that infants' lack of success on searching tasks is due to a conceptual limitation.

Following the method used by Baillargeon, Wynn (1992) has attempted to demonstrate that infants possess rudimentary arithmetic abilities. Infants aged 5 months were shown toys placed successively behind a screen. When the screen dropped, either the number of toys that had been placed behind the screen appeared (the "possible outcome" condition) or there were more or less toys (the "impossible outcome" condition). Infants looked longer at the unscreened display when the outcome was impossible rather than possible. Wynn argues that infants have "true mathematical concepts" and that they are predisposed to interpret the physical world in terms of discrete objects that can be added or subtracted. If Wynn is correct, this would be a sensational result—demonstrating that human infants can add and subtract quantities such as $1 + 1$ and $2 - 1$. But, as Wynn herself notes, other interpretations exist. For example, infants may simply be demonstrating an ability to perceive continuous quantities in forming expectations about how much of a substance has been concealed.

The experiments of researchers such as Baillargeon and Wynn have shown how habituation techniques can be used as a method to communicate with infants. In general, the younger the child, the more likely an habitual or repeated presentation of the task will create disinterest. A long delay between concealing an object and the opportunity for retrieval may induce infants to fall back on an earlier hiding place where the object has been found on previous occasions (Diamond, 1985). A new and unexpected situation may recapture infants' attention and permit a more genuine appraisal of their abilities.

Nevertheless, habituation techniques are not perfect measures of cognition in infancy. Although habituation seems an advance on research that relies on search patterns, it does not yield an unambiguous interpretation of how infants reason about objects (Carey, 1994). Even if infants look significantly longer at one display than another, this does not mean that they are contemplating the unexpected and are actually surprised. An improved measure of their understanding may demand a qualitative rather than a quantitative approach in which infants' facial expressions are recorded as a more direct indication of surprise. Expressions such as surprise, sadness, anger, and happiness can be reliably scored (Ekman, 1994; Izard, 1994) and, as discussed next, the scoring of expressions has become the cornerstone of research on imitation in infancy.

IMITATION OF FACIAL EXPRESSIONS

An understanding of object relations may emerge from a capacity in newborns to learn through imitation. In a series of experiments reported in 1977, Meltzoff and Moore tested the proposition that infants between 12 and 21 days of age can imitate both facial and manual gestures. Six infants in a first experiment were shown the non-reactive, passive face of an experimenter for a 90-second period. Then four gestures were each repeated four times in a random order during a 15-second stimulus-presentation period immediately followed by a 20-second response period in which the experimenter resumed a passive face. The infants were observed to imitate the gestures of the experimenter: finger movements, opening of the mouth, and protrusion of the tongue and lips.

A second study was designed to rule out the possibility that interaction between the experimenter and infant might have resulted in a form of "pseudo-imitation": that is, the infants' own random gestures might have altered those of the experimenter until their behaviour coincided with behaviour resembling imitation. Infants were shown the experimenter's mouth opening and tongue protrusion gestures for 15 seconds while sucking attentively on a pacifier. They imitated the gestures when the pacifier was removed. In a similar manner, Tiffany Field and her colleagues (Field, Woodson, Greenberg, & Cohen, 1982) found that newborns imitated an experimenter's happy, sad, and angry expressions. As Reissland (1988) has shown, such responses do not seem limited to white North American or European babies since babies born in rural Nepal also exhibit imitation of facial expressions. There may be something about the human face that elicits an imitative response, as in the first month of life infants will make a special effort to turn to look at a true depiction of a human face compared to a loose or scrambled configuration of facial features (Johnson, Dziurawiec, Ellis, & Morton, 1991)

Not all the data clearly indicates imitation in early infancy (see Lewis & Sullivan, 1985; McKenzie & Over, 1983). Yet there is now widespread agreement that babies can imitate by 6 months of age, long before Piaget's estimate of between 8 months to a year. In fact, it can be speculated that a capacity for representation which may facilitate infants' responses is present at birth. In a study of hand–mouth co-ordination, Butterworth and Hopkins (1988) filmed the spontaneous motor activity of 15 newborns. They found that the mouth was open "in anticipation" of the arrival of the hand and that this movement was not related to guidance by the eye.

IDENTIFICATION OF VOICES AND SOUNDS

If infants can imitate at an early age, when might they be able to identify voices and sounds? To address this question, DeCasper and Fifer (1980) asked the mothers of 10 infants (younger than 3 days of age) to read Dr. Suess's book, *To Think That I Saw it on Mulberry Street*. Their voices were tape-recorded. By sucking on a nipple in long and short patterns of bursts, the infants could control whether they would hear the story read by their own mother or another mother. Infants showed a significant preference for their own mother. Since postnatal mother–infant verbal interaction did not relate to their responses, DeCasper and Fifer interpreted the data to indicate that infants' preference for the mother's voice develops in utero.

Using the sucking technique, it has also been shown that somewhat older infants can distinguish between different sounds in a categorical fashion much as adults do. Eimas and Miller (1980) presented 2- to 4-month-olds with synthetic speech patterns consisting of combinations of the stop consonant [b] and the semivowel [w]. An increase in the number of high amplitude sucking responses per minute was taken as a measure of their ability to discriminate between stop consonants and the semivowels. The infants' rate of sucking increased with the transition in the acoustic information. In addition, as in adults, the ability to discriminate sounds was influenced by the duration of the transition and the length of the syllables. More recently, using a modified version of the high amplitude sucking technique, newborns have shown some ability to represent differences in a set of syllables (Bertoncini, Bijeljac-Babic, Jusczyk, Kennedy, & Mehler, 1988). Such research has been used to investigate how infants come to perceive sounds in their native language and how early speech perception contributes to children's language acquisition (Werker & Desjardins, 1995).

Newborns also have some ability to make connections between vision and sound. Perhaps the most interesting demonstration remains the series of experiments conducted by Mendelson and Haith (1976). For example, babies aged 1 to 4 days were placed on their backs facing up to a television camera. They then heard 10 auditory stimuli such as the following:

> Hello Baby. It's really nice to see you here today. Believe it or not, you're on television right now. If the folks back home could only see you, wouldn't they be surprised? I hope that you'll keep your eyes open nice and wide and please. Baby, try not to move your head around too much. That's the only way we'll get a good videotape of you. If you co-operate really well you'll have the satisfaction of knowing that you've helped Science find truth and understanding. And remember, Baby, "Truth is beauty, beauty truth." Thank you for trying so hard, Baby. Have a nice day.

In response to this message, infants turned their heads and looked towards the location of the sound. They demonstrated a capacity for using sound to guide their visual exploration.

By the age of 4 months, there is an expectation that sounds correspond to sights. In the first of four experiments, Spelke (1981) presented 3- to 4-month-olds with pairs of films. During an initial familiarisation procedure, they watched kangaroos and donkeys bouncing to a soundtrack synchronised to either a gong or a thumping sound. Then, in a test period, the sounds were placed out of synchrony. The infants looked first at the animal that had previously bounced in synchrony. Later experiments confirmed that the ability to match sound with sight can be transferred to new information and is not specific to the spatial position of visual stimuli.

MATCHING TOUCH WITH VISION

The ability of infants to use touch as a basis for visual recognition was shown in a series of experiments by Bryant, Jones, Claxton, and Perkins (1972). In a first experiment, 60 infants between 6 and 11 months of age were given a task consisting of three phases. The infants were initially shown two objects that were out of reach on a table: one object was a complete shape (e.g. a cube) and the other was incomplete (e.g. a cube with a piece missing). In the second phase, they were given one of the objects to hold, unseen, containing a bleeper activated by a mercury switch when tilted. In the third, test phase, the pairs were presented again and the number reaching for the previously held object was observed. In this experiment and a subsequent one, infants often reached for the object that they had felt in their hands. A significant number made the match from touch to vision. Though the extent to which infants can differentiate among information that comes from the eye, ear, or hand is unclear, cross-modal matching ability in infants at this age accords with reports that such infants can often recognise and distinguish between familiar and unfamiliar stimuli over considerable time intervals (Rovee-Collier, 1993; Rovee-Collier, Sullivan, Enright, Lucas, & Fagen, 1980).

Meltzoff and Borton (1979) demonstrated that even young infants aged from 26 to 33 days can match across modalities. In a first experiment, 32 infants were given a small hard rubber pacifier to place in their mouths for 90 seconds. Then the stimulus was removed. The babies' visual preferences were tested by presenting them with two shapes made from dense styrofoam and painted orange. One shape matched that of the small hard rubber pacifier and the other was different. During a 20-second test, infants preferred to look at the object that they had previously explored orally. The results were replicated in a second experiment using a different group of infants and a different experimenter.

Similarly, Gibson and Walker (1984) gave 12-month-olds either a hard or an elastic, spongy substance to explore orally for 60 seconds. The infants preferred to look more at a visual depiction of the familiar substance than at the alternative choice. In more recent work, Kaye and Bower (1994) had infants as young as 12 hours of age suck on a pacifier using the sucking technique employed by DeCasper and Fifer in infants' discrimination of their mothers' voice. By sucking on a nipple in long and short patterns of bursts, the infants could control whether they would see an image of the shape of the nipple that they were presently sucking or see a differently shaped nipple. According to Kaye and Bower, infants showed a significant preference for the image that corresponded with the nipple that they were sucking.

PERCEPTION OF NUMBER AND CAUSAL RELATIONS

In line with Wynn's (1992) research on infant arithmetic, the ability to detect changes in small numbers and to identify correspondences between seeing numbers and hearing a sequence of sounds has also been demonstrated in several series of experiments. Starkey and Cooper (1980) gave infants with a mean age of 22 weeks (range, 16 to 30 weeks) arrays containing two, three, four, and six dots. Once the infants habituated to these arrays, they were given other ones containing a different number of dots: the two-dot array was replaced by three dots, the three-dot array by two dots, the four-dot array by six dots, and the six-dot array by four dots. In the case of the two- and three-dot arrays, the infants dishabituated and looked significantly longer at the new stimuli. Similar results have been reported based on a sample of newborns with a mean age of 53 hours and a range of 21 to 144 hours (Antell & Keating, 1983).

Starkey, Spelke, and Gelman (1983) have further established that infants prefer to look at arrays of objects that correspond in number to sound sequences. In their experiments, 7-month-olds viewed pairs of slides of two or three heterogeneous objects (e.g. a memo pad and comb vs. a bell pepper, animal horn, and scissors). Two or three beats of a drum accompanied each slide presentation.

The infants attended to the two-object array longer when it was accompanied by two drumbeats, and the three-object array when it was accompanied by three drumbeats. These findings are compatible with the notion that knowledge of arithmetic develops from an early sensitivity to correspondence between number.

Other work by Leslie and Keeble (1987) has suggested that 6-month-old infants may already have the capacity to perceive cause-and-effect relations. In two experiments, infants were shown films of apparently causal events and non-causal events. In the film of the causal event, a "direct launching" was depicted: a bright red brick moved a bright green brick on impact. In the film of the non-causal event, the green brick moved as a delayed action. About a minute after the infants had habituated to the sequence of filmed events, the direct and delayed launching events were reversed by switching the projector to run backwards. As predicted, the group of infants who had watched the direct launching increased their looking to the reversed sequence more than the group who had watched the delayed reaction.

According to Leslie and Keeble, infants are sensitive to causal relations and can discriminate causal from spatiotemporal relations. As part of a modular organisation of the perceptual system that operates in the absence of prior relevant knowledge, the early perception of causal relations may lay the foundation for the later development of causal understanding.

CHANGING VIEWS OF CHILDREN'S KNOWLEDGE: A WORKING MODEL

Piaget often examined child development through observing infants' reaching strategies or interviewing preschoolers and primary school children. On this basis, he mounted a case for early conceptual limitations. Alternatively, the child might be understood in the manner of a young philosopher who cannot yet express his or her intelligence in motor development or through the use of vocabulary. The British short story author Roald Dahl (1959) writes of the case of a philosopher who had died. However, his brain had been preserved and remains attached to an eye. The philosopher retains his knowledge of the world and his earthly pretences (for example, to read newspapers such as *The Times* of London). Yet he cannot speak and the only way he can communicate is by moving the pupil of his eye up and down.

The infant, unable to speak, immature in its physical growth, and susceptible to long periods of sleep, may still have a capacity to understand that is closer to Dahl's philosopher than to Piaget's notion of a very young creature who generally lacks a concept of objects. Indeed, the physical immaturity of infants influences their participation in experiments in the first place. To secure a sample for a study often requires that two or more infants must be tested for every one infant that can be included in the results. For instance, as reported by Bertoncini et al. (1988, p. 25) in one of their experiments on infants' representations of speech sounds, it was necessary to test 174 infants to obtain a sample of 48 (mean age = 10.2 weeks). Many of the excluded infants cried, while others fell asleep or ceased to give a sucking response during the course of the experiment.

Nevertheless, although we cannot attribute anything like full-blown knowledge to infants (and do not assume that they can read newspapers), at least judging from those who can and do participate in experiments, they are far more precocious than Piaget originally described. Their "Dahl- like" abilities stand in opposition to Piaget's contention that they lack object permanence as well as to the belief of William James (1890/1960) that the world of infants is one of "blooming buzzing confusion".

The list of infants' achievements in experiments is extensive (Spelke, 1994). They can make connections between touch, sound, and vision. They can identify voices and their attention is captured by objects that are made to disappear. They perceive differences in number, and would appear to be sensitive to causal relations. All of this underscores their ability to represent the world, and points to the early existence of a capacity or mental "architecture" for dealing with abstract concepts. They may have an inborn set of functions that can be recombined in subtle ways during the first year of life to analyse phenomena such as number and object relations.

Of course, with increasing age, infants become more aware in their analysis of changing situations (Mandler, 1987, 1992). Yet the use of techniques of habituation and recovery of interest—though these themselves cannot be given an unqualified endorsement—has yielded a more genuine appraisal of knowledge in infancy.

My point in this excursion into recent research on infancy is that even very young children are equipped with an abstract understanding. To make sense of the world, they have "storage drawers" of knowledge—a set of functions—that structure their thinking and behaviour. Infant research indicates that the dilemma of how to treat the early potential of children must be taken seriously and cannot be dismissed as preposterous. Such work to date does not yet clearly show that the more individual infants display abstract knowledge, the more these individuals will use this knowledge in some way when they can talk. Still, it raises several questions about the existence of conceptual limitations in child development: To what extent can infants become preschoolers who do not have the ability to think abstractly about number, causality, objects, and persons? Can so many primary school children have the same lack of ability? The evidence from experiments on infants provides grounds to hypothesise answers. With carefully conceived but simple experiments, it is possible to uncover pre-existing knowledge on tasks requiring abstract concepts. That is not to say that children actually use the correct, or best, abstract strategies to solve problems, only that they often have the capacity to do so. To support this capacity, attention is required on how the conversational world of children differs from that of adults.

The working model of development which emerges is that young children have a substantial *implicit* knowledge or conceptual competence. This may not be revealed in conversations with investigators because the measures designed to test what children know require procedural or language interpretation skills that are beyond their grasp or experience. On many tasks, they may lack plans or procedures to translate their understanding into performance even though they have at least an implicit, skeletal knowledge of the correct response. However, even if children do have these procedures, they need to share adults' use of conversational rules to interpret the meaning and purpose of questions in the way intended by the investigator. Too often, experimenters' models of child development have taken these assumptions largely for granted. Therefore, it is important to consider the nature of conversation with children.

If development is not necessarily restricted by conceptual limitations in the manner proposed by Piaget, an alternative account is needed for young children's lack of success in experiments. The model proposed here is that children frequently can succeed on measures of their abstract understanding if these are formulated in a "child-friendly" language. Support for my position that their weak performance on standard developmental measures can often be explained in terms of their interpretation of adults' use of conversational rules comes from a variety of sources: work on children's number and measurement abilities (discussed in Chapter Two), experiments on their ability to detect causal relations and to represent and recognise objects, events, and viewpoints relevant to eyewitness testimony (Chapters Three, Four, and Five), studies of friendship, popularity, and concepts of gender (Chapter Six), and research on the understanding of authority and the acquisition of academic skills (Chapter Seven). This evidence (summarised in Chapter Eight) has significance for education and child care. What follows is an examination of how children appreciate the meaning and purpose of the questions put to them.

2 Communication with Children on Number and Measurement Problems

CONSERVATION AS A THEORETICAL BUILDING BLOCK

Probably the most notable demonstration of young children's capacity for understanding in the tradition established by Piaget has come from his conservation experiments. For Piaget (1952, 1970), children under approximately 7 years are non-conservers; they judge transformed quantities by focusing on perceptual changes in appearance rather than on features that remain invariant such as number. Suppose they are given two rows of six buttons, each arranged on a one-to-one correspondence. An experimenter asks if the two rows have the same amount and children ordinarily respond that the rows are the same. The rows are then transformed so that one is now shorter and denser than the other. The question is asked again. Non-conservers say that the numbers are unequal and may choose the row which is longer. According to the Piagetian interpretation, they lack an understanding of "invariance", the concept that quantities remain the same despite perceptual changes. This is evidence for a preoperational stage of development. At the age of approximately 7 years, children now correctly conserve and enter into a stage of concrete operations.

However, over 65 years ago, Piaget (1929) in his book *The Child's Conception of the World* wrote of difficulties in asking children questions. To promote the diagnosis of authentic reasoning abilities, his rule was to encourage "the flow of spontaneous tendencies" in advocating that "every symptom" of the child's thought should be placed in its "mental context". Questions ideally should be asked in the manner and form of the spontaneous questions actually asked by children of the same age and under. In efforts to avoid "systematic errors" inherent in the "pure experiment" in which children may give artificial responses, Piaget was particularly concerned with the effects of repeated questioning and lengthy interviewing. He sought to deal with this problem by presenting countersuggestions (i.e. "Another child told me that the two rows still had the same"), to let the child talk for a few minutes and return to the subject indirectly later, and to pursue the connection with the child's other convictions. He advocated that the interviewer probe the roots of the suspect answer and then ask the question in as many different ways as possible. But, while he believed that "suggestion may thus be avoided by means of patience and analysis", Piaget (1929, pp. 27–28) did concede a "much more serious difficulty": "that of distinguishing from among the results of the examination the point to be regarded as the child's original contribution and that due to previous adult influences". This problem is of crucial importance in experiments on child development but was never squarely confronted, let alone resolved, in Piaget's research programme. His attempts to come squarely to grips with this issue were rather casual.

Nevertheless, although it is not easy to determine how children answer questions in the way that they do, there is a first theoretical leap in research based on Piaget's approach. Using a form of "clinical method" consisting of interviews with children, Piaget and his followers have interpreted the results of conservation studies to illustrate that young children centre on perceptual aspects of transformations and ignore invariant features. They cannot compensate by integrating information from two or more dimensions of a problem. For example, they do not take into account density as well as length in comparing the numbers of candies or counters set out in parallel rows and often judge that the longer row has more irrespective of its number. If water is poured from a short, wide beaker into a longer, narrow one, they determine the amount often by focusing on one dimension only (i.e. height) rather than compensating with another (i.e. width). In this respect, Piaget concluded that children are "egocentric" and cannot consider more than one dimension or point of view in making judgements of physical quantity.

A second leap in the argument comes when applying children's lack of success on measures of cognitive development such as conservation to theories of social development. If they are egocentric and cannot conserve, then what are the implications for their friendships and their ability to consider others' points of view? Further, what are the implications for sex-role concepts that require the conservation of gender attributes across superficial perceptual transformations in dress? For example, do boys think that they will turn into girls if they wear girls' clothing, or do they believe that gender is invariant and is unrelated to dress style? As will be seen in Chapters Five and Six, many writers (including myself) have at one time or another maintained that cognitive development as described by Piaget is a prerequisite for concepts of friendship and gender.

These two leaps are implicit in Piagetian research on social development. Problematic though it is, interpreters of Piaget have taken a third leap: that education should be matched to children's stage of development or, at least, delayed until they have attained the "cognitive prerequisites" to demonstrate a readiness to acquire academic skills such as arithmetic as well as to understand others' viewpoints.

This chapter concerns the critical first leap that young children genuinely share the purpose underlying questions on cognitive tasks such as measures of conservation and that their incorrect responses are not simply due to the language of the experiment. The assumption has gained considerable acceptance in much neo-Piagetian research on cognitive development and has provided a theoretical foundation for work in social development (the second leap) and education (the third leap). For example, in his generally thought-provoking and well-written textbook, Robert Siegler (1986, p. 3) introduces a discussion of how children process information by referring to an often cited study by DeVries:

> Some of the most interesting parts of children's thinking are the parts where children differ most markedly from adults. DeVries (1969) provided a particularly compelling example of such a difference. She was interested in 3- to 6-year-olds' understanding of the difference between appearance and reality. The children were presented with an unusually sweet-tempered cat named Maynard and were allowed to pet him. When the experimenter asked what Maynard was, all of them knew he was a cat. Then the experimenter put a mask on Maynard's head, in plain sight of the children. The mask was that of a fierce-looking dog. The experimenter asked, "Look, it has a face like a dog. What is this animal now?" DeVries found that many of the 3-year-olds (unlike the 6-year-olds) thought that Maynard had become a dog. They refused to pet him and said that under his skin he had a dog's bones and a dog's stomach.

According to Siegler, "It is simply stunning that a human being, even a very young one, would think that a cat could turn into a dog." While he cautions that differences between the responses of 3-year-olds and older children should not be overemphasised and that young children display adult-like abilities in many situations, no consideration is given in his textbook to another possibility. Children at 3 years of age have little experience in conversation with adults. Instead of assuming that an experimenter wishes to discover what children know about the distinction between the appearance of an animal and its true identity, they may seek to comply with the perceived force of the question. Rather than reveal their authentic conservation of the identity of animals despite superficial perceptual changes, they may seek to flatter an adult for an entertaining display.

(Perhaps, we may add, "it is simply stunning" that adults would so uncritically accept, in a serious model of development, that young children truly and fully believe that a cat could turn into a dog.)

EXPERIMENTS AND LANGUAGE: CONSERVATION OF NUMBER AS A STARTING POINT

In contemporary critiques of research on cognitive development, the issue of "demand characteristics" inherent in the conservation experiment has not gone unnoticed. In an incisive pair of exploratory studies with 6-year-olds, Rose and Blank (1974) tested the hypothesis that non-conservation is influenced by the language used in the experiment—specifically, that repetition of the question (e.g. "Are there the same number in both rows or does one row have more?") misleads children to change their answers and respond incorrectly. Rose and Blank found that children gave significantly more conservation responses when only one question was asked after the rows had been transformed than in a standard two-question condition. This is similar to the effect we see in adult conversations where repeated questioning (for example, "How are you?" Response: "OK." Repeated question, "How are you?") results in response switching or, perhaps in some cases, annoyance at having to repeat the answer. However, Rose and Blank's findings have met with equivocal support in replication studies (for example, Neilson, Dockrell, & McKechnie, 1983; Samuel & Bryant, 1984) and, in any event, were largely restricted to 6-year-olds' judgements of small numbers of items.

Because conservation has become such a theoretically key issue, it requires a fresh investigation. There are experiments that can be carried out to consider whether children's failure on conservation problems is due to a deep limitation in understanding or to the nature of a methodology that can provoke children to respond inconsistently. To address this problem, we examined children's appreciation of repeated questioning in experiments with 4-, 5-, and 6-year-olds (Siegal, Waters, & Dinwiddy, 1988). As in most of our experiments, the children came from middle-class areas of Brisbane, located near the University of Queensland. Our conservation project was designed with two purposes: (1) to examine children's responses using a one-question procedure on forms of conservation length tasks; and (2) to determine their attributions for conservation and non-conservation answers in one-question and two-question conditions.

A total of 180 children participated in our first experiment. Within each age group, half were randomly assigned to a condition where they were tested by a one-question procedure, and half to the traditional or standard two-question testing condition often used by Piagetians.

The children were shown two displays each consisting of two parallel rows of buttons. Each row consisted of 20 buttons 1cm in diameter. The display used for the standard testing condition consisted of rows of pink and purple buttons. For the one-question condition, rows of red and blue buttons were used. The initial

(Array A) and post-transformation (Array B) location of the buttons for both displays are shown in Fig. 2.1.

Why would we use two rows of 20 buttons? As others have noted (for example, Halford & Boyle, 1985), these numbers preclude the use of counting as a problem-solving strategy. The numbers and positions of the counters also avoid the possibility that children could make judgements by a kind of default strategy should one of the rows appear more salient before a transformation; when asked initially to identify which row has more, children's choice of row was at a chance level of 50%. Therefore, the displays provided a simple test of consistency in their judgements under one-question and standard conditions of numbers in rows that have been perceptually rearranged but remain the same with nothing added or taken away.

To record pretransformation judgements, the children were given a small flip-top box containing pairs of buttons (either red and blue or purple and pink, matched according to the testing condition). Each child was given "two trials":

Array A   **Array B**

FIG. 2.1   The two arrays used in the first conservation of number experiment (from Siegal, Waters, & Dinwiddy, 1988).

one trial on each display in which Array A was transformed into B. Half the children in each age group first received the standard condition and the other half received the one-question condition.

In the standard condition, the displays were placed directly in front of the child who was seated at a table opposite a female experimenter. The child was told: "Here are two big rows of buttons. This row has pink buttons in it and this row has purple buttons in it. Point to the row which has more buttons." The order of mention of the rows was alternated on successive standard trials as was the original left or right positioning of each row in the display. The child was then given the box containing the pairs of buttons and told: "You think the purple (or pink) row has more. So take that (colour) button from the box and hold it in your hand. Now watch carefully what I'm doing." The experimenter rearranged the rows, alternatively transforming the left and right row first on subsequent trials. Then she repeated the request to "point to the row which has more buttons" and asked the child, "Did you pick the pink (or purple) row before? Let's see. What's in your hand?"

In the one-question condition, the child was told to "think about which row (blue or red) has more buttons. But don't tell. If you think the blue row has more, take that button from the box. If you think the red row has more, take that button from the box. But don't show me. Hide it in your hand." Again, both the order of mention and left or right positioning of the rows was alternated on successive one-question trials. After the child chose a button privately, the experimenter transformed the array. The child was asked to compare the rows and reveal his or her initial selection of button as in the standard condition. No feedback was given on responses.

Conservation judgements under each of the two testing conditions for the three age groups, together with the numbers of children who conserved on both trials, are shown in Table 2.1. As predicted, the children tested on the first trial under the one-question condition gave significantly more conservation judgements on this trial than did those tested under the standard condition. Given the criterion for successful conservation of consistent judgements before and after the counters were rearranged, 78% of all the children tested under the one-question condition could be considered conservers: 63% of the 4-year-olds, 77% of the 5-year-olds, and 93% of the 6-year-olds. By contrast, only 23% of those tested under the standard condition on the first trial reached this criterion. On the second trial, as expected, more conservation judgements were given in the standard format if one question instead of two questions had been asked in the first trial. For each of the three groups, performance under the one-question condition was impaired by experience in the first trial with the standard procedure.

Significantly more children in each age group conserved on both trials when tested first in the one-question condition than in the standard one. By this criterion, 59% of all children tested in the one-question condition followed by

TABLE 2.1
Correct Responses in the First Experiment on Conservation of
Number

Condition	Group		
	4 Years	5 Years	6 Years
One-question (trial 1)	19	23	28
Standard (trial 2)	16	19	23
Conserved on both trials	13	17	23
Standard (trial 1)	5	6	10
One-question (trial 2)	10	13	21
Conserved on both trials	3	4	10

NOTE: From Siegal, Waters, and Dinwiddy (1988). In each
condition, there were 30 children from each age group.

the standard were classifiable as conservers compared to only 19% of those
tested in the reverse order. Of the children who conserved on the first trial, 67%
of the 4-year-olds, 72% of the 5-year-olds, and 87% of the 6-year-olds conserved
on the second trial, indicating that the answers of the children who did conserve
were unlikely to be random. Therefore, as in the studies of Rose and Blank
(1974), the one-question condition elicited significantly more conservation (i.e.
consistent) answers than did the standard two-question condition. Moreover,
prior experience with the one-question procedure enhanced subsequent
performance on a standard trial, suggesting that it served to clarify the
requirements of the task.

However, there are two possible objections to the interpretation that the
children in our first experiment were giving consistent, conservation answers.
First, those tested by the one-question procedure may have desired to share their
secretive button choice with the experimenter. Rather than conserving, they may
have merely repeated their initial choice when the post-transformation request
for a response was made. Second, some children tested in the one-question
condition may have offered perseverated judgements since no other perceptual
bases for post-transformational judgements were available.

In our second experiment, we sought to rule out these possibilities by asking
children to make attributions for others' performance under one- and two-
question conditions. Recognising that attributions for the performance of others
are not the same as attributions for one's own performance, our aim was
straightforward: it was to test further the hypothesis that they interpret repeated
questioning to require that the initial answer should be switched.

Following the method used in several earlier studies (Fluck & Hewison, 1979;
Gelman & Meck, 1983), we asked children to evaluate the answers of puppets in
a detection task. The puppets were shown as subjects in videotaped conservation

experiments. The children's task was to give causal attributions for the puppets' responses. If children interpret a repeated request as a cue to change answers, they should assign "external" attributions (for example, "to please someone else") to puppets' lack of conservation in the standard two-question condition, and "internal" attributions (for example, "really thought was true") to conservation responses or, possibly, to non-conservation in a one-question condition.

There were 32 children in our second experiment. Each one was initially alerted to the possibility that choices can be made to please others by instructions derived from Asch's (1958) classic series of conformity experiments. The experimenter read two stories to the children. These contained two practice requests for attributions. For example:

> Sally was playing with a few of her friends at kindergarten when the teacher came up to the children and showed them two blocks, one big and one small. The teacher asked each child to point to the biggest block. The first child pointed to the smaller block, and so did the others. Then it was Sally's turn. She pointed to that block too. Do you think Sally pointed to the small block because (a) she really wanted to please the other children and be like them or because (b) she really thought that block was the biggest? (All the children chose "a".)
>
> The teacher showed the same blocks to another group of children who were playing with Louise, and asked them to point to the smallest block. The first child pointed to the big block, and so did the others. Then it was Louise's turn. She pointed to the other block instead. Do you think Louise pointed to the small block because (a) she wanted to please the other children or because (b) she really thought it was the smallest block? (All the children chose "b".)
>
> So you see, sometimes people do things just to please others, and sometimes they do things because they really think what they do is true.

The children then viewed four videotaped segments depicting the answers of puppets on the conservation of number arrays used in the first study. The puppets were shown tested by a female experimenter, twice under one-question conditions and twice under standard conditions. For the two segments in each condition, one puppet was a conserver and the other one was a non-conserver. The presentation order of the segments was varied systematically.

After viewing each segment, the children were asked if the puppet had responded "just to please the grown-up" or "the way the puppet really thought was true", representing external and internal attributions respectively. Each child was then required to indicate the certainty of his or her choice by pointing to one of three triangles of increasing size representing "not sure at all" (smallest triangle), "half sure" (middle-sized triangle), and "very sure" (largest triangle). All children had used the scale correctly in sample cases given in the instructions. Ratings were given scores ranging from 0 to 5. A response of "very sure, internal" was scored as 0 and one "very sure, external" was scored as 5. "Half sure, internal", "not at all sure, internal", "not at all sure, external", and "half sure, external", were scored as 1, 2, 3, and 4 points respectively.

For puppets' non-conservation responses in the standard condition, the percentage of children's external choices—"just to please the grown-up"— amounted to 69% and was significantly above a chance level. Only in this condition did they give external attribution ratings (mean of 3.47 out of a maximum possible 5.00). The percentage of external choices was below chance level at 25% for conservation response in the standard condition and at 28% for responses in the one-question condition. Attributions for non-conservation in the one-question condition where the children had no clear basis for inferring causality, either through correct responses or repeated questioning, were at a chance level of 44%.

Experiments like these require qualifications. Since the objective was to examine children's consistency under repeated questioning and to avoid their use of counting and other extraneous problem-solving strategies, our conservation tasks departed somewhat from those originally used by Piaget (1952). Moreover, we must note that no necessary connection exists between children's own answers on conservation tasks and their attributions for others' responses. In the first experiment, a minority of children, especially 4-year-olds, did not conserve and, in the second experiment, there were some who did not give external attributions for others' non-conservation answers in the traditional, two-question format. Although repeated questioning may jeopardise children's performance on many tasks, asking only one question does not guarantee that all will respond correctly.

Bearing these considerations in mind, our results are in agreement with Rose and Blank's original findings and were replicated in two subsequent experiments on conservation of length where preschoolers could indicate that a straight line and a line bent into the shape of a crescent were the same length (Siegal et al., 1988, Experiments Three and Four; see Fig. 2.2). As illustrated in Fig. 2.3, there is striking similarity between children's attributions for puppets' responses in conservation of number and length experiments.

Therefore, while children are often able to respond correctly in standard, two-question conservation of number or length experiments, they may change their answers because they are prompted to do so by repeated questioning. The majority give external causal attributions for non-conserving responses in the standard procedure. By contrast, they conserve and give internal causal attributions in a one-question condition. These results do not offer direct support for the proposition that unsuccessful performance in *individual* children is due to repeated questioning, but they provide data to entertain this hypothesis as entirely plausible. As a *group*, children's apparent lack of understanding on conservation measures is strongly influenced by repeated questioning.

FIG. 2.2   A puppet in a videotaped conservation of length experiment.

EXPLANATIONS FOR PERFORMANCE

This is only one illustration of how at least some children may be misled by the questions asked in experiments. It establishes that their non-conserving (or inconsistent) responses on measures of cognitive development can be influenced by their interpretation of the experimenter's intent. Through repeated questioning, adults can mislead children to give inconsistent answers. These answers in turn mislead adults to accept a theory of cognitive development that does not faithfully reflect the depth of children's understanding. Such interactions support the model of development which proposes that children's knowledge is obscured by a clash of conversational worlds.

One scenario of non-conservation under the standard two-question procedure is illustrated in Fig. 2.4. However, there are several, more specific, explanations that lead to hypotheses for children's answers to questioning forms which stray from conversational rules.

Explanation One: Switching Under Uncertainty

According to this explanation, which was favoured by Rose and Blank, problems designed to establish what children know can contain language factors that affect communication. On such problems, repeated questioning can mislead

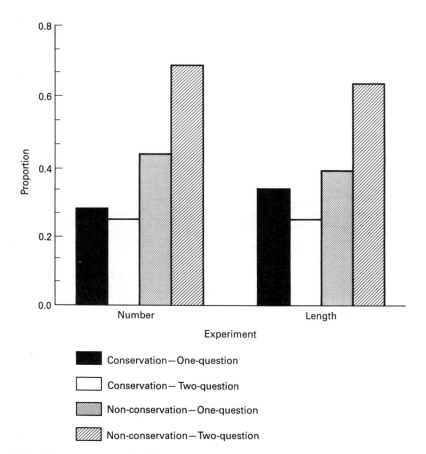

FIG. 2.3 Proportion of children's external causal choices for puppets' responses in conservation of number and length experiments (from Siegal, Waters, & Dinwiddy, 1988).

children to provide inconsistent answers by implying that the first answer was not acceptable and should be switched. Clarification of instructions should facilitate performance.

Consistent with this explanation, Schiff (1983) has maintained that children as young as 3½ years can conserve length where care has been taken to avoid linguistic confusion, and Rochel Gelman (1982; Gelman & Gallistel, 1978, pp. 13–14) has claimed that 3-year-olds rapidly acquire number conservation responses in training studies designed to clarify the nature of the task.

For example, Gelman (1982) attempted to illustrate 3-year-olds' ability to conserve number by directing their attention to toy turtles in rows placed in one-to-one correspondence. The children were asked to count the number of items in one of the rows. The row was then covered and the children were asked, "How

FIG. 2.4 A possible context of non-conservation answers.

many are under my hands?" The question was repeated for the other row. When one of the rows was transformed, the children now retained their initial response and conserved. Yet although this procedure might have uncovered a pre-existing but fragile understanding, there is the possibility that the children did not genuinely conserve and did not understand that the same number remained regardless of the transformation. This procedure might have simply signalled to the children that it is all right to give the correct (or same) answer.

More recently, Gelman (1993; Gelman, Meck, & Merkin, 1986) has suggested that repeated requests on counting tasks underestimate children's numerical competence, and have maintained that preschoolers' counting mistakes under repeated or ambiguous instructions reflect an inexperience at "stepping outside a particular interpretation of an utterance and selecting another" (R. Gelman et al., 1986, p. 27). Consider the example of an adult's comment such as "Did you get a haircut?" that immediately follows a child's haircut. Although it is obvious that the child did receive a haircut and, in this sense, the comment is irrelevant, preschoolers may not be easily able to attribute to the adult an alternative motive of sarcasm or sauciness (see, for example, Ackerman, 1981). They may be puzzled or unsettled by the lack of co-operation shown by the adult in commenting upon what is obviously the case.

As Gelman and her colleagues have maintained, children's responses to repeated questioning may reflect a lack of experience or confidence in the answer. Similarly, Hughes (1986, p. 46) has claimed that uncertainty underlies responses on simple arithmetic problems. He gives an example from an interview with a child called Amanda (3 years, 11 months):

MH: How many is two and one? [Long pause. No response.] Well how many bricks is two bricks and one brick?
Amanda: Three.
MH: Okay. So how many is two and one?
Amanda: [Pause.] Four? [Hesitantly.]
MH: How many is one brick and one more brick?
Amanda: Two bricks.
MH: So how many is one and one?
Amanda: One. Maybe.

According to Hughes, "Amanda clearly saw no connection between the questions concerned with bricks and the more abstract questions—indeed, she seems to be using a strategy of giving a different response to the latter. It is as if she is thinking, "Well, I don't understand this question but I know it's not the same as the previous one, so I'll try a different answer."

Young children may not share the purpose and relevance of direct questions about number. They may suspect some sort of trick or ulterior motive that undermines their confidence in what the correct answer should be in response to the experimenter's questions. To overcome this insecurity and to confirm the number of objects or counters in a row, they often need to count—and indeed correct, consistent conservation responses in standard two-question conditions that may otherwise prompt children to change their initial answer are associated with spontaneous counting (Sophian, 1995). But children do not count spontaneously even though, under the surveillance of an experimenter, they can be instructed to use this ability to detect the number of a quantity (Cowan, Foster, & Al-Zubaidi, 1993; Sophian, Wood, & Vong, 1995). One interpretation of this result is that young children are not initially confident in their counting abilities. Nevertheless, in two ingenious experiments, Starkey (1992) presented children aged 18 to 48 months with a task in which they placed objects in a set sequentially into an opaque searchbox. They then observed an experimenter add, subtract, or perform no operation on the set in the box. The children could correctly search and remove all the objects in the box. Thus in a naturalistic situation that avoided a direct question to count the numbers of objects and thus did not require them to share the scientific purpose and relevance of the task, children display numerical reasoning even before they attain the verbal ability to count.

This insecurity in the face of an inscrutable conversational setting can be seen as mirroring the insecurity of infants in experiments. For example, the lack of object permanence in Piaget's studies of infants may in part be attributed to an unfamiliar situation in which they can respond by focusing their attention on the location of the mother. Presson and Ihrig (1982) placed 30 9-month-olds in a spatial location procedure in which the task was to respond to pictures of animals and people. The infants used the mother as a landmark to guide their responses. When the mother's position was stable and did not provide a cue to repeat a previous response, they were able to find the correct location of the pictures.

Explanation Two: Insincerity

An alternative explanation for children's lack of success is that, in at least some cases, they are certain and confident of the answers after all. Yet they may not state their convictions because of unfavourable perceptions of the experimenter's questioning or the task itself.

For example, Perner, Leekam, and Wimmer (1986) have suggested that, because young children know that the experimenter already knows the answer, they regard standard conservation questions as insincere. Their incorrect responses reflect an insufficient analysis of a well-meaning experimenter's reason for asking the same question twice rather than an inability to conserve. When told to give their response to a second, naive experimenter who had not heard their first answer, the majority of 4- to 6-year-olds now conserve. Older children have a more advanced appreciation of intentions in conversations. They conserve in any event because they can understand the "second order epistemic intention" of the experimenter—that he or she wants to know whether children know. To account for non-conservation, Perner and his co-workers substitute an inability in early childhood to understand the mind of the experimenter for the lack of a logical ability to disregard perceptual appearances. (This may be rather strong. Instead of an inability to understand the mind of the experimenter it may simply be inexperience at recognising others' intentions in response to certain questioning formats and domains of knowledge. See Chapters Four and Five.)

Therefore, care must be taken to prevent an uncritical acceptance of the conclusion that non-conservation answers are necessarily due to an uncertain conceptual understanding. Under prolonged or repeated questioning, some children may not grow less confident of the answer. They only change their response because of the perceived insincerity of the experimenter or the unattractive nature of the task. As it happens, conservation problems may not capture the hearts and minds of young children. A quick finish may allow a return to more attractive activities. Even if repeated questioning is avoided, children may regard some tasks as unattractive and respond in ways that do not provide insight into their authentic understanding.

Explanation Three: The Overattractive Task

Explanations One and Two dwell on the more negative aspects of questioning children in interviews. However, language explanations for why children do not display the depth of their understanding may take a more positive tone. For example, a task may in fact be too attractive, particularly if the answer seems obvious. Preschoolers can interpret certain forms of questioning to require age-typical or "cute" answers, whereas older children, who see themselves more as adults, do not interpret questioning in this way. An example that may fit this explanation comes from research on children's gender concepts or "conservation" of gender (see Chapter Six).

Explanation Four: Trust in the Experimenter

These possibilities do not exhaust reasons for why children's lack of success on cognitive tasks may not reflect a conceptual limitation. Yet another explanation involves the naive approach to the task which can be seen in terms of a "trust in the experimenter" hypothesis. An example that fits this explanation comes from research on children's conceptions of contagion and contamination in which children must understand that adults could offer them a contaminated drink in order to determine their knowledge of the causes of illness (see Chapter Three).

Explanation Five: Word-use in Relation to Distinct Domains of Knowledge

The fifth explanation is that children's lack of success merely indicates cases in which they do not share how adults use words in relation to distinct domains of knowledge. It has been argued that preschoolers cannot easily be granted an understanding of words such as "more", "less", and "same" (Donaldson & Balfour, 1968; Karmiloff-Smith, 1977). Moreover, Cummins, Kintsch, Reusser, and Weimer (1988) have proposed that some primary schoolers' difficulties with word arithmetic problems (e.g. "Mary has three marbles. John has four marbles more than Mary. How many marbles does John have?") are due to their misunderstanding of the uses of words such as "some" and "altogether" and linguistic forms such as "How many more X's than Y's?"

This issue cannot be considered in isolation from the domain of conversations with children. Hirschfeld and Gelman (1994, p. 21) characterise a domain as "a body of knowledge that identifies and interprets a class of phenomena assumed to share certain properties and to be of a distinct type" and which "functions as a stable response to a set of recurring and complex problems faced by the organism". Domains serve as guides for describing and explaining the world. These encompass descriptive and explanatory classification criteria that channel intelligent learning selectively in order that children can construct a coherent body of knowledge.

Examples of domains that serve as guides in this way are the domains of number (i.e. counting) and food (i.e. the edible–inedible distinction to be discussed in Chapter Three). Language and conversation itself is a domain that intersects with other domains of knowledge. Hunt and Agnoli (1991) observe that words which have many meanings ("polysemous words") can be less effective in directing the attention of a listener as intended than are words with single meanings. This ambiguity in word use creates difficulty in translating across languages. It further suggests that children with limited conversational experience are unlikely to display the depth of their understanding should they interpret words with multiple meanings in adult conversation as if these have a single meaning—one that the investigator has not intended. In conversation experiments, for example, they may interpret questions such as, "Which row has more?" to mean, "Which row covers more area (and is longer)?" rather than the intended, "Which row has the greater number of counters irrespective of their spatial location?" In investigations on understanding the means by which diseases are transmitted, even adults may interpret questions such as "Can germs grow bigger?" to mean "Can a colony of germs grow bigger?" rather than the intended, "Can individual germs grow bigger?" (Au & Romo, 1996). The domain of language and conversation in a highly polysemous language such as English amounts to a complex guide for interpreting and classifying the meanings in questions. Thus it is hardly surprising that children who have just acquired conversational ability in English are liable to misinterpret words that point to the intended purpose and relevance of questions.

Forms of questioning that follow conversational rules avoid such difficulties and are more likely to succeed in eliciting correct answers from children than forms that require children to follow the conversational implications of an experimenter's questions. Although problems with how language is used in various domains of knowledge do not provide a full explanation of children's apparent inability to understand abstract concepts in science and mathematics, the hypothesis has been far from adequately exploited (see Chapters Five and Six).

TOWARDS THE ADJUDICATION OF ALTERNATIVE EXPLANATIONS: CONVERSATIONAL AWARENESS IN YOUNG CHILDREN

In cognitive science, a useful distinction has often been made between a symbolic representation of goals, beliefs, and knowledge and the "functional architecture"—a metaphor derived from computer research—required to interpret the symbols into meaning (Pylyshyn, 1984, pp. 30–31). Two people whose beliefs and goals are the same may be functionally distinguishable if they have, for example, different memory retrieval mechanisms or degrees of alertness.

In Piaget's analysis, children and adults share beliefs about the purpose of comparisons in experiments. Age differences in conservation answers are due to differences in the schema or functional architecture required to use concepts such as invariance in number. Young children are at a preoperational stage. In adapting to the environment, they later come to share the same logic and concepts as adults. By contrast, the results of our conservation tasks suggest that adults and children may often have similar logic and concepts but differ on the nature of the language used in the experiment. Rather than sharing the experimenter's purpose, children may be anticipating that they should give particular answers. They may be uncomfortable with the task in the first place and be induced to respond incorrectly, or they may be confident and know the answer but respond incorrectly because they read insincerity into the motives of the experimenter. Alternatively, even if they do understand the experimenter's purpose, they may give incorrect answers to seek attention or to shorten or prolong the experiment.

Piaget's clinical interview method does not circumvent these alternative explanations. Consequently, children's beliefs about conservation—even if these do turn out to be rather fragile—may actually be no different than those of adults. In this respect, adults and children may be functionally indistinguishable. However, adults and children may differ in their beliefs about the meaning of words or the purpose underlying repeated or unconventional questioning. Therefore, children may respond in a seemingly illogical manner.

As Carey (1985b, p. 200) points out, the specification of an initial state of cognitive development is a prerequisite for a theory of learning. A description of the child's initial state must come before or proceed together with an examination of mechanisms of change. A major distinction that can be drawn here is between the child's capacity to use concepts such as invariance in number, and knowing when to employ them. Children's "initial state" as shown in experimental contexts may reflect not so much their lack of ability to use abstract concepts but their interpretation of the experimenter's intent in communication.

Much of children's early relationships with their caregivers centres on learning how, when, where, and with whom to converse. During this period in their language acquisition, they have caregivers who make allowance for their early conversational inexperience. According to research carried out in many societies, these adult speakers generally shorten their utterances and do not say more or less than is necessary to sustain conversation, they are clear, relevant, and informative in referring to objects and events in the here and now, and they are concerned to correct truth value in the child's speech rather than errors of syntax (Brown & Hanlon, 1970; Cross, 1977; De Villiers & De Villiers, 1978, pp. 192–198; Ferguson, 1977). As a consequence, children assume that a speaker's messages will be motivated by co-operativeness, non-redundancy, truthfulness, relevance, and clarity—conventions of communication that have been noted by philosophers of language. These are rational, systematic rules that "constrain" our conversations.

In his exposition of speech conventions, Grice (1975, p. 45), a philosopher, formally states a "co-operative principle" that underlies effective communication: "Make your conversational contribution such as is required at the stage at which it occurs, by the accepted purpose or direction of the talk exchange in which you are engaged." In accordance with this principle, he lists four rules or maxims that may be described, briefly, as the maxims of quantity: "Speak no more or no less than is required"; quality: "Try to speak the truth and avoid falsehood"; relevance (or relation): "Be relevant and informative"; and manner: "Avoid obscurity and ambiguity".[1]

As Grice has pointed out, these rules create a "logic in conversation" that involves knowledge of the implications contained in natural language. In communication between adults who are conversationally experienced, it is usually mutually understood in these settings that the rules may be broken to make what Grice refers to as "conversational implicatures." For example, adults know that speakers may be uninformative and state the obvious for purposes of irony (e.g. stating that "It's another sunny day" in referring to the weather of a habitually rainy locality) or that they may be redundant and speak more than is required (e.g. repeatedly asking, "How are you?") to probe an initial answer out

---

[1]There are a number of complexities in the study of pragmatics in language. However, although critiques of Grice's approach are offered by Brown & Levinson, 1987; Cohen, 1971; Leech, 1983; Sperber & Wilson, 1986; and Wilson, 1994, the rules proposed by Grice can be regarded are promissory notes or "conversational rules of thumb" which precede a general theory of collective action (Clark, 1987). As widely acknowledged (Clark, 1992; Hilton, 1990, 1995; Levinson, 1989), this framework allows insight into the nature of communication processes.

of politeness or curiosity in order to establish that this is the respondent's genuine opinion. Moreover, to be fully informative would often violate the quantity rule to speak no more than is required. For example, if a person complains that he has a headache, a friend may respond that there is a drugstore around the corner. The implications are that the walk to the drugstore is short, that the drugstore is open at the time, that it sells tablets to alleviate headaches, and that these tablets are publicly available to be sold to the sufferer if he can pay as a member of the community. To state all this explicitly would be to breach the quantity rule since the implications are likely to be mutually understood among conversationally experienced speakers.

In this way, effective communication between speakers and listeners involves a common grounding in knowledge of time, location, and community membership that permits a mutual mental representation of contexts for comprehension (Clark, 1992, pp. 60–77; Clark & Brennan, 1991; Graumann, 1995). Reasoning and problem solving are importantly influenced by this grounding (e.g. Falmagne, 1990; Occhipinti & Siegal, 1994; Politzer & Nguyen-Xuan, 1992; Scholnick & Wing, 1995). However, even in conversations between adults, the listener is liable to be misled if a rule is set aside and there is a lack of common grounding in communication (e.g. Schegloff, 1987).

By the age of 3 years, the speech habits of children reflect a common grounding and are often in line with conversation as prescribed by the Gricean maxims. They converse fluently with others and demonstrate substantial ability in adjusting speech to the characteristics of listeners such as their age and their access and attention to previous information (Baldwin, 1993; Braine & Rumain, 1983; Gelman & Shatz, 1977; Shatz & Gelman, 1973). They speak in less sophisticated ways to children younger than themselves and use more complicated forms of language when conversing with adults. Moreover, by the age of 3 years, children in Western societies learn as part of the culture to take turns in conversation and to pause until the person has completed his or her message (Broerse & Elias, 1994). They have acquired considerable expertise in saying what they mean (Snow, Pan, Imbens-Bailey, & Herman, 1996), and can often use a knowledge of their own and others' mental states in conversing with other children and adults (see Bretherton & Beeghly, 1982; and the chapters by Dunn, 1994, Shatz, 1994, and Wellman & Bartsch, 1994, in Lewis & Mitchell, 1994).

Nevertheless, the early process of becoming a conversationalist does not prepare preschoolers for specialised settings in which conversational rules are set aside. The need to follow the conversational implications of a speaker who has set aside the rules may place the understanding of children who are inexperienced in conversation at risk.

In particular, contrary to the rules to be relevant and to speak no more than is required, an experimenter may pose questions where the answer is obvious or repeat questions when an answer has already been given. Young children may not recognise that the purpose underlying departures from conversational rules is to establish their understanding of concepts. Instead, they may act on a mistaken implicature. For example, they may assume that repeated questioning (that sets aside the quantity rule to speak no more than is required) implies a rejection of their first answer and is an invitation to switch the second time around regardless of whether that answer was correct. Moreover, contrary to the quality and manner rules to be truthful and avoid ambiguity and obscurity, children can be asked questions that require them to be sceptical of the experimenter's sincerity or to share the use of certain key words. Again, they may respond incorrectly not because they do not know the answer but because they misinterpret the experimenter's purpose or use of language. In some cases, communication may be jeopardised by their perception that the experimenter is not even observing the basic principle that speakers co-operate with the listener.

The communication gulf between adults and young children can be illustrated by comic incidents in conversations between adults. Take an example from the Marx Brothers where one adult says to another, "Where can I get hold of you?" and the response is, "I don't know. I'm ticklish all over!" This gulf in misperceiving the experimenter's intent in questioning is probably more pervasive in adult–child communication. But it is also more subtle since children are less experienced in conversation and may have difficulty in blocking out an implicature that the experimenter did not intend. Furthermore, compared to adults, they may be less likely to retort spontaneously in response to questions and to offer repairs for improving communication. For instance, recall Piaget's method of using countersuggestions to probe for certainty in answers: to tell children that another child has said the opposite. By contrast, children may not share the experimenter's purpose. Even though counter-suggestions are still used in carefully devised experiments to test for the certainty of responses (e.g. Sophian, 1995), preschoolers may extract meaning from their personal knowledge of others and strain to import the own relevance; as Anne-Nelly Perret-Clermont (Siegal, 1991, p. 26) points out, their response to such a suggestion may be tacitly based on the presumed answer to the question, "Is he a dumb or smart kid?"

SPONTANEOUSLY DECIDING WHICH ONE HAS MORE

The watershed between "knowing how", or at least having the "capacity to know how", and "knowing when" to apply a strategy for solving a problem remains at the crux of cognitive development. It is not enough to give a child a particular problem, record failure, and then conclude that the child does not know. It can only be ventured that he or she might not share the experimenter's purpose or use of language in questioning. Once this purpose and language is shared, children can be shown when to apply an appropriate strategy. A good example comes from the studies of children's measurement abilities.

According to Piaget (Piaget, Inhelder, & Szeminska, 1964), children under the age of approximately 7 years are unable to use a measuring device to compare the length of objects. They are not capable of inferring that an intervening measure such as a stick or rod can be used to check the heights of two towers of blocks set on stands at different levels.

Bryant and Kopytynska (1976) challenged this position. They reasoned that young children's apparent inability to use measurement devices is not due to the absence of some underlying conceptual mechanism. Rather, children often do not recognise when these devices need to be used. To succeed on measurement tasks, they need to know that a direct comparison by eye is unreliable and that a measurement device is required. In Bryant and Kopytynska's studies, 5- and 6-year-olds accurately compared the depth of holes in blocks of wood after an experimenter pointed out the presence of a measuring rod. Therefore, children may indeed have the necessary skill to make inferences but at times they do not always realise when this skill is needed.

My analysis of children's understanding of the conservation task is in agreement with these results. There are many explanations for non-conservation that can be framed in terms of a gap in communication between children and experimenters. Children may have the skill to conserve quantities but, caught in this gap, the skill is not translated into success. Bryant (1985) further contends that young children's difficulties in the addition and subtraction of quantities are rooted not so much in their lack of mathematical ability but in the realisation that certain number skills are required. Children may need to be shown that concepts of number have a function in solving problems.

Possibly there is some biologically or maturationally influenced upper bound in children's capacity to process information on cognitive tasks (see, for example, Case, 1985, pp. 377–381). However, the existence of these may in fact serve to promote development; for example, possible capacity limitations in working memory may assist children to avoid missing causal relations by amplifying relations that would be otherwise overlooked (Kareev, 1995). Moreover, despite similarities in maturation, children vary greatly in their performance. Apparently rapid changes in their information-processing ability might turn out to be a byproduct of rapid changes in their responses to requests using unconventional forms of language that violate Grice's rules or maxims for in conversation. Any conceptual limitation that is proposed as rooted in maturation must be scrutinised in terms of the ability to understand implications in conversation as this ability can have an entirely separate basis in maturation and neuropsychological development and may mask an underlying capacity for understanding (Siegal, Carrington, & Radel, 1996). For this reason, the first purpose in experiments must be to describe the initial state or "know-how" in children's cognition under optimal conversational conditions. A next step is to find procedures by which this state can develop.

RECOVERING FORMERLY OBSCURED CAPACITY IN CONTEMPORARY DEVELOPMENTAL RESEARCH

During the 1980s and 1990s, many psychologists have sought to recast Piaget's findings on cognitive development into a somewhat different theoretical orientation. Two of these efforts seem especially noteworthy: the studies of Flavell, Flavell, and Green (1983) and of Siegler (1981, 1995). The former approach concerns children's knowledge of the distinction between perceptual appearance and "reality" (i.e. the invariant properties of objects); the latter characterises their inability to conserve number in terms of "rule-complexity" and "microgenetic analysis".

The intriguing work of Flavell et al. (1983) follows in the tradition of the DeVries (1969) study on children's inability to distinguish perceptual appearance from reality. For Flavell and his colleagues, there are two types of conceptual difficulties in their understanding of the appearance–reality distinction. When asked to report reality, they instead report appearance. This difficulty is termed "phenomenism" and is said to be characteristic of non-conservation in young children. The converse is "realism" where they report reality when asked to report appearance.

In a series of three experiments, Flavell and his co-workers gave 3- and 4-year-olds problems in which they were asked to report, say, on the appearance and real composition of an object. For example, the children were shown an object that looked like an egg but was actually a stone painted white. They were then asked pairs of questions about the object while viewing it under three conditions: clear plastic (identity), dark plastic to make it look blue (colour), and a magnifier/minifier to make it appear to change in size. The questions were, "When you look at this with your eyes right now, does it look like a stone or does it look like an egg? What is this really, really? Is it really, really a stone or is it really, really an egg?" Many 3-year-olds did not make the distinction between appearance and reality. In the identity condition, they gave reality answers to both questions (realism) and in the colour and size conditions they gave appearance answers (phenomenism). Flavell et al. (1983, p. 117) interpreted the results to indicate a "general metacognitive limitation concerning mental representations". While young children use such representations, they are said to be less knowledgeable about their source and less aware of the origins of appearances. They do not easily process indirect or second-hand information.

Contrary to Piaget, the Flavell experiments have shown that preschoolers as young as 4 years of age often do have the capacity to distinguish perceptual appearance from reality. However, before focusing on conceptual difficulties, as limited as these may be, it is necessary to note that children might not share the experimenter's purpose in questioning or know when to apply an appropriate strategy. At the age of 3 years, they might distinguish between appearance and reality but they do not have the manner to convey this distinction. In the procedure used by Flavell, they may be trying to supply satisfactory, desirable "cute" answers to a continuous flow of questions on one topic that may be tacitly perceived as redundant or having obvious answers and so to contravene the quantity and relevance rules. In an effort to please, a child may be implicitly attributing to the experimenter the ability to change the properties of objects. He or she may then be excused.

Consider one further aspect of the experimental context: Children have friendships and relations with other children and these may affect their responses. They may not indicate a deep, explicit knowledge of the distinction between appearance and reality (or knowledge on many other measures for that matter) owing either to the apprehension or attraction of communication with the grown-up (consistent with Explanations Two and Three discussed previously). The latter possibility is illustrated in Fig. 2.5. To be sure, there is a further recent body of evidence that has been interpreted to support the claim of "conceptual difficulties" in 3-year-olds. This will be discussed in Chapter Four.

Using a novel approach in experiments with children aged 3 to 9 years, Siegler attempted to characterise development in terms of an acquisition of increasingly powerful rules for problem solving. Unlike Piaget, his "rule assessment" approach does not often presume a structured whole or similarity in children's performance across different tasks that amounts to a conceptual limitation. To some extent, it also recognises that tasks which reduce children's dependence on language comprehension provide a clearer indication of their understanding than responses in a Piagetian interview. However, it steers clear of the need to consider conversational rules.

According to Siegler, children's ability on number conservation problems can be interpreted as involving the acquisition of four rules:

Rule I in which children concentrate on the dominant dimension (i.e. the length of the rows).
Rule II where they also consider the subordinate dimension (i.e. row density) when values on the dominant one are equal.
Rule III in which they consider both dimensions but do not know how to resolve conflicts between the two.
Rule IV when conservation is obtained.

At Rule I, children are able to solve problems involving rows of counters with density held constant by focusing on the dominant dimension of length. At Rule II, they can focus on density with length held constant. Children at Rule III consider both density and length but cannot consider conflicts such as between a row of four matched with a shorter, denser row of five.

FIG. 2.5 A child giving an appearance answer when asked to report reality: An illustration of the possible context of "phenomenism" errors on an appearance–reality task that children perceive to be attractive.

While Siegler found mixed support for the use of these rules, the children were presented with problems in which the pretransformation state contained two rows of four equally spaced counters. They first judged whether the numbers were the same and then had to repeat their judgement after a counter was added or subtracted or the rows were lengthened or shortened. Therefore in every case, Siegler's tasks amounted to a two-question format.

Even if the effects of repeated questioning did not exist, rule-complexity did not very strictly predict the children's performance. The 4-year-olds' responses on comparing small number sets were particularly puzzling. They solved less than half the problems in which there was a conflict between density and length but nothing was added or subtracted. As Siegler (1981, p. 54) comments, the finding is not explainable in terms of counting, pairing, or "subitising" (estimating numbers perceptually without the use of a cognitive strategy). He ends up by offering the interpretation that children may believe a quantitative comparison is not necessary where a transformation without addition or subtraction takes place. This suggestion is in keeping with the observation that children have some understanding of abstract concepts; they can often measure and conserve but need to be shown when these skills are needed. At the same time, repeated questioning can contravene the quantity rule in conversation. In the absence of the salient cues of addition and subtraction, it may mislead children to change their initial responses.

More recently, Siegler (1995) carried out a "microgenetic" study to examine the path, rate, breadth, variability, and sources of change in children's answers on conservation of number problems. In this study, 45 children aged from 54 to 73 months were given problems similar to those used in his 1981 research. The children received 12 problems in each of four pretest sessions and four training sessions for a total of 96 presentations in all. All the children who had participated in the training were classified by Siegler as having performed unsuccessfully in the pretest sessions. In the training sessions, the children were divided into three groups of 15: one group was given feedback on their responses, a second was given feedback and asked to explain their reasoning, and a third group was asked to explain the reasoning behind the experimenter's judgements of the correct answer. The group that was asked to explain the experimenter's reasoning (e.g. "nothing was added or taken away so the numbers in the rows remain the same") significantly outperformed the other two. Siegler noted that the path, rate, breadth, and variability of change was gradual and characterised by considerable individual differences across children rather than by a developmental sequence or stage-like progression. The source of change was seen in terms of encouragement to take on the perspective of the experimenter in coming to understanding the basis underlying conservation (in the form of "cultural learning" as termed by Tomasello, Kruger, & Ratner, 1993).

In the present account, the importance of taking on this perspective serves to clarify the relevance and purpose underlying the tremendous amount of repeated questioning in Siegler's study. It provides an alternative account for the superior performance of the children requested to explain the experimenter's reasoning as well as of the great variability in the responses of children in all the groups on the 48 training problems in response to repeated questioning. Yet despite the possibility of response-switching, disinterest, or fatigue, Siegler (1995, p. 259) actually explicitly advocates repeated questioning on the same set of problems as "useful for microgenetic studies in general" in order to examine the rate and breadth of change.

In view of methodological issues concerning children's interpretation of the relevance and purpose of conversation initiated by experimenters in an effort to determine what children know, the general difficulty is one of a lack of communication in natural language. On the basis of interviews or experiments that depart from conversational rules, we may wrongly conclude a limitation in understanding. Accordingly, it must be recognised that negative evidence on children's problem solving is almost inevitably vulnerable to weakness for they may simply have misunderstood the question or have interpreted the experimental context to require a particular answer. Positive results from experiments on children's knowledge are more informative for these show what children do, or what they are capable of doing, even though they may not have a full-blown understanding.

To establish children's knowledge of abstract concepts such as invariance in number is a matter that might be seen to require repeated or prolonged questioning or the use of certain forms of language. But through these sincere attempts to gain insight into processes of development, an experimenter may inadvertently neglect children's appreciation of the purpose and meaning of language and infer that they share the pragmatic force of an adult's questioning.

The difference between the the abysmal performance shown by children in experiments carried out in the Piagetian tradition and the results of experiments in which preschoolers are guided by the experimenter's questions to successfully judge the reasons underlying puppets' correct or incorrect performance on questions about conservation can be seen as due to the transparent purpose of the latter methodology. Following Bos (1937), Rogoff (1990, p. 183) astutely points out that joint efforts between the experimenter and the child in determining the basis for another's choice avoids confronting the child with the sole responsibility of ensuring that his or her first answer to a direct question is the correct one. Children can take a more open, freer, and critical approach to their answers in that the purpose and relevance of the problem takes place within a collaborative atmosphere.

In research carried out using traditional Piagetian methodology, children may be uncertain of the answer to the task in the first place and be induced to respond incorrectly, or they may be confident and know the answer but respond incorrectly because they read insincerity into the motives of the experimenter. Even if they do understand the experimenter's purpose, they may give incorrect answers to seek attention or to shorten or prolong the testing session. Then we have the problem that the experimenter's use of words may not yet map on to their experience. These are complex issues that can be approached by diagnosing the nature of the co-operation contained in the discourse of the experiment as well as that which is implicit in the task itself. Innovative methods of eliciting knowledge from children are required that are sensitive to their experience in communication and which avoid an excessive reliance on the sophisticated conversational implicatures used by adults.

Even infants have an appreciation of the identity of persons and objects. At an early age, they know that it is the same person or object that reappears despite perceptual changes. Because this "skeletal" knowledge constrains children to acquire theories about the mental and physical world, the architecture of children's minds does not rule out an implicit knowledge of abstract concepts such as invariance in number, though this understanding can be obscured in settings where well-meaning experimenters set aside conversational rules.

Therefore, children's interpretation of language in experiments cautions against the use of conservation as a building block to take leaps in theories of child development. Should techniques of conversation be seen as irrelevant or redundant, children may be misled to answer incorrectly. At least in some cases, they may in turn mislead the adult into believing that they are inherently limited in their conceptual development. In this way, a well-meaning methodology can obscure an appreciation of development and instead inadvertently produce cases of "misleading children". A more solid foundation comes from their success on tasks where well-meaning experimenters have not strayed from conversational rules.

3 Detecting Causality

Piaget claimed that children's knowledge of cause and effect relations is limited to what they see. In *Judgement and Reasoning in the Child* (Piaget, 1928, p. 4), he characterised their ideas about causality to be restricted by "syncretism":

> the spontaneous tendency . . . to take things in by means of a comprehensive act of perception instead of by the detection of details, to find immediately and without analysis analogies between words or objects that have nothing to do with each other, to bring heterogeneous phenomena into relation with each other, to find a reason for a chance event; in a word, it is the tendency to connect everything with everything else.

If asked to complete the beginning of a sentence such as "The man fell off his bicycle because . . . ", children under 5 or 6 years will respond "because he broke his arm" rather than, say, "because he lost his balance". On this basis, Piaget denied that young children can detect causal relations. In providing additional evidence from tasks devised in later work with Barbel Inhelder (Inhelder & Piaget, 1958), he contended that their thinking is muddled and chaotic, and that their propositions about events are juxtaposed together instead of causally linked.

Not only did Piaget judge young children to be incapable of clearly identifying causal relations but he contended that they assign internal states and motives to inanimate objects. For example, in his early work, Piaget (1929) asked children questions such as "Can a bench feel anything if someone burnt it?" or "Are bicycles alive?" He interpreted their answers to indicate that young children's notions of causality are primitive and reflect an inability to distinguish between subjects and objects. They believe that any object may possess consciousness at a particular moment, especially a thing that can move, like a bicycle.

Piaget also used children's responses in his clinical interviews to illustrate the primitive state of their ideas about causality. His approach is well represented by their explanations for the appearance of shadows and for the origin of dreams. For example, Piaget (1930, p. 184) reported an interview with a 5-year-old named "Stei" on the nature and cause of shadows:

Interviewer: You know what a shadow is?
Stei: Yes, it's the trees that make them, under the tree.
Interviewer: Why is there a shadow under the tree?
Stei: Because there are a lot of leaves. The leaves make it.
Interviewer: How do they do it?
Stei: Because they are pink.
Interviewer: What does that do?
Stei: It makes a shadow.
Interviewer: Why?
Stei: Because inside [the leaves] it is night, inside.
Interviewer: Why?
Stei: Because it's day on top. The leaves are big and it is night inside them. [Stei is shown his shadow on the ground]
Interviewer: There is a shadow there?
Stei: Yes, the chair does it.
Interviewer: Why does the chair make a shadow?
Stei: Because it's black underneath. It's dark.
Interviewer: Why?
Stei: Why, because it is dark under the chair, because it's a chair and there is an edge and that keeps the shadow under the chair.

For Piaget, young children typically believe that a shadow is a substance emanating from the object but participating with the night. They realistically attribute animistic qualities to leaves in projecting shadows. Only with increasing age do children know how shadows are projected and deny that objects cast shadows at night.

Similarly, Piaget proposed that young children misunderstand the nature of dreams; they believe that dreams originate from outside and remain external to the self. For example, Piaget (1929, p. 118) reports an interview with a 7-year-old named Mort:

Interviewer:	Where do you see dreams?
Mort:	Against the wall.
Interviewer:	Should I see them if I was there?
Mort:	Yes.
Interviewer:	Where do they come from?
Mort:	From outside.
Interviewer:	What sends them?
Mort:	People.
Interviewer:	What do you dream of?
Mort:	A man being run over.
Interviewer:	Is he in front of you when you dream, or inside you?
Mort:	In front of me.
Interviewer:	Where?
Mort:	Under my window.
Interviewer:	Should I have seen him if I had been there?
Mort:	Yes.
Interviewer:	Did you see him in the morning?
Mort:	No.
Interviewer:	Where did this dream come from? Did you make it, or someone else?
Mort:	Someone else.
Interviewer:	Who?
Mort:	A man my father knows (the one who was run over).
Interviewer:	Does he make all the dreams?
Mort:	Only that one.
Interviewer:	And the others—
Mort:	Other men.

According to Piaget, older children believe that dreams originate and take place within the head. Even so, children under the age of 7 or 8 years may mistake the experimenter's purpose in asking questions about causal relations. Should they perceive the questions to contravene the conversational rules of relevance and quality (to be informative and sincere), they may offer silly or "cute" answers instead of the correct ones of which they are capable. Yet, interviewing that is liable to involve such questioning has at times continued to be used as a sole or primary technique to obtain information about child development.

For example, in some very interesting work reminiscent of Piaget, Frank Keil (1979, pp. 109–110) reported children's answers to a sequence of interview questions on the nature of dreams during an interchange between an experimenter and a child aged 4 years 2 months:

E (Experimenter):	Can dreams be tall?
C (Child):	Yeah.
E:	How tall?
C:	Big, big, big [spreads arms].
E:	Where are dreams?
C:	In your bedroom.
E:	In the daytime?
C:	No, they're outside.
E:	Could you see a dream?
C:	Yeah.
E:	How?
C:	They're red.
E:	What are they like?
C:	They're made out of rock.
E:	Could they be heavy?
C:	Yeah, and they can't break either.
E:	What do they look like?
C:	They look like rocks. Like they're asleep on the grass. And the kids go outside and they see the things asleep.
E:	Are dreams alive then?
C:	No, they're not dead either. They just got grass on them.

To demonstrate a systematic pattern of errors in children's early knowledge of "conceptual distinctions", Keil (1983) used this type of interview technique in a later series of three studies. Based on their responses, he maintained that young children are not easily able to distinguish between predicates (e.g. "happened yesterday") that apply to events and those that apply to physical objects (e.g. "shiny").

For example, in a first study, children in kindergarten and grades 2 and 4 were asked to judge 63 sentences as "OK" or "silly". These consisted of all combinations of three physical object terms (chair, rock, car) and three events (trip, party, storm) with nine predicates, some of which were applicable to physical objects and others to events. The test was to judge sentences like "The rock is heavy" as OK and those like "The car has ended" as silly. Kindergarten children were more likely than older ones to judge incorrectly the application of physical object predicates to events as acceptable (for example, "The storm is upside-down"). When this type of mistake occurred, it took the form of a consistent pattern across all combinations of physical object predicates and event terms. By contrast, a misapplication of event predicates to physical object terms occurred occasionally for some children. Keil's interpretation (1983, pp. 356–366) was "that there is a stage in concept differentiation in which the child knows very well what physical objects are but is confused about the nature of many events and about their distinguishing properties".

Using a similar method, Carey (1985b, p. 91) reported that many 4-year-olds believe that a mechanical monkey eats (40%), sleeps (30%), and has bones (30%). More recently, Simons and Keil (1995) gave children numerous pairs of photographs and models of natural kinds such as sheep. For example, in one pair, a sheep was shown with "animal insides" such as a heart, liver, and intestines and, in the other, with "machine insides" such as gears and cogs. The children were asked questions such as, "Which of the drawings shows a real sheep?", "Which shows a real sheep with sheep insides?" A significant number of 4-year-olds chose the sheep with machine insides to represent a real sheep.

However, a closer look at this method of assessing children's knowledge of concepts suggests an alternative explanation. For example, in Keil's (1983) study, the children were repeatedly questioned not only on the 63 sentences but on sentences involving polar opposites of the predicates. The youngest children were seen individually, often in four half-hour sessions, and the occasional kindergarten child had to be dropped from the research because of a refusal to continue in all the sessions. Keil's rationale for the use of this technique was to ensure that responses were not influenced by fatigue or uncertainty. But alternatively, from the child's point of view, the experimenter's attempts to elicit "silly" judgements may have been perceived as a contravention of the quantity rule and interpreted as an invitation to give silly answers. Since children are liable to perceive violations of conversational rules in questioning about their causal knowledge, at least some may have misunderstood the experimenter's purpose and have given pretend answers instead of correct ones.

Given the type of interview questions, children may conclude that sentences like "The dream is tall" or "The storm is upside-down" (or that pictures of a sheep that might be seen to have swallowed machinery in Simons and Keil's study) are novel or cute and therefore consistently OK. By contrast, sentences containing combinations of physical object terms and event predicates such as "The rock has ended" hold no such attraction. Similarly, in Carey's (1985b) research, the genuine belief of some children may have been that dolls and mechanical monkeys are inanimate objects just as a stone, a vehicle, or a garlic press. The possibility remains to be tested, for example, in studies where children are asked to give attributions for the correct and incorrect choices of peers.

The position of Keil is related to Piaget's (1970) hypothesis that young children have difficulty with tasks which require a knowledge of part–whole or "inclusion" relations. To illustrate, children may be shown bunches of flowers, many of them roses, and asked, "Are there more roses or more flowers?" Typically, they say that there are more roses.

Piagetians have taken children's responses on class inclusion problems to demonstrate that they are at a preoperational stage in their ability to understand concepts. Since a knowledge of inclusion relations and how animate and inanimate objects ought to be included in classes is essential to detect causal events in nature, some of Keil's work might be regarded as evidence for a limitation in children's understanding of scientific concepts. At the same time, however, responses on inclusion problems demonstrate once more how children are sensitive to unconventional or unfamiliar forms of language that depart from conversational rules.

Might this concern lead to reservations about the evidence which suggests that young children have difficulties in inclusion relations? Carol Smith (1979) approached the issue by examining the effects of presentation order on their responses. In a series of experiments, 4- to 6-year-olds were asked questions on the inclusion of persons and objects into classes. Some of these referred to items where X was a subset of Y (e.g. "Are all boys people?"); others concerned items where X was a superset of Y (e.g. "Are all animals cats?"). Similar to Keil's material that required a "silly" answer, the X and Y items were disjointed in a third set of questions (e.g. "Are all spoons bumblebees?").

Smith took care to ensure that the children included in her studies understood the words "all" and "some". In paying special attention to the effects of prolonged questioning on the 18 "quantified inclusion" questions given to the children in her first study, she discovered significant differences between performance on the first half of the questions and the second. On the first half, most of the children answered correctly. Performance on the second half fell off sharply, particularly for the younger children. However, contrary to the hypothesis that young children have a general conceptual limitation as shown by a consistent difficulty with all the class inclusion problems, errors were usually on only one type of item. In her follow-up studies, Smith reduced the number of questions and found that even 4-year-olds performed significantly better than would be predicted by chance. Similar results have come from related studies (e.g. Freeman & Schreiner, 1988).

As shown by the pattern of responses on Smith's measures, the basic format of children's representation of concepts may be the same as in older children and adults. Their difficulties may be in drawing out the consequences of this representation or in misinterpreting the force of the experimenter's intent. As Smith (1979, p. 454) remarks, children who made mistakes were frequently answering the wrong question (for example, Experimenter's question: "Are all animals dogs?" Child's response: "Yes, 'cause I know what dogs are." Experimenter's question: "Are all robins birds?" Child's response: "No, 'cause there are other kinds of birds.")

For children to express an explicit knowledge of inclusion relations in interviews with adults requires extensive conversational experience. A team of psychologists working in Scotland (McGarrigle, Grieve, & Hughes, 1978) has shown that 4- to 6-year-olds have much difficulty when comparing one row of four cows (two black and two white) with a second row of four horses (three black and one white). When asked to say whether there were more black horses or more cows, only 5 of 48 children gave the correct answer that there were more cows. However, as the Scottish psychologists point out, the children's responses do not necessarily point to a lack of knowledge about classes. Their presuppositions of what the task requires them to do are tied to the salient features of their environment (in this case, colour). They have little experience of the formal usage of language used by adult questioners that is rounded on the implicit message, "Ignore the colours that you see. Just think about the logic of my question." To novices on inclusion problems, colour may seem the most reasonable way to compare quantities. After all, they could well reason, why would an adult show a child objects of different colours if colour was not a good way to compare quantities?

In this way, as may often be the case in experiments, many questions which require children to make judgements about causality and classification can inadvertently violate the rule of ordinary conversation that a speaker's messages should be relevant. If listeners are inexperienced in the world of adult conversation, they may strive to grant relevance to an otherwise senseless question and respond as if the speaker really meant that the properties of the objects to be compared are relevant to the correct answer. It cannot be assumed that children share the experimenter's definition of the attributes relevant to the task.

In view of the research that points to preschoolers' ability to distinguish between the properties of animate and inanimate objects, a conversational reinterpretation of the results of this aspect of Keil's research program is a distinct possibility. But at the least, although there remain several grounds to challenge Keil's analysis of conceptual development (see Carey, 1985b), he has drawn attention to the importance of studying children's knowledge of ontology or basic categories of existence. In at least some cases, children can be capable young scientists in detecting causal relations and classifying objects and events.

CHILDREN AS YOUNG SCIENTISTS

Recently, the early ability to understand causal relations and to distinguish between the properties of animate and inanimate objects has been intensively re-examined. The results serve to question Piaget's assertion that young children lack causal knowledge as well as Keil's notion of a limitation in their ability to differentiate concepts.

One of the most intelligent studies of causality has been carried out by Shultz (1982b). To take Shultz's Experiment 3 as an example, children aged 3, 5, 7, and 9 years were given three problems. They saw: (1) an electric blower and a lamp directed toward a spot of light on the wall; (2) an electric blower and tuning fork directed toward a candle light which was then extinguished; and (3) a lamp and tuning fork directed toward the opening of a wooden box which began to resonate audibly.

Even many of the 3-year-olds were able to determine the cause of the effect. They told the experimenter that the lamp created the spot of light on the wall, the electric blower extinguished the candlelight, and the tuning fork made the sound come from the box. The children were able to identify the blower as irrelevant to the spot of light, the tuning fork as irrelevant to the candle, and the lamp as irrelevant to the sound from the box. Shultz concluded that young children can understand cause and effect relations in a sophisticated "generative" sense rather than as the simple covariation of two events at the same point in time. (For a further discussion, see Shultz, Fisher, Pratt, & Ruff, 1986.)

To determine whether young children can distinguish between the properties of animate and inanimate objects, Bullock (1985) gave 3- to 5-year-olds and adults four films depicting either an inanimate object (a multicoloured stack of wooden blocks or a plastic wind-up worm) or an animate object (a 2-year-old girl or a rabbit). The objects were first stationary on a flat surface and then moved until a bowl of crackers was reached. The children were asked questions about each object such as "Can (x) grow bigger?", "If we forget to give (x) food, will it get hungry?", "If (x) breaks, can we fix it with glue?" Most of the 4- and 5-year-olds performed like adults. Although the 3-year-olds made a greater number of errors, the majority were still able to stipulate whether an object was alive or not. Similarly, even 4-year-olds make a distinction between the possibility of restoring an inanimate object such as pencil with a broken tip and a natural kind produced by an animate object such as a rotten peach. They recognise that the pencil can be repaired by gluing on the tip but that the peach cannot be made fresh even through washing and refrigeration (Springer, Ngyuen, & Samaniego, 1996).

Christine Massey and Rochel Gelman (1988) have further established that 3- and 4-year-olds are able to use the distinction between animate and inanimate objects in deciding whether an object can move by itself. Children were given glossy photographs of unfamiliar mammals (e.g. a sloth, a pygmy marmoset), non-mammalian animals (e.g. a praying mantis, a freshwater crayfish), statues of animals (e.g. a figurine with insect-like eyes), wheeled vehicles (e.g. an electric golf caddy, an antique large-wheeled bicycle), and rigid objects consisting of more than one part (e.g. a robot). Instead of mistakenly using general or prototypical animal parts and shapes to guide their judgements of self-movement, the children were able to make correct inferences based on the visible movement-enabling features of each object. They were able to distinguish objects that can initiate their own movements from those for which movement must depend on an external source.

In recent years, this pattern of findings has gained impressive support from a number of sources. For example, Susan Gelman and Kathy Kremer (1991) compared the responses of 4- to 8-year-olds on a "direct question" task with those on an "open-ended question" task. In the direct-question task, the children were given three types of item: "remote natural kinds" (sun, moon, stars, ocean, clouds, thunder) that Piaget had used in his studies, familiar natural kinds (dogs, birds, apples, flowers, dirt, salt), and artifacts (cups, hammers, dolls, shoes, cars,

TVs). They were asked to say whether people made (or make) each item and to justify their responses. In the open-ended question task, the children were asked the same questions posed by Piaget such as, "Where do clouds come from?" Under direct questioning, even children as young as 4 years demonstrated an understanding of how natural kinds are produced by nature in contrast to artifacts that are produced by people.

In a follow-up series of studies carried out by Hickling and Gelman (1994) that also used a direct questioning technique, children aged as young as 4½ years were generally able to identify that same-species plants are the sole originator of seeds for new plants of that species. Similarly, according to a series of experiments reported by Springer (1995) using direct questioning, 4- and 5-year-olds who understand that human babies grow inside their mothers (77% of the total number of 56 children in his first experiment) possess a "naive theory of kinship" in that they could use this knowledge to predict the properties of offspring. They can say that a baby which is physically dissimilar to the mother will likely share her stable internal properties (e.g. "grey bones inside her fingers") and lack transitory properties (e.g. "scrapes on her legs though running through some bushes").

Children appear especially well-equipped to understand the course of human biology. Inagaki and Hatano (1993) examined children's understanding that some bodily characteristics such as eye colour are not modifiable in contrast to the modifiability of bodily characteristics such as the speed of running and mental characteristics such as memory. Most 4- and 5-year-olds were able to distinguish accurately among the modifiability of these three categories, and almost all were able to say that they could not stop their heartbeat or stop their breathing for a couple of days.

Hatano and Inagaki (1994) have perceptively observed that children's grasp of human biology is adaptive in that it performs three functions. First, it enables children to form predictions about the behavior of familiar natural kinds such as mammals regarding food procurement, sheltering, and reproduction. Second, it enables children to make sense of biological phenomena such as animals and plants that become unhealthy when they are fed too little or too much or with inappropriate food. Third, it helps children to learn rules for taking care of animals and plants, as well as themselves. Their knowledge of internal bodily functions constrains their choices of the variety and quality of food.

Culture and conversation are powerful influences on whether children actually display such an understanding. In a recent series of studies that has taken issue with the claim that young children have an explanatory framework in the domain of biology (Solomon, Johnson, Zaitchik, & Carey, 1996), children aged 4 to 7 years were asked to indicate whether a child born to a biological parent but adopted by another would be more like one than the other in his or her physical traits and beliefs. Not until 7 years of age did children report that physical traits are associated with the biological parent and beliefs with the adoptive parent. However, as the investigators themselves concede (Solomon et al., 1996, p. 161), the younger children may have interpreted these questions in terms of their perceived desirability that change could occur from the situations that they have experienced whereas, at least in Western culture, older children and adults have the "metacognitive" understanding to recognise that the purpose and relevance of the questions is to detect what they know about nature and nurture. If so, young children, in paying homage to the adoptive parent, might say that a child adopted by this parent would "change" in the similarity of both its physical traits and beliefs to this parent.

This interpretation is supported by the intriguing research carried out by Sheila Walker (1992) on the "preservation of identity" judgements of Yoruba adults in Nigeria. In her research, each adult was given five pairs of stories in which one member in each pair had the significance of a ritual in Yoruba culture and the other did not. Walker gives the example of ritual and nonritual members of the pair "chicken/turkey". In the ritual case, the sacrifice of a chicken is deemed necessary by the Yoruba to drive out a child's illness; however, in the story presented to the subjects, a turkey is used that is disguised as a chicken. In the nonritual case, the sale of a chicken is deemed necessary to produce a nice profit; chickens are disguised as turkeys for sale. In either instance, the Yoruba were asked to judge the identity of the changed item. They reliably indicated that the altered ritual item actually changed in its identity (e.g. the turkey was changed into a chicken for the purpose of sacrifice) whereas the altered nonritual item did not (e.g. the chickens disguised as turkeys for the purpose of profit remained chickens).

Thus despite the competence of children and adults to distinguish between appearance and reality and to identify causal relationships in the domain of biology, their actual performance in judging the probability that change will occur is often directed by their cultural experience and expectations together with the format and context of the questions that are asked.

JUDGEMENTS OF TIME

According to the "principle of priority", causes must precede their effects. Since to understand causality it is necessary to be conscious of how sequences of events lead to psychological states, children's early grasp of causal relations presupposes a knowledge of the priority principle. This knowledge is shown in their awareness of random and deliberate phenomena, their understanding of the words used to describe time, and their estimation of distance and duration.

The research of Kuzmak and Gelman (1986) suggests that children can distinguish between random and deliberate events. In their study, 3- to 7-year-olds were shown two physical phenomena: a marble cage game in which marbles would trickle out haphazardly at random, and a marble tube game in which a marble at the end of the tube would roll out if released by a knob. For each problem, the children were asked: "When you play with this game here, do you know which colour is going to come out? Yes or no?"

Correct responses were given by children aged 4 and older. While the 3-year-olds did not differentiate between the random and determinate phenomena, they did not treat either event as predictable. As Kuzmak and Gelman suggest, the youngest children may have just misunderstood the question. Similarly, in two experiments, Sophian and Huber (1984) found that 5-year-olds showed an appreciation of the priority principle while the performance of 3-year-olds was at a chance level. However, the younger children experienced prolonged testing. In fact, in Sophian and Huber's first experiment, they were asked to make 64 judgements. Under these conditions, the children may not have revealed their understanding of causality.

Whatever the interpretation of experiments on knowledge of the priority principle, by the age of 5 years, children have a grasp of words used to describe time such as "yesterday" and "tomorrow" and "always", "never", and "sometimes". For example, in an early study by Harner (1975), children aged 2, 3, and 4 years were seen on two successive days. On the first day, they played with a set of toys and saw a bag with toys for the next day. On the second day, the children saw three sets of toys: those from yesterday, those for tomorrow, and "today's toys". The experimenter's requests were, "Show me a toy from yesterday" and "Show me a toy for tomorrow". The 2-year-olds did not comprehend differences in the three groups of toys. The 3-year-olds appeared to understand that "yesterday" did not refer to today's toys, and "yesterday" was better understood than "tomorrow". By the age of 4 years, "yesterday" and "tomorrow" were understood equally well.

In a similar series of experiments on the acquisition of words such as "never", Kuczaj (1975) gave preschoolers (mean age, 4 years) pairs of sentences such as "The boy always drives the car. The girl never drives the car." The children were then asked, "Who drives the car?" In response to this procedure, most children treated "never" as a negative. Words such as "always" and "sometimes" were often correctly regarded as a positive.

In keeping with children's knowledge of causality and their comprehension of time words, several experiments have now demonstrated the early ability to make accurate judgements of duration. Levin (1982) reported a series of experiments in which preschoolers were able to infer relative durations from differences in starting and ending points. For example, children were shown two lights and were asked to judge whether the lights were lit for the same time and, if not, which light was on for the longer time. The majority of preschoolers could respond correctly, although performance declined when the lights were presented with interfering cues such as differential brightness and size. These results undermine Piaget's claims that young children judge time simply by taking account of either starting or ending points and that they lack the ability to integrate the two points together.

Wilkening (1981) presented three age groups (5–6 years, 9–10 years, and adults) with a set of three tasks to examine the abilities to integrate information about velocity and time, velocity and distance, and distance and time. For example, in the task on velocity and time integration, a frightful-looking toy dog was made to bark for 2, 5, or 8 seconds. The children and adults were required to estimate the distance travelled by a turtle, guinea pig, and cat during each time interval by placing pictures of the animals along a miniature drawbridge. In sharp contrast to Piaget, all age groups were able to integrate velocity and time according to the multiplying model: judged distance = time × velocity. The greater the time and the quicker the velocity of the animal, the longer the estimated distance.

On the two other tasks, there were clear developmental differences. Compared to the 9- and 10-year-olds and adults, the 5- and 6-year-olds were less able to judge time on the basis of the distance travelled by the three animals, or to differentiate which of seven animals (a snail, turtle, guinea pig, mouse, cat, deer, and horse) could cover various distances (70, 140, and 210cm) in relation to different time intervals. However, in the former task, time information was not "visually present". The children could only respond by pressing a key to let a toy dog bark for a certain time. An overload on the child's memory may have prevented the use of a sophisticated multiplication strategy. The memory demands of the latter task were also high; the children were required to judge the comparative speeds of seven different animals for each of three distances.

More recent studies have established that young children are able to distinguish the durations of everyday activities. For example, Wilkening, Levin, and Druyan (1987) found that, by the age of 6 years, children can use counting as a strategy to estimate time in successive events. Friedman (1990) gave 3- to 9-year-olds a task in which they could point to sandglasses of different sizes in order to represent the duration of five events depicted on cards: drinking milk, shopping, a family car trip, one cartoon show, and sleeping at night. While performance improved between 3 and 6 years, even 3-year-olds estimated true normative durations at an above chance level. In later research, Friedman (1991) showed young children may not have knowledge of days, weeks, or months, but they can judge which of two events occurred first in time and can identify the time of day in which an event has occurred.

Reliable evaluations of others' actions on accurate estimates of time intervals. As Wilkening (1982, p. 110) has astutely observed:

> From the point of view of an applied developmental psychology, for example, it is of interest to know under what conditions children can integrate time, distance, and velocity in everyday life decisions . . . how children combine two or more velocities of objects moving at different directions at different distances, when estimating time of collision or safe passing.

These judgements require perceptual estimations as well as knowledge about time, velocity, and distance.

Although in everyday situations children may accord less recognition to the constraints of time, it is also noteworthy that adults themselves often bend time to suit the circumstances. Perhaps the most vivid illustrations of real-life distortions of time can be found in literature. In many novels, time has been stretched or condensed. This feature is not limited to the works of Joyce and Proust. Borges (1964) in his story *The Secret Miracle* graphically depicts how a second could be stretched into a year through the will of a condemned man facing execution in Czechoslovakia during the Second World War.

EXPERIMENTS ON CHILDREN'S KNOWLEDGE OF HEALTH AND ILLNESS

Thus, although children do better on causal tasks with increasing age, even preschoolers show more than a limited capacity to understand causality in the domains of physics and biology and to recognise the time intervals and principle of priority in causal relations. They often succeed at a level that exceeds what would be expected by chance alone. Many of their shortcomings may also have less to do with a limitation on their ability to understand causal relations than with the language used in experiments. When questions have been devised to avoid redundancy and to promote relevance, the research often contradicts Piaget's original position with implications that are applied as well as theoretical.

A key applied issue concerns the nature of children's conceptions of health and illness. On the one hand, should it be accepted that young children generally mistake appearances for reality and that they are unable to detect cause and effect, there would be little point in informing them about health-related matters. On the other hand, evidence that young children have an understanding of the nature of illness would have significance for education and preventive health.

Two major perspectives on children's ability to grasp the mechanisms underlying contagion and contamination have been formulated. First, Bibace and Walsh (1981) proposed a Piagetian stage analysis of children's knowledge of the causes of illness. Children between 2 and 6 years of age account for illness by immediate temporal or physical cues. People are said to catch colds from magic, or from the sun, trees, or God. Later children say that colds are caught when someone else goes near them and when touched by sick persons. Finally, at approximately 11 years of age, they give "formal-logical" explanations. There is a differentiation between external and internal causal agents. While a cold may be transmitted by an external agent, the illness is located within the body. Children may describe colds as transmitted by viruses and consisting of blockages in the sinuses and lungs.

In fact, according to Bibace and Walsh, young children may regard all illness as contagious and believe that toothaches, as well as colds, can be caught by proximity to a sick person. Since children cannot reason about causality, they may view illness as punishment. Bibace and Walsh go on to suggest that the clinical usefulness of a Piagetian theory for the prevention and treatment of illness in children is to promote empathy with the irrational childish fears of the young and to communicate children's immature understanding to health professionals. For example, health workers should be told that closeness to a sick person may be unnerving and, because children have only a limited appreciation of the nature of contagion, they may request to be moved away lest they catch the illness themselves.

By contrast, according to an adaptive-evolutionary perspective (Rozin, 1976b; Rozin & Schull, 1988), children's understanding should be facilitated in domains where problem solving is clearly related to survival such as in the domain of food and contamination. A key example of a domain related to survival concerns solving problems that are relevant to food and safety. Organisms in striving for survival and reproductive fitness confront specific problems such as food procurement. Solutions to these problems require an adaptive, specialised intelligence. During the course of evolution, intelligence in specific problem-solving domains becomes more accessible to conscious awareness. For example, the problem of procuring a safe diet involves the intelligence to assist and compete with companions in detecting and extracting foods. It concerns both the foraging and social relational processes that have been viewed by primatologists to influence the evolution of intelligence (Cords, 1992; Milton, 1988). Because food selection in omnivores is fundamental to survival, the problem of recognising edible foods and possessing an awareness of health-endangering contaminants must be solved early in development. Intelligence in this domain is an adaptive specialisation that involves a preparedness for knowing what to identify as safe to eat, even in the absence of surveillance from caregivers who cannot constantly monitor children's food intake and provide vigilance against the deceptions of others.

Rozin (1990) has defined sensory-affective (taste, smell, and appearance), ideational (culturally appropriate or symbolic), and anticipatory (beneficial or dangerous) criteria for classifying a food as edible or inedible. In solving problems in the domain of food and contamination which is highly relevant to their own concerns (in line with the Gricean maxim of relation), children are constrained to acquire a knowledge of these classification criteria and are apt to recognise that the purpose of questions is to determine their ability to detect edible substances and to reject those that are inedible. Therefore, even 3-year-olds should often be able to distinguish reality from appearance in recognising that a food that looks edible may be in reality contaminated and liable to result in illness.

These two proposals have together generated considerable research on children's understanding of contagion and contamination. Guided by the Piagetian account of Bibace and Walsh, Kister and Patterson (1980) investigated children's understanding of contagion and their belief in punishment or "immanent justice" explanations for illness. The participants in their study were 15 healthy children in each of four groups: preschool, kindergarten, second grade, and fourth grade. The interviewer used a cold as an example of a common contagious illness, a toothache as an example of a common non-contagious illness, and a scraped knee as an example of a common accident. In each instance, the children were given questions such as "If a boy (or girl) your age went to school one day, and the girl sitting next to him had a cold (or two other ailments), would he have to be careful so he wouldn't catch the cold from her? Why (not)? Can the boy catch the cold?" If the child answered in the affirmative, the following questions were asked. "Let's say the boy really didn't want to get the cold. Would it be better for him to sit next to the girl with the cold, across the room from her, or does it make a difference where he sits? Why (not)?"

The children then received questions to determine whether they interpret illness to be punishment for naughtiness. The interviewer said, "Once a boy your age disobeyed his mother. Was that a nice thing to do? Well, that afternoon, he got a cold (or other ailment). Do you think he got a cold because he disobeyed his mother? What made him get a cold? Let's pretend he didn't disobey his mother. Do you think he would get a cold anyway? Why (not)?"

Using this method, the children in preschool (mean age = 4 years 8 months) and kindergarten (mean age = 5 years 6 months) appeared to generalise contagion to ailments such as a toothache and scraped knee. They did not seem to understand the role of distance in the transmission of contagious illnesses. In stark opposition to the work of Shultz and others, Kister and Patterson concluded that young children are biased to regard all contiguous events as causally related. Even on a control story in which the boy who had helped his mother later lost some money, 11 of the 15 preschoolers affirmed a causal relationship when asked questions such as, "Did he lose the money because he helped his mother?" Most importantly, children who offered incorrect responses were very likely to give punishment explanations for the causes of illness.

In addition, Rozin, Fallon, and Augustoni-Ziskind (1985; see also Rozin & Fallon, 1987, pp. 34–35) have claimed that young children do not easily understand the invisible nature of contamination. In their study, an experimenter dropped substances such as a used comb and a grasshopper into glasses of juice. In line with the results of an earlier interview (Fallon, Rozin, & Pliner, 1984), a considerable number of 4- to 6-year-olds drank the juice on request.

On this basis, it could be concluded that young children do not understand contagion and contamination as causes of illness. Instead they may express a belief in immanent justice. However, as Rozin et al. (1985) have cautioned, the effect of social pressure on responses is difficult to evaluate. In this respect, the evidence has often come from studies in which children have been subjected to forms of prolonged or unconventional questioning that may be perceived to depart from the quality rule in conversation to be sincere. Under this procedure, children's inconsistent responses again may not reflect the depth of their understanding. Rather than lacking knowledge of the causes of illness, they may simply have misinterpreted what they were required to do. For example, children may know that a drink which has been in contact with a foreign object can be harmful and they may reject the object as food. At the same time, they may not be aware that a grown-up could offer children a contaminated drink and insincerely imply—in violation of the quality rule—that the drink is safe in a well-meaning effort to test their understanding. In studies to ascertain whether they believe that illness is punishment, they may attempt to comply with the suggestion of an adult interviewer: Adults are so powerful that children who are naughty will inevitably be punished. For these reasons, it is premature to conclude that young children do not have the ability to distinguish between contagious and non-contagious ailments, to understand the nature of contamination, and to discount immanent justice as an explanation for illness.

Even if some children do have a genuine belief in immanent justice and illness as punishment, there is another objection to the form of Piagetian analysis which has been adopted by researchers such as Kister and Patterson: immanent justice is by no means a mode of explanation limited to children. Shweder (1977, 1986), an anthropologist, stresses forcefully that many adults as well as children believe in magical or unnatural explanations for events and that these beliefs are rational in a world where resemblance is not a good predictor of the likelihood that an event will occur or coincide with another. He provides a rather macabre anecdote to illustrate the extent to which children have unnatural explanations for cause and effect relations (Shweder, 1977, p. 637). This is not for the squeamish: "A little boy . . . tried to prove that spiders hear with their legs. After cutting off spider's legs, he yelled, "Jump". The spider did not jump. So the little boy said, "You see, I was right. Spiders hear with their legs."

During the 19th century, adults often professed similar, primitive views about the nature of illness that were tied to visible events. They believed that cholera epidemics in the United States were due to punishment for leading an immoral lifestyle, and such beliefs are present today among many adults in both industrial and non-industrial societies as explanations for the spread of venereal disease and AIDS (Brandt, 1987; Murdock, 1980; Rosenberg, 1962). Both children and adults may be prone to immanent justice explanations in an environment where alternatives are not available or are unappealing (Nemeroff & Rozin, 1994), and researchers may seriously entertain the proposal that, to some extent, magical thinking is universally present in normal adults. Yet an adaptive intelligence must to some extent be present to avoid the catastrophic consequences of illness on health and survival.

UNDERSTANDING CONTAGION AND CONTAMINATION

I sought to re-examine children's knowledge of contagion and contamination in a series of three experiments (Siegal, 1988a). Since direct, prolonged questioning on notions about health and illness may result in a contravention of the quantity and quality rules in conversation and a misinterpretation of the task requirements, the children were asked to evaluate others' explanations for illness, to indicate the likelihood that illness would occur, and to predict their own preventive health behaviour. Different children were included in each experiment.

In Experiment 1, children considered immanent justice, contagion, and contamination as causes of illness. I hypothesised that they would be able to differentiate accurately between contagious and immanent justice explanations for contagious and non-contagious ailments and to identify foreign substances as sources of contamination. The 120 participants were divided into three groups of 40. The mean ages in years and months (with ranges in parentheses) were preschool, 4.11 (4.6 to 5.4), grade 1, 5.9 (5.5 to 6.2), and grade 3, 8.3 (7.6 to 8.7).

The experiment consisted of two phases. Half the children received one phase first, and half the other phase first. In the first phase on contagion, the experimenter showed each child four videotaped segments of puppets in a random order (see Fig. 3.1 for an example). In two of the segments, the puppets were shown to be suffering from a cold. In the other two, they were shown to be suffering from a toothache. In one instance for each of the ailments, the puppets told an adult female questioner on the videotape (who was not the same person as the experimenter) that they caught the ailment when playing with a friend; in the other, the puppets claimed that they caught the ailment through naughty

FIG. 3.1 A puppet on videotape complaining to an experimenter about a toothache and explaining its cause.

behaviour that included playing with a forbidden pair of scissors. After each segment, the children were asked two questions: (1) "Is the puppet right or wrong?"; (2) for the segments on immanent justice, "Can children get (the ailment) by being naughty?" for the segments on proximity, "Can children get (the ailment) by playing with a friend who had (the ailment)?"

In the second phase on contamination, the children were given three situations in a random order. An insect, comb, and spoon were shown to fall accidentally to the bottom of a glass of milk just as a child (the same age and gender as the subject) was about to drink. The situations were illustrated with a real dead cockroach, comb, and spoon. The spoon did not look dirty but its actual cleanliness was not specified. The comb was obviously used with dandruff clearly stuck to it. The cockroach was obviously authentic and could be readily identified by all the children; it was used since pilot work suggested that contact with insects such as flies and grasshoppers may not be sufficient to affect Australian adults' judgements about contamination.

The experimenter asked the questions before and after she removed the object from the milk and placed it out of sight. The questions before removal of the object were: "Would the child get sick if she (or he) drank some of the milk with an (x) in it?" If yes, "A little or a lot?" The next question was, "Would you want to drink milk that had an (x) in it if a grown-up told you that you could?" The questions after the object was removed were: "Would the child get sick if she (or he) drank some of the milk now that the (x) had been taken out?" If yes, "A little or a lot?" Next question: "Would you want to drink milk that had an (x) taken out of it if a grown-up told you that you could?"

The responses in the contagion phase of Experiment 1 are shown in Table 3.1. The children often accepted the explanation that colds can be transmitted by proximity and rejected an immanent justice explanation. For all groups, correct answers for both types of explanations for colds were above a chance level. In the case of toothaches, the responses of the preschoolers and first graders did not exceed chance. In these two age groups, the knowledge that toothaches are not transmitted through proximity was correlated significantly with their rejection of immanent justice as a causal factor. As Kister and Patterson (1980) observed, a belief in immanent justice explanations may be associated with the absence of knowledge about contagion.

In the contamination phase of the study, the children demonstrated expertise (see Table 3.2): 39 out of 40 preschoolers said that they would not drink milk with a cockroach inside and 34 said they would not drink even when the cockroach was removed. Most children claimed that to drink milk with a dirty comb inside or removed would make the child either a little or a lot sick. The majority would not drink the milk themselves in either of these two circumstances. It seemed, although further study is needed to investigate this possibility, that some of the few children who said that they would drink the milk that had been in contact with a cockroach or dirty comb intended to shock the

TABLE 3.1

Children Responding Correctly in the Contagion Phase of Experiment 1 on Conceptions of the Causes of Illness

| Group | Cold | | | | Toothache | | | |
| | Proximity | | Immanent justice | | Proximity | | Immanent justice | |
	No.	%	No.	%	No.	%	No.	%
Preschoolers								
Puppet right or wrong?	33	83	29	73	22	55	23	58
Can children catch it that way?	37	93	29	73	21	53	25	63
Grade 1								
Puppet right or wrong?	33	83	29	73	23	58	24	60
Can children catch it that way?	38	95	30	75	23	58	21	53
Grade 3								
Puppet right or wrong?	40	100	38	95	37	93	37	93
Can children catch it that way?	38	95	36	90	38	95	38	95

NOTE: From Siegal (1988a). $N = 40$.

TABLE 3.2

Responses of the Children in the Contamination Phase of Experiment 1 on Conceptions of the Causes of Illness

| | Cockroach | | Comb | | Spoon | |
	In	Out	In	Out	In	Out
Preschoolers						
Not sick	4	7	12	17	20	29
A little sick	2	5	9	7	7	6
A lot sick	34	28	19	16	13	5
Not drink yourself	39	34	33	24	27	15
Grade 1						
Not sick	0	1	6	15	30	32
A little sick	6	12	18	14	6	7
A lot sick	34	24	16	11	4	1
Not drink yourself	39	37	37	32	20	8
Grade 3						
Not sick	1	2	6	7	39	39
A little sick	13	18	22	27	1	1
A lot sick	26	20	12	6	0	0
Not drink yourself	39	38	37	33	6	1

NOTE: From Siegal (1988a). $N = 40$.

experimenter. Surprisingly, 13 out of 40 preschoolers claimed that a child who drank milk with the spoon inside would become very sick. Many of these spontaneously volunteered that they would be afraid of swallowing the spoon! With the spoon removed, the number decreased to five.

Altogether, the children in our sample had a substantial knowledge of contagion and contamination as causes of illness. I carried out two additional experiments to determine whether they can distinguish between explanations for contagious ailments and accidents and to re-examine responses to milk in contact with a spoon. According to Kister and Patterson (1980), if physical contact is salient, young children are likely to infer a causal relationship between any two contiguous events and may fail to distinguish between contagious and non-contagious ailments and those caused by accidents. Therefore, in a second experiment, preschoolers were asked to evaluate a child's explanation for a scraped knee and for contiguous events that could not have been causally related.

The participants in Experiment 2 were 12 boys and 12 girls with a mean age of 4 years 11 months (range, 4.6 to 5.6). They were presented in a randomised order with three stories about a child who had a scraped knee. In one story, the central figure incorrectly gave a contagious response and in a second, a correct non-contagious response. The third story acted as a control; it was used to test Kister and Patterson's assertion that young children infer causality in events that covary. The experimenter told the children, "Here are stories about some other children. I want you to tell me whether they were pretending or giving the right answer." To guard against order effects in which children might repeat back the last thing said to them without considering both response alternatives, the order of the premises was reversed for half the children. (Was he just pretending or could this be the right answer?). The actual gender of the story characters was the same as the boys and girls questioned. The male versions of the stories were:

1. A boy named Fred who was about your age had a scraped knee. A grown-up asked Fred how he got his scraped knee. Fred said he got it from sitting next to another boy with a scraped knee. Could this be the right answer or was he just pretending? (Contagious response—pretending.)

2. A boy named Bill who was about your age had a scraped knee. A grown-up asked Bill how he got his scraped knee. Bill said he got it from falling off a swing on to a sharp rock. Could this be the right answer or was he just pretending? (Non-contagious response—right answer.)

3. A boy named John who was about your age had a shirt with spots of wet purple paint. A grown-up asked John how he got spots of paint on his shirt. John said he got it from falling off a swing on to a sharp rock. Could this be the right answer or was he just pretending? (Control story.)

Of the 24 children, 22 judged correctly that the child who claimed he received the scraped knee through sitting next to another child with a scraped knee was pretending; and 19 felt that the child who said the scraped knee was caused by falling off a swing on a sharp rock could have been telling the right answer. Of the five other children who claimed that the child was pretending, only one was incorrect on either of the two other stories. Almost all of the children (22 out of 24) attributed pretending to a child who claimed that the wet paint was due to falling on a sharp rock.

These responses were all above a chance level. At least in the case of a scraped knee, children do not ordinarily generalise their concept of contagion to include accidents. Contact alone does not guarantee an explanation involving contagion. Further, similar to Shultz's (1982b) results, young children do not regard a temporal concurrence of events to necessitate causation.

Experiment 3 examined preschoolers' understanding of contamination in the spoon and milk situation of the first experiment. I expected that, if the cleanliness of the spoon was clarified, they would be likely to indicate that there would be no ill-health effects from drinking the milk. The participants were 10 boys and 10 girls with a mean age of 4 years 10 months (range = 4.6 to 5.6). They saw an experimenter wash a spoon and then say, "This is a very clean spoon. It has just been washed in hot water with soap suds, rinsed with clean water, and dried. Suppose that the spoon fell in the milk that a little boy (or girl) about your age was about to drink." The remainder of the procedure was similar to the contamination phase of Experiment 1. The children were asked questions before and after the spoon was said to have been removed by a grown-up. The questions before were "Would the child get sick if he (or she) drank some of the milk which had a spoon in it being careful not to drink the spoon? A little or a lot? Would you want to drink milk that had a spoon in it if a grown-up told you that you could?" Then the children were told, "Suppose the spoon were taken out. Would the child get sick if he (or she) drank some of the milk now that the spoon had been taken out? A little or a lot? Would you want to drink milk that had a spoon taken out of it if a grown-up told you that you could?"

With the spoon inside, 17 of the 20 children indicated that the child would not get sick by drinking the milk, 3 said that the child would be a little sick, and only 5 said that they would not drink the milk themselves. With the spoon removed, the comparable numbers were 18, 2, and 5. These results were clearly superior to those in Experiment 1, although responses were not unanimous. A small number of children may have been overly careful, and it remains to be determined whether some may have been mindful of possible allergies or reactions to milk.

The results of the three experiments are limited to a knowledge of contagion and contamination as causes of illness. Some ailments such as toothaches may have an internal or maturational basis, and research is required to probe children's understanding of internal body functions and their consequences (Eiser, 1985). Further, although the children in the studies often responded correctly, a minority did not; individual differences in knowledge about health-related matters merit additional attention.

Bearing these considerations in mind, children's knowledge of contagion and contamination has been underestimated in previous studies. Contrary to Bibace and Walsh (1981) and Kister and Patterson (1980), many preschoolers can identify contagion and dismiss immanent justice as an explanation for colds. They can understand that a scraped knee is a non-contagious ailment. At least in Western societies, immanent justice may be a factor in explanations for ailments such as toothaches only if the illness is not easily within personal experience and another explanation is not salient. Conversely, children without having experience or been provided with explanations for illnesses such as AIDS may draw the conclusion that these are caught in the same way as a common cold (Au & Romo, 1996).

The possibility is left open that even younger children would have some capacity to display a knowledge of the consequences of ingesting contaminants. In one further experiment (Siegal & Share, 1990, Experiment 1), we sought to test the hypothesis that 3-year-olds are sensitive to the invisible nature of contamination in a naturally occurring context and, accordingly, can make evaluations and inferences for others' false responses and choices about contamination. The participants were 48 children with a mean age of 43 months and range of 36 to 47 months. The experimenter spent about a week in the children's day care centres prior to testing in order to become acquainted with them. The experiment consisted of three phases in which the children were seen individually. Within each phase, the orders of the stories, questions and alternatives were counterbalanced. The actual names of the story characters were the same sex as the children.

In the first phase on contamination labelling, the experimenter told the children in the course of natural conversation during their snack time, "Here's some juice. Oh! It has a cockroach in it." The cockroach (*Periplaneta americana*) floated to the top. The experimenter removed it from sight without a trace and asked, "Is the juice OK or not OK to drink?"

In the second phase, the experimenter gave the children two stories and asked them to evaluate the responses of others. Story A was: "A grown-up poured juice into a glass with a cockroach in it. The cockroach floated on top and then the grown-up threw it away. He asked John, a boy your age, whether the juice would be OK to drink or whether it would make him sick? John said that the juice would be OK to drink. Was John right? Would it make him sick?" Responses to the last question were used as the evaluation measure. Story B was the same except that a child said the juice would make him sick.

In the third phase on inferences for others' false choices, the children were shown two glasses and told, "Here is some chocolate milk and here is some water. A cockroach fell into the chocolate milk. It floated on top. A grown-up pulled it out and threw it away. A boy named Jim came along to ask for a glass of chocolate milk which was his favourite drink. Jim didn't know the cockroach had fallen in. Which glass did Jim want? Which glass should the grown-up give him?" The experimenter displayed two signs and continued, "Jim wanted to tell other children that one of the two drinks would make them sick. He had two signs: 'happy face' and 'sad face'. Which one should he choose to tell the children? You take the 'sad face' and put in front of that drink to tell them not to drink it." To establish the stability of contamination labelling, about two weeks later, a different experimenter who was unaware of the initial responses re-enacted the first phase using a different drink.

Table 3.3 shows that performance in all phases was above a chance level. Contrary to the notion that young children lack the capacity to comprehend the nature of contamination, 77% consistently responded that the juice was not good, 83% correctly evaluated the responses of other children to the incident in both stories, 67% correctly inferred that, while a child may want a chocolate drink, he or she should be given an alternative, and 75% chose a "sad face" without prompting as a warning against the drink. In all phases, the ages of the children were not correlated with the responses.

Although Rozin et al. (1985) have maintained that young children do not readily understand the invisible nature of contamination, most preschoolers in our Australian research were unwilling to pronounce an apparently safe glass of milk as harmless after a foreign substance had been removed. Part of this

TABLE 3.3
Children Responding Correctly in the Experiment on Contamination Sensitivity
in 3-year-olds

	%	No.
Labelling		
Responding on the first test that the juice is not good to drink despite appearance (removal of cockroach)	85	41
Responding on the second test that the juice is not good to drink despite appearance	85	41
Consistent on both tests	83	40
Consistent in indicating that the juice is not good	77	37
Evaluations		
"No" to a child's response: (A) the juice is OK	88	42
"Yes" to response: (B) the juice would cause sickness	90	43
"No" to response A, "yes" to B	83	40
Inferences		
Child wants chocolate drink	77	37
Child should be given another drink	83	40
Responding both that a child wants a chocolate drink but should be given an alternative drink	67	32
Choosing "sad face" without prompting and correct use of sign to warn others	75	36

NOTE: From Siegal and Share (1990), Experiment 1. $N = 48$.

discrepancy may be due to the different methods and foreign substances employed by Rozin and his colleagues in their American studies and to the comparatively ubiquitous nature of insects, and especially cockroaches, in the Australian environment.

Nevertheless, results that support children's ability to grasp the mechanisms underlying contamination have now been reported in several American studies. In these studies that have employed a methodology which has avoided direct, prolonged questioning, efforts have been made to determine whether young children's responses to contamination merely reflect what they have been told by adults or indicate an understanding of invisible germ particles that act as a mechanism that causes illness. Thus in research designed to identify what preschoolers understand about germs, children as young as 3 years have been shown to often understand that particles of a substance such as sugar continue to exist in liquid even when these are invisible to the eye (Au, Sidle, & Rollins, 1993). The work of Rosen and Rozin (1993) further suggests that young children (69% of their sample of 3-year-olds and 100% of their sample of 4- and 5-year-olds in Philadelphia) understand that substances such as soap suds are inedible and retain their dangerous properties even when invisible in water. Similarly, Kalish (1996, Study 3) asked 3-year-olds to choose which of two food items would make a story character sick when considering a food that looked harmless but was actually contaminated in contrast to a food that appeared contaminated but was actually harmless. Only 1 child of the 12 in his experimental condition was able to link germs with illness explicitly by saying "germs make you sick" in response to the question, "What is a germ?" However, at a level that far exceeded what would be expected by chance, the children were able to identify the apparently clean item as the food that would cause illness.

Although such results suggest that even some 3-year-olds have a tacit knowledge of germs as invisible illness-causing mechanisms, the results of other studies give rise to caution. For example, to test whether children's understanding of contamination is restricted to the material contact of a substance to a noxious stimulus, Springer and Belk (1994) presented two groups of children aged 3–4 years and 7–8 years with three stories. In the first story, which concerned material contact, the children were told:

> There was a little boy who had a glass of juice in front of him that he wanted to drink. A bug flew into the room and fell right into the juice. The little boy took the bug out of the juice, and the juice looked okay. So the little boy drank the juice. Do you think the little boy would get sick from drinking the juice?

The second story concerned the proximity of a substance to a noxious stimulus (in which a bug was said to be present but not to have touched a glass of juice) and the third in which the noxious substance was not present but was said to be only mentioned aloud by a story character while looking at the juice (termed the "nominal story").

Whereas virtually all children in both age groups affirmed that the little boy would get sick from drinking the juice in the material contact story, a few 3- and 4-year-olds also said that illness would result in one of the other two conditions. Springer and Belk point out that the responses of the 3- and 4-year-olds could be interpreted in terms of a conservative, adaptive strategy by preschoolers or in terms of a response that interprets the sickness question to refer to the disgust of an association of food with noxious substances rather than mere physical illness.

Only further research can sort out the degree to which preschoolers have the capacity to understand that germs are invisible, animate particles that could influence health through material contact. A next step to take following the Springer and Belk study would be to have preschoolers evaluate the conflicting responses of two children in the associational contamination and nominal stories to determine whether the children's conservative judgements in response to single stories creates a bias that masks a knowledge that contamination can only create illness through material contact.

Children cannot be credited with a full-blown understanding in this domain and the research does not yet show conclusively that the sensitivity of 3- and 4-year-olds to contamination forms the basis for an early microscopic theory of illness. Even so, the findings of studies to date converge to support the adaptive-evolutionary view that children are constrained towards learning about causal processes that result in contamination. Since to obtain nutrients is an activity that is a prerequisite for fitness and survival, children are likely to possess an implicit knowledge of contagion and contamination that can be drawn out with preventive health instruction from parents and caregivers. My proposal is compatible with the position that young children are equipped with a skeletal implicit knowledge of abstract concepts such as causality. In specific domains of knowledge such as the domain of food and contamination, this knowledge may be brought to the surface should experimenters attend to using child-friendly techniques that consist of questions that abide by the rules of conversation and convey elements of sincerity, non-redundancy, relevance, and clarity.

Children's understanding of contagion and contamination has implications for education but not necessarily in the manner envisaged by the followers of Piaget. Bibace and Walsh (1981) claimed that instruction about health should be matched to the children's stage of development because they do not have the cognitive prerequisites to benefit from causal knowledge. Our studies contradict this account and suggest that knowledge of the causes of illness is within the grasp of young children. Moreover, even preschoolers have an implicit theory of child care and advocate reasoning as a form of intervention against physical harm (see Chapter Seven). Therefore, they should be receptive to methods of verbal instruction, possibly through the use of picture books that graphically illustrate the causes of illness (Berger, 1985).

Rather than maintaining that instruction about health and illness is most likely to be successful where information is "matched" to the particular concerns shown by children in a Piagetian stage when they do not understand causality, children's early causal knowledge may be used as a basis for preventive health education. Adults' appreciation of what children can or do know about contagion and contamination should promote communication with children on health matters. My hope is that this possibility will draw recognition to an area which cries out for attention. As Kleinman (1986, p. 226) has pointed out, psychology and related disciplines have been neglected in primary medical care despite the "epidemiological reality" that over 50% of clinical practice deals with the psychological and social aspects of illness. Here is a solid application of developmental psychology to health education and prevention.

4 Representing Objects and Viewpoints

SEEING AND KNOWING

Piaget used the term "egocentrism" more broadly than to describe the ability of children who do not conserve. His claim was that egocentrism permeates young children's thinking and is a severe, general limitation on their knowledge of the world. He contended that they rely purely on the perceptual point of view when judging the visual perspectives of others and that they are not capable of understanding how another's viewpoint differs from their own. According to Piaget and Inhelder (1956, p. 209) in *The Child's Conception of Space*, children's understanding of the physical world is "at first completely egocentric", and it is the same egocentric orientation that prevents them from understanding others' perspectives, interests, intentions, and feelings.

In the 40 years since Piaget and Inhelder's book appeared, a great variety of tasks have been used to measure the ability to represent objects and viewpoints in taking the perspective of others. Children have been shown displays of pictures, toys, or blocks and asked to match photographs to the perspectives of different observers around a table. They have also been required to report on the percepts of an observer wearing sunglasses tinted a different colour than those worn by the children themselves (for reviews of these tasks, see Ford, 1979, 1985 and Waters and Tinsley, 1985). However, the most prominent of all perspective-taking measures has been the "three-mountains" task.

In the description supplied by Piaget and Inhelder (1956, pp. 210–211), this task consists of a pasteboard model, 1m square at the base and 12–30 cm high (see Fig. 4.1). When seated in front of the model at the initial position (A), children view a small green mountain with a little house at the summit, a higher brown mountain topped with a red cross slightly to the rear of the green one, and the highest mountain which is grey with a snow peak. By pointing to photographs, for example, they can indicate what an observer views from different perspectives on the model (B, C, and D). Piaget and Inhelder (1956, p. 213) proposed that, on this type of task, children under 7 years are confined to reproducing their own point of view, "When a number of objects are involved, as in the case of the group of mountains, it is found that the child fails to realise that different observers will enjoy different perspectives and seems to regard his own point of view as the only one."

One of the simplest and most elegant re-examinations of children's perspective-taking was carried out by Borke (1975). Children aged 3 and 4 years were shown objects on a rectangular turntable, including a replica of the three-mountains task and a display consisting of a small lake with a toy sailboat, a miniature horse and cow, and a model of the house. They were introduced to Grover, a *Sesame Street* character, and told, "Grover is going to play this game with us. He will drive his car along the road. Sometimes Grover likes to stop and

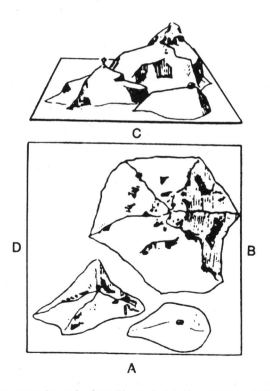

FIG. 4.1 The three-mountains task (from Piaget & Inhelder, 1956, p. 211).

look out of his car . . . When Grover stops to look out of his car, I want you to turn the scene that moves so you are looking at it the same way Grover is." On test situations, Grover was parked at each of the three sides which presented a view different from the child's. The task was to turn the display to match Grover's perception.

The children in Borke's experiment were able to answer questions about others' visual perception of objects. The majority could perform successfully on all the displays, except for 3-year-olds on the three-mountains task. Borke's results would seem to be inconsistent with Piaget and Inhelder's contention that young children are incapable of taking others' viewpoints. Her interpretation was that toy figures can be discriminated more easily than the configurations of the three mountains.

Nevertheless, Borke's findings have apparently been contradicted in subsequent studies. For example, Liben (1978) asked 3- and 4-year-olds to report on percepts of coloured blocks as seen by the self and an experimenter. Rather than rotating a turntable to represent the display, they were required to point to a card that "shows the way the blocks look". The children had substantial difficulty with this task. Liben explained her results in terms of a distinction between two developmental levels of knowledge about visual perception put forward by Flavell, Everett, Croft, and Flavell (1981) that build upon Piaget and Inhelder's proposal. At a "Level 1", young children may infer that another's viewpoint does not coincide with their own although they egocentrically do not recognise how these viewpoints are different. At a "Level 2", not only do children know that others have different viewpoints of simultaneously visible objects but they can now indicate how these viewpoints differ.

As evidence, Flavell and his co-workers requested 3-year-olds to report the appearance of an object visible to the self and experimenter in upside-down and right-side-up perspectives. For example, the children were shown a horizontally placed picture of a worm lying between a red blanket and a blue blanket. They were asked to say how the worm appeared to the experimenter, who was seated opposite, i.e. if it was lying on the red or the blue blanket. Three-year-olds did not show clear evidence of Level 2 understanding in this study.

Building on this pattern of results, Flavell and his colleagues have arrived at the position noted at the end of Chapter Two that young children have little or no understanding of the distinction between appearance and reality (Flavell, 1993; Flavell et al., 1983; Flavell, Green, & Flavell, 1986). This position has been influential in some accounts of how children come to represent the mental and physical world (e.g. Perner, 1991, pp. 94–96). According to Flavell, 3-year-olds are limited in their ability to distinguish between the true nature of a substance and its appearance under, for example, coloured filters or masks and costumes.

For example, in the first of a very extensive series of experiments in Stanford, California (Flavell et al., 1986), 24 children with a mean age of 3 years 8 months (range = 3.3 to 4.0) were given familiar or "easy" appearance–reality tasks. In one appearance–reality (AR) task, milk was shown in a glass with a red filter wrapped around it. The children were asked, "What colour is the milk really and truly? Is it really and truly red or really and truly white? Now here is the second question. When you look at the milk with your eyes right now, does it look white or does it look red?" Care was taken to randomise the order of the alternatives presented so that, again, the children's responses could not simply be a matter of repeating back the last alternative.

Of the 24 children, only 11 correctly identified the milk to look red but to be white really and truly. Similarly, in a second study, an experimenter questioned 3-year-olds on numerous tasks including one in which an adult female is seen to put on a disguise as a bear. The children were asked, "When you look at her with your eyes right now, does she look like Ellie or does she look like (for example) a bear? Here is a different question. Who is over there really and truly? Is she really and truly Ellie or is she really and truly a bear?" Only 52% (a chance level) of responses on the disguise tasks were correct. Two types of error were equally common on this task: saying that the adult both looked like and truly was a bear (a phenomenism error), or that she looked like and truly was Ellie (a realism error).

Keil (1989) has incisively pointed out that children's difficulties on appearance–reality tasks may not reflect their intrinsic inability to deal simultaneously with two representations in general but rather their lack of knowledge about how to deal with the apparent contradiction between the two. He remarks that "even adults find some contradictions unfathomable because they lack an explanation" (p. 249). Of course, at least with regard to conversationally inexperienced young children, a major part of the difficulty might not be in their ability to reason about their everyday encounters with reality and the phenomenal world of appearances but with questions about such contradictions. If so, phenomenism (reporting appearance when asked for reality) and realism (reporting reality when asked for appearance) might indicate that some children may misinterpret the experimenter's purpose to test whether they understand the distinction between appearance and reality. Should they applaud the effectiveness of a disguise, they may give phenomenism answers and report on the appearance of an object when asked for reality. Should they perceive the disguise to be ineffective, they may give "realism" answers to both questions.

We have reported evidence that children often understand the distinction between appearance and reality with respect to common liquids and are able to make inferences and attributions for the false beliefs and answers of others. In these three experiments, we aimed to allow the children to respond in an atmosphere guided by conversational rules.

In our Experiment 1 (Siegal, Share, & Robinson, 1989), the participants were 48 3-year-olds (range 35–47 months, mean age 42 months) seen in individual sessions. Following the procedures used in the previous Flavell studies, all children initially received pretests for language and memory to ensure that the terms used by the experimenter were understood. The testing itself consisted of three phases:

1. *Labelling.* This AR task was the milk-colour labelling problem used by Flavell et al. (1986, Study One) as part of a series of 24 measures. An experimenter showed the children a clear glass of milk. She poured the contents into a blue-filtered glass so that only a blue liquid was visible and asked, "What colour is the milk really? Is it truly white or truly blue?" (Reality question.)" When you look with your eyes right now, what colour is the milk? Does it look white or look blue?" (Appearance question.)

2. *Inferences.* In this phase, the children were asked to make inferences based on the false phenomenist beliefs of a friend who did not share AR information. They were shown two glasses and told: "Here is some milk in a blue glass. It looks like juice but it is truly milk. Here is some cream in a clear glass. It looks like milk but isn't really. If a friend came along to ask you for a glass of milk, which one would you give her?" (Reality question.) "Which one would the friend think was milk?" (Appearance question.)

3. *Causal attributions.* Half the children responded to the story: "A grown-up poured milk into a blue glass with a blue lid on top. She asked Sally, a girl your age, what colour the milk was truly. Sally said the milk was truly blue. Did she say that because she really and truly thought that the milk was blue or was she pretending?" The other half responded to a story that was the same except that a girl said the milk was truly white. The actual names of the story characters in the experiment were the same sex as the children.

To control for order effects, the three phases were counterbalanced across children in the six possible orders. As well, the orders of the questions and alternatives were counterbalanced within each phase.

As shown in Table 4.1, the numbers of those who answered both AR questions correctly in the labelling and inference phases were above what would be expected by chance alone. There were no significant order effects. All children attributed pretending to the response that milk in a blue glass is blue in reality and a true belief to the response that the milk is white.

In Experiment 2, responses on a single AR task were compared with those on multiple tasks under a prolonged form of questioning that children are liable to perceive as contravening the conversational rules to be non-redundant, sincere, relevant, and informative. Forty-eight children were assigned to one of two conditions. In a single task condition, half (range 38–46 months, mean age 43 months) were given the milk-colour labelling task as in Experiment 1. In a multiple task condition, the remainder (range 39–47 months, mean age 43 months) responded to AR questions on four groups of four labelling tasks; here

TABLE 4.1

Responses to the Appearance and Reality Questions in the Labelling and Inference Phases of Experiment 1

	Labelling		Inferences	
	%	No.	%	No.
Correct on both	85	41	71	34
Appearance answers to both questions (phenomenism)	8	4	10	5
Reality answers to both questions (realism)	4	2	15	7
Incorrect on both	2	1	4	2

NOTE: From Siegal, Share, and Robinson (1989). $N = 48$.

the milk-colour task always followed at least one other. The presentation of the task groups was counterbalanced in the 24 possible orders.

As predicted (see Table 4.2), 18 out of 24 children answered both AR questions correctly on the milk-colour task in the single condition. Yet only 10 out of 24 were correct in the multiple condition; many responded that milk in a blue glass is blue in reality as well as appearance. Six of the children in the multiple condition received a colour AR task first (i.e. a pink kangaroo under a blue filter) and almost all (5 out of 6) were correct. Of the 18 who received the same task later, only 5 succeeded. There was a significant negative relationship between the ordinal position of the tasks and correct responses on both AR questions. In fact, when the AR tasks were presented in the last and next-to-last positions (in the 15th and 16th orders), no child was correct on both. Thus towards the end of a lengthy session of prolonged questioning, some children may be so muddled that they tend to gave incorrect answers to any question.

In further support of the position that unconventional questioning can impair communication, each child was asked at the conclusion of the session, "Would

TABLE 4.2

Responses on the Milk-colour AR Task in Experiment 2

	Single-task		Multiple-task (prolonged questioning)	
	%	No.	%	No.
Correct on both	75	18	42	10
Appearance answers to both questions (phenomenism)	25	6	42	10
Reality answers to both questions (realism)	0	0	13	3
Incorrect on both	0	0	4	1

NOTE: From Siegal, Share, and Robinson (1989). $N = 24$.

you like to stop now or go on?" Only two children in the single condition declined to proceed in contrast to ten in the multiple condition.

We devised a follow-up experiment (Siegal & Share, 1990, Experiment 2) to determine whether even younger children may have an implicit knowledge of the distinction between appearance and reality. Information about food such as its taste is conveyed through touch, and representational ability for tactile information is present in very early childhood (Flavell, Flavell, & Green, 1989; Gibson & Walker, 1984; see also the experiments on infants discussed in Chapter One). For this reason, 2-year-olds may be knowledgeable about appearance and reality in the case of food, especially in employing the early contamination sensitivity that was discussed in the previous chapter.

The 48 children in this experiment ranged in age from 30 to 42 months, with a mean age of 35 months. Six others were not included, five of whom were silent during questioning and one who indicated a dislike for jam or Vegemite (a pungent, popular Australian breakfast spread).

The children were first shown jars of Vegemite and jam and asked to say which one, if either, they liked to eat more. All but two preferred the Vegemite. They were then randomly assigned in equal numbers to one of two conditions. Owing to the more limited attention and memory of the 2-year-olds, the procedure only required children to label a slice of bread as edible or not. In the experimental condition (age range = 31–41 months, mean = 36 months), they were told as a matter of course during their snack time, "Here's some bread. Oh! it's mouldy." (This statement was delivered in a slightly surprised, non-frightening tone.) The mould did not possess more than a trace odour and, in pilot testing with adults and children, we determined that smell could not be used to detect the presence of concealed mould on bread containing Vegemite. Therefore the children could not have been guided in their responses by a persistent odour.

To half of the children, the experimenter said, "Is it OK or not OK to eat?" She spread Vegemite (or jam for the two children who preferred jam) over the entire surface of the bread and asked, "Now is the bread OK or not OK to eat?" Since, as noted in Chapter Two, repeated questioning may induce children to switch their responses on many cognitive tasks possibly by suggesting that their initial answer was incorrect, the other children were asked the question only once after the Vegemite had been spread.

In the control condition (age range = 30–42 months, mean = 33 months), the children were told as a matter of course during their snack time, "Here's some white bread." Again to half of the children, the experimenter said, "Is it OK or not OK to eat?" She spread Vegemite on the entire surface and asked all the children, "Now is the bread OK or not OK to eat?"

Children in the experimental condition rejected the mouldy bread with Vegemite at a level above what would be expected by chance. Of the 24 children, 20 (10 out of 12 in each of the single-question and repeated-question subgroups) rejected the bread when the mouldy portion had been concealed by Vegemite; 10 out of 12 consistently rejected the bread on both questionings. By contrast, out of the 24 children in the control condition, only 3 (1 in the single-question subgroup and 2 in the repeated-question subgroup) rejected the white bread with Vegemite that was free of mould; no child in this condition consistently rejected the bread on both questionings. Even those as young as 30 months were able to identify an apparently edible substance as not good to eat.

The results of our three experiments do not address the issue of processes by which children seek out AR distinctions. Outside familiar areas such as food, AR knowledge may be more fragile. In addition, the false belief questions in our Experiment 1 differed somewhat from those employed by others in previous research (see Perner, Leekam, & Wimmer, 1987, discussed in the next section).

Bearing these considerations in mind, many complications stand in the way of accepting the account of Piaget and the more recent variation offered by Flavell on the lack of appearance–reality knowledge in young children. In natural conversation, 3-year-olds overall demonstrated a clear understanding of the distinction between appearance and reality with regard to common foods and liquids. Not only could they indicate that a drink which looks blue in appearance is white in reality, but they were able to make inferences and attributions for others' false beliefs and answers. Even 2-year-olds may have an implicit understanding of the distinction between reality and the phenomenal world of appearances. The children's performance indicates more than a rote understanding, and provides further support for my position that they abstract concepts of the properties of objects.

Whereas these findings cast doubt upon the presence of a conceptual limitation that is rooted in phenomenism and realism, AR knowledge may not be explicitly disclosed in reaction to forms of questions that are liable to contravene the quantity and relevance rules. Such forms can involve a repeated or prolonged series of questions, or other cases where children perceive questions to have answers that are obvious, silly, pointless, or impossible to obtain.

In response to AR questions, children may answer incorrectly in evaluating the effectiveness of the experimenter's attempts at providing deceptive appearances. Especially during unconventional or prolonged questioning on AR colour tasks, they may be induced to say that an apparent deception is so good that it is real; hence, milk really and truly is blue when placed under a blue filter or, to take another example (Keil, 1989), a horse really and truly becomes a zebra when painted with black and white stripes and when taught it to eat and behave in a zebra-like way.

The unconventional nature of questioning on such tasks and the child's lack of experience with the purpose of these procedures renders this possibility a good one. A similar account can be given for a realism pattern on object identity tasks. For example, should 3-year-olds evaluate a sponge which apparently looks like a rock as a less than adequate facsimile, they could quite justifiably respond both that the object looks like a sponge and is a sponge in reality. Indeed, as shown in our Experiment 2, after having experienced prolonged questioning on AR tasks, many children if given the opportunity would choose not to proceed any further. This scenario is illustrated in Fig. 4.2.

The effects of prolonged or other forms of unconventional questioning on children's responses may also occur on AR training tasks as well as on perspective-taking measures. Although Flavell, Green, Wahl, and Flavell (1987) have reported that attempts to train children's AR knowledge are largely unsuccessful, many training tasks can also involve unconventional questioning. Training may be ineffective for that reason. In a recent study, Gauvain and Greene (1994) found increases with age in correct responses on AR tasks but also reported that 2-, 3-, and 4-year-olds were similar in their success in describing and differentiating the appearance and function of deceptively appearing objects in a show and tell task. In this sense, the children did not make substantial realism or phenomenism errors. Gauvain and Greene claim that younger preschoolers may be less motivated than older preschoolers to answer challenging adult requests such as in the case of AR questions.

How methods of questioning influence children's responses on measures related to AR knowledge is unclear and obviously requires further study. Nevertheless, by the age of 4 years, children certainly do have some capacity to represent different perspectives and viewpoints, and thus to display what Flavell has termed "Level 2" knowledge. Not only can children as young as 3 years of age often identify that someone else has a different perspective but at times they can indicate the nature of these different perspectives.

However, DeLoache (1987) has taken a novel direction in research that, she speculates, is supportive of Flavell's position that young children have little or no understanding of the distinction between appearance and reality. She has intriguingly argued that there is a sense in which children's ability to represent the locations of objects in space changes very rapidly and abruptly. In a first experiment, two groups of 16 children, the first with a mean age of 31 months and the other with a mean age of 38 months, were shown a furnished room and its scale model located in an adjoining room. An experimenter explicitly described the correspondence between the two toys to be hidden and the furniture that served as hiding places. The children were told that the larger toy was in the "same place" as the miniature toy that was concealed by the furniture of the scale model. They had four trials to retrieve the larger toy from the room. An impressive difference emerged between the two age groups. The older children could retrieve the object very well in the analogous location while few of the younger ones could do so. Yet both age groups could retrieve the miniature toy in the original scale model at the end of each trial, providing evidence that the younger children had not simply forgotten the original hiding place. In a second experiment, children with a mean age of 31 months could use a photograph to retrieve a toy successfully in the room but still could not use the scale model.

FIG. 4.2 A child giving an appearance answer when asked to report reality: An illustration of the possible context of "phenomenism" errors on an appearance–reality task that children perceive to be unattractive.

According to DeLoache, children under 3 years of age may not be able to maintain a dual orientation to a model, treating it only as an object rather than a symbol. Since the children's success at using a symbol to find an object changed so abruptly with age, she proposed a maturational explanation. Even so, there are at least three possible reservations to accepting this interpretation of a conceptual limitation with an allegedly maturational underpinning.

First, no attention was devoted to the usual child-care environment. Quite possibly, all of the older children were "veterans" in day care while the younger ones were newly enrolled. The quality and quantity of day care has an effect on children's understanding of persons and situations (see Chapter Six for a further discussion) and is associated with measures of perspective taking (Klemchuk, Bond, & Howell, 1990). As younger children are liable to lack extensive day-care experience, they may have been uncomfortable in following the instructions of a strange adult who continually referred to an unfamiliar type of model.

Second, even if this was not the case for some children, it may have been that the younger ones were mostly correct on the first trial and tired under repeated questioning. They may have been uncertain of the answer in the first place and induced to respond inconsistently, they may have perceived the experimenter's well-meaning repeated requests as insincere, or the task to be unattractive (Explanations One and Two in Chapter Two). Therefore, rapid changes in representing the model as a symbolic guide to locate objects may be seen as rapid changes in understanding departures from conversational rules.

Third, again with respect to possible violations of rules for communication, young children may not share the experimenter's meaning of the "same place". Once they entered the room, the miniature hiding place of the model was absent and the experimenter's instructions may have been seen as ambiguous and irrelevant. While the children's knowledge of "the same" was examined through (undefined) "independent comprehension checks", these may not have been sufficient to ensure that the children did understand the meaning.

Owing to the unprobed effects of children's understanding of conversational rules and their perceptions of tasks that require the representation of objects, the conclusions which can be drawn from research in this area remain uncertain. In more recent research (DeLoache, 1991; Marzolf & DeLoache, 1994), it has been shown that even children aged 2.5 years can often use a model that is dissimilar in scale to locate an object in a room if first provided with experience in viewing either a familiar symbol such as a picture to represent the object's location or a model that is highly similar in scale to the room (or cleverly "shrunken" to approximate the scale of the room) to be represented. The more familiar the model as a medium of representation and or more similar the model in dimensions, the easier the task as the room and model are seen as more alike. Insight into the use of symbolic relations through these familiar experiences may achieve a "symbolic sensitivity". This sensitivity involves an awareness of the experimenter's purpose in using pictures and models to demonstrate a correspondence between spatial relations. To answer questions on symbolic representation, children have to recognise the relevance and purpose of the information contained in pictures and models that are intended by experimenters to demonstrate a correspondence between spatial relations (Goswami, 1995; Suzuki, 1994; see also Zelazo & Reznick, 1991, p. 732).

Why then do preschoolers seem to have persistent difficulties on perspective-taking tasks? Based on a series of experiments with children aged 3 to 5 years, Newcombe and Huttenlocher (1992) report that preschoolers can identify the location of an object from the vantage point of a hypothetical observer. This task avoids a conflict between the actual frame of reference that the child uses to view an object and an imagined frame of reference. Thus children may be "egocentric" in the very limited sense that the self is habitually used as a landmark in coding information. This strategy usually serves children well in everyday life as it prompts them to remember object locations that can be lost through movement of the self as a reference point. However, the same strategy sometimes affects children's ability to suppress their own more salient viewpoint in favour of another. In reconciling the relevance of what they are shown to the question, they may be reluctant to consider a representation other than that provided by their own actual frame of reference.

A "THEORY OF MIND" IN THE CHILD?

Therefore, despite Piaget's notion of egocentrism, young children may after all have some knowledge of the properties of objects viewed from alternative perspectives. They understand that the visual perception of others often does not correspond with their own. In distinguishing between the real properties of objects and their phenomenal appearances, they may represent the location of concealed objects even if they may not actually employ this understanding in their responses to experimenters' questions. Yet proficiency in visual perspective-taking ability may not easily be generalised to understanding the mental states of others for it cannot be assumed that the requirements for perspective-taking are identical in the social and physical realms.

Glick (1978) and Shultz (1982a) point out that, although the differences between the physical world and the world of persons are not as clear-cut as they may seem, the behaviour of objects is often more stable than that of persons. The social behaviour of persons is only known probabilistically. Sustained interaction between persons is a key focus of social behaviour. Persons both create and react to external events and may be more sensitive to contexts than is the behaviour of objects.

Still, regardless of these apparent differences between social and physical or non-social cognition, young children have at times proved themselves adept at judging perspectives in social settings. Though adults often talk about concepts in children's minds, to claim that children have a "theory" or "theories of mind" presupposes that there is a valid theory that can be clearly defined. Yet what "mind" actually is remains an issue of ongoing controversy. In essence, experimental research subsumed under the rubric of "theory of mind" has dealt with two major questions: (1) Do children know that their beliefs may be different from the false beliefs of others? (2) Can children understand the nature of their own false beliefs?

Do Children Know That Their Beliefs May be Different from the False Beliefs of Others?

DeLoache (1987, 1991) and Flavell (1993) have linked their position that young children are severely impaired in their representational abilities to the extensive work has been carried out by Perner and his colleagues in England. For example, Perner et al. (1987, Study Two) saw 32 children with a mean age of 3 years 5 months (range 3.1 to 3.9). Each child, together with a friend, was taken to a room. The experimenter promised to show each individually what was in a box inside the room and told the friend to wait outside for a turn later. Inside the room with the door closed, the children saw a Smarties box. Even though they thought it contained Smarties candies, they saw that the box had a pencil in it. The children were asked a control question for memory, "Can you remember what's inside here?" (correct response: pencil), and two test questions: (1) "But what did you think was in here?" (correct response: Smarties) and (2) "What will (name of friend) think is in here?" (correct response: Smarties).

Although most were able to answer the first question that referred to one's own false belief, only about half on the second question were able correctly to attribute a false belief to the other child. Perner and his colleagues claimed that, while young children can engage in pretend play, only those older than 3 years consistently possess knowledge of the distinction between appearance and reality and can assign "conflicting truth value" in understanding how others may entertain false beliefs.

Yet there are several other possibilities that remain to be tested systematically. First, some children may have switched their response from question to question (pencil, Smarties, pencil) in an effort to accommodate their answers to the experimenter's sequence of questions. Second, some children may have interpreted the final test question to mean "After he (or she) sees it, what will (name of friend) think is in here?" After all, why would a grown-up ask this question unless the information will be shared with all children waiting their turns? In keeping with conversational rules, children may be assigning their own perception of relevance to questions on false beliefs.

Wellman and Bartsch (1988) have suggested a third possibility. They have argued that 3-year-olds often do understand how false beliefs lead to actions. Instead, the difficulty lies in the understanding of "explicit" false beliefs. For example, children can be asked to respond to stories in which a character explicitly desires to find an object which is really in one location, but the character believes that it is in another (wrong) location: "Jane wants to find her kitten. Jane's kitten is really in the playroom. Jane thinks her kitten is in the kitchen." When asked "Where will Jane look for her kitten?" many 3-year-olds answered, "In the playroom" instead of "In the kitchen."

In a fashion that is reminiscent of Piaget's (1970) emphasis on egocentrism, Wellman and Bartsch proposed that young children do not fully appreciate that desires can be unfulfilled owing to the location of identities in the external world. Though they can often determine how behaviour follows from beliefs, preschoolers weight desires over beliefs when these are in conflict. In support of this explanation, Wellman and Woolley (1990) have reported that, while 2-year-olds and young 3-year-olds fail false belief tasks, they succeed on tasks that involve predicting behaviour on the basis of desires and Wellman and Bartsch (1994) have reported that 2- and 3-year-olds talk more about desires than about beliefs.

Nevertheless, children's greater talk about desires (i.e. the satisfied or pleasurable states that would be obtained through achieving a goal) as compared with beliefs (i.e. the propositions which they and others have accepted) does not mean that they are without a knowledge of beliefs. Children may express their desires to others verbally because they wish others to meet these desires whereas they may have no similar need to express their beliefs. Instead, it may be that on the explicit false belief tasks used by Wellman and Bartsch, as on Perner et al.'s (1987) tasks, children assign their own perception of relevance to the test question. On such tasks, children are required to recognise that the purpose is to test whether they can detect how the beliefs held by others may be initially false. They are required to follow the implications of the language of test questions such as, "Where will a person (with the false belief) look for the object?" to mean "Where will the person look first?" However, children who are inexperienced in conversation may not recognise these implications and not display the depth of their understanding of mental states on false belief tasks. They may reinterpret the test question to mean, "Where will Jane have to look to find the cat?" and end up by answering this question rather than the one that the experimenter assumed to have asked. If so, the original test question may have amounted to a departure from the quantity rule in conversation to speak no less than is necessary for effective communication.

As Fodor (1992) notes, 3-year-olds may approach tests of their knowledge of beliefs with a "very simple theory of mind" which consists of this general heuristic: "Predict that the agent will act in a way that will satisfy his desires." In the child's early experience, reliance on this heuristic will often lead to success in their interactions with others and they will have no need to consider the falsity of beliefs. Nevertheless, according to Fodor, children are prompted to discard this heuristic when they realise the possibility that no unique behavioural prediction corresponds to desires. When the outcome of a desire is seen to be ambiguous, they are capable of using a second, more sophisticated heuristic, "Predict that the agent will act in a way that would satisfy his desires if his beliefs were true." The "selection processor" theory of mind model proposed by Leslie (1994) incorporates Fodor's observations. It identifies the child's assumption as shown in their pretend behaviour that the content of a belief normally reflects relevant current facts about behaviour. For example, even 2-year-olds know that two cups without liquid are both empty. But when they are told to pretend that both cups are full and then see one cup tipped over, they will say that the other cup contains the liquid even though both continue to be empty. In their pretence, children focus on the here and now, indicating that pretence is "opaque" in the present tense.

To enable children to consult their memory for information on the false contents of beliefs that may take place in the past or future, Leslie (1994) maintains that help is required in the form of specific questions and contexts. These aids permit the child to resist the "pre-potent" tendency to base their belief predictions upon a present state of affairs. Without such aids, the purpose may appear to be something more familiar and straightforward that resembles Fodor's first very simple theory of mind heuristic: to test whether children can predict the behaviour of others in achieving a goal. The question, "Where will Jane look for her kitten?" may simply be interpreted as "Where does Jane have to look (or go to look) for her kitten in order to find it?" rather than "Where will Jane look first for her kitten?", which is the conversational implication intended by the experimenter who has assumed that the child shares the purpose of the task. Once the question is explicitly formulated to dispense with the need to share the implication, children perform well.

Support for this position comes from the use of explicit questions on explicit false belief tasks. When asked questions such as "Where will Jane look first for her kitten?" Siegal and Beattie (1991, Experiment 2) found that 83% of preschoolers could often correctly predict the consequences of holding a false belief. Leslie (1994; Surian & Leslie, 1995) has replicated this result, reporting that 88% of 3-year-olds passed the "look first" question on such tasks. In both instances, children demonstrated that they understood the meaning of "first" and that they were not using a kind of "dumb strategy" in ignoring beliefs by simply interpreting "first" to mean that they should point to a different location than the one that would allow the story character to fulfil her desires. The children in Siegal and Beattie's research passed a "true belief–look first" task in which they were asked where a story character would look first for his pet when the believed location of the pet corresponded with the real location rather than an alternative one. Leslie reports that children respond correctly when asked to predict the first search strategy of a character who saw that an object had moved locations.

Though a similar pattern of findings has emerged from studies that have used a variety of questioning techniques to prompt a consideration of time and place in children's answers to questions about false beliefs (Freeman & Lacohée, 1995; Lewis & Osborne, 1990; Mitchell & Lacohée, 1991), the issue has recently been re-examined by Clements and Perner (1994). In their study, children aged between 2 years 5 months and 4 years 6 months were given a story about two mice. One of the mice put some cheese in a blue box to have later when he woke up from sleep. In the meantime, the other mouse found it. She picked up the cheese and put it a red box to have later for her tea. The children were told that the first mouse was about to wake up. They were asked to answer the question regarding the location of the cheese, "I wonder where he's going to look?" Then they were told, "(The mouse) wants to get the cheese" and asked a second time where the mouse will look. Half the children were asked, "Which box will he open?" and the other half "Which box will he open first?"

For reasons that were not given, responses to the first question were analysed only in terms of the direction of the children's gaze as recorded on videotape rather than in terms of their verbal answers. On this first measure, children above 2 years and 11 months responded correctly that the mouse would look in the blue box whereas, on the second question, fewer children at all ages—though more of the 4-year-olds—answered correctly that the mouse would look in the blue box, even when the word "first" was used in the question.

To explain this result, Clements and Perner invoke an interesting proposal from the work of Goldin-Meadow, Alibali, and Church (1993) that children in a "transitional" stage of cognitive development may display an initial grasp of the solution to a problem through gestures that do not match their incorrect verbal answers. These gesture–speech mismatches reflect a time in which children display uncertainty about their responses, and signal their readiness to learn (and provide a measure of what they can learn) with the guidance of a capable adult or peer (Vygotsky, 1978). In appealing to this model, Clements and Perner maintain that children have only an "implicit" representation of false belief and that they cannot yet explicitly make a verbal judgement of a situation that does not conform to reality.

Nevertheless, the discrepancy between initial gesture and subsequent response reported by Clements and Perner can also be explained in terms of conversational theory. In their task, unlike those used by Siegal and Beattie, the children were asked twice to indicate where the mouse would look. This procedure therefore involved repeated questioning in setting aside the Gricean quantity maxim to speak no more or no less than is necessary for effective communication. As noted in Chapter Two with regard to conservation experiments, having answered the first question correctly, preschoolers who are liable not to recognise the purpose of the experimenter's questions may have been prompted to change their answer on the second question to demonstrate what they perceived was the response that the experimenter was seeking. They may in effect be reasoning, "Why would (the experimenter) ask me again? She must want me to change my mind. I'll show her where the mouse has to look to find the cheese." Whereas the Clements and Perner study used a different type of story and form of questioning than that used by Siegal and Beattie and is not directly comparable, the effects of repeated questioning remain to be investigated for, on tasks similar to those used by Clements and Perner, most 3-year-olds answer correctly on a first trial but frequently err on a second trial (Siegal & Peterson, 1994, pp. 437–441).

Thus children who can predict the consequences of holding false beliefs may not reveal their knowledge because they do not share the purpose and relevance of the experimenter's questioning rather than because they weight desires over beliefs. Such results suggest that children's difficulty can be considered in terms of pragmatic factors as opposed to a conceptual limitation in which they cannot conceptualise how another's false belief can lead to an undesired outcome. Explicit questioning techniques that do not require children to follow the conversational implications of questions serve to appraise more accurately whether there is a conceptual limitation in their theory of mind. In this respect, there is a need to avoid complex question structures where the relevant critical information is lost in a remote subordinate clause. For example, the question "When Jane *first* goes to find her kitten, where will she look?" is less likely to succeed in eliciting children's correct responses on explicit false belief tasks than "Where will Jane look *first* for her kitten?" Nevertheless, very young children might still not be credited with a complete, adult-like understanding of mental states and display the same patterns of responses that are shown by adults who themselves do not always take into account the falsity of beliefs in considering behaviour (Mitchell, Robinson, Isaacs, & Nye, 1996).

Can Children Understand the Nature of Their Own False Beliefs?

Gopnik and Slaughter (1991; see also Gopnik, 1993), have taken Perner et al.'s views a step further in claiming that children are so preoccupied with their own current mental states that, not only do they lack an understanding of others' beliefs, but they have little insight into their own past beliefs. In a belief task devised by Gopnik and Slaughter, 3-year-olds were shown a closed crayon box. They initially reported to the experimenter that the box contained crayons. The experimenter then demonstrated that birthday candles were inside. The children scored no better than chance on the experimenter's questions, "When I first asked you, before I opened up the box, what did you think was in the box then? Did you think there were candles inside or crayons inside?"

But having just viewed the candles inside the box, children are likely to use this single piece of physical information (candles in the box) to answer rather complex "double-barrelled" questions about beliefs that require the simul-taneous consideration of two possible choices. In this sense, the task is similar to Newcombe and Huttenlocher's (1992) analysis of Piagetian perspective-taking problems as setting up a conflict between actual and imagined frames of reference. In reconciling the relevance of the context to the question, they may regard the introduction of the physical information placed before them as pivotal. After all, they might reason, why would an adult go to the trouble to create and disclose the information unless the implication was to use it in answering the test questions? In doing so, children would simply reinterpret the questions about beliefs as the straightforward question, "What do you think is inside the box?" The 3-year-olds would likely have answered more correctly had they received the single, short question, "What did you *first* think was in the box?" and care taken to ensure that they regarded each alternative as equally relevant.

Gopnik and Slaughter contrast responses on their belief task to those on a pretend task where 3-year-olds easily answered questions about pretending that a stick was first a spoon and then a magic wand, "When I first asked you, before we moved over here, what did you pretend the stick was then? Did you pretend it was a spoon or a wand?" However, from an early age, children recognise that pretending is detached from physical reality, unlike thinking that can be either detached or non-detached and continuous. They could not incorrectly re-interpret the questions about pretending to mean "What do you pretend the stick is?" because of their detachment from the two induced pretend states and because the experimenter had not highlighted physical information that could lead one of the pretend states to be construed as more relevant to the answer.

Similarly, in a series of studies carried out by Wimmer and Hartl (1991), most 3-year-olds who saw one unexpected physical object in a deceptive box task gave incorrect responses to the test question, "Listen, when in the beginning I took the box out of my bag and showed it to you, what did you think was in here?" However, when in a "change of state" task, the children were shown two pieces of physical information in which the expected contents (matches) were replaced by unexpected ones (sweets), most children answered the test question correctly possibly because either alternative could now be regarded as relevant.

Because false beliefs arise from a sequence of events, test questions often refer to the past or future. Yet young children do not easily recognise the purpose underlying questioning about false beliefs and their habit is to assume from previous conversational experience that questions refer to the present. Thus they may still have a strong inclination to reinterpret test questions in this fashion unless special efforts are taken to align their initial interpretation with that intended by the experimenter through simple, clear messages.

For example, Pratt and Bryant (1990) have shown that double-barrelled questions (e.g. "Do you know what is in the box or do you not know what is in the box?") used in tasks such as those devised by Gopnik and Slaughter are hard for children to comprehend and are prone to interruptions and responses before the experimenter poses the second alternative. A possibility that requires investigation is that children may assume that, because an experimenter has gone to the trouble of mentioning an alternative, it must be relevant and therefore worthy of choice. Yet even fairly advanced or cumbersome questioning forms may reveal an understanding of false beliefs if these are accompanied by a physical setting that is attractive and relevant. Mitchell and Lacohée (1991) gave 3-year-olds practice in "posting" a pictorial representation of their predictions of the contents of deceptive boxes. When the posting was relevant to the representation of their initial belief, most children responded to the test question, "When you posted your picture in the postbox, what did you think was in here (the deceptive box)?" by distinguishing false beliefs from reality. By contrast, when the posting procedure was irrelevant to their initial representation and thus irrelevant to the test question, most did not succeed. Mitchell and Lacohée interpret this result as demonstrating that children's understanding of beliefs is dependant on physical representations and that such understanding dissipates when beliefs are not accompanied by a physical counterpart. However, the relevant posting procedure may have also conveyed to the children the importance of using their initial representation to answer the test question, thus clarifying the relation of the temporal aspect of the question to their previous belief and enabling the children to answer correctly. If this is the case, their previous understanding of beliefs may endure even in the absence of a relevant physical representation. Yet it may not be disclosed in response to forms of questioning that appear to focus on the contents of a deceptive box.

As Pratt and Bryant (1990) point out, children act as if they understand their own beliefs as well as those of others. This observation is consistent with reports by Bretherton and Beeghly (1982) that 2-year-olds often talk about internal states in conversation with their mothers and by Woolley and Wellman (1990) that 3-year-olds spontaneously distinguish between the real and non-real properties of objects and actions. Of course such observations do not demonstrate that young children have an adult-like ability to understand the nature of beliefs and to distinguish between reality and appearance. Nevertheless, there is a striking discrepancy between these findings and the results of many theory of mind studies which require children to understand the purpose and implications of questions if they are to succeed.

This discrepancy is shown clearly in studies by Sullivan and Winner (1991, 1993) in which children's spontaneous comments contrasted with their answers to experimental test questions. For example, when asked to substitute unexpected contents such as string in a box of crayons or pencils in an "M & Ms" candy bag, children aged 3 to 3½ years frequently made comments such as "No one will know we put pencils in here!" But these same children often responded incorrectly to a series of probes: "What did you think was in the bag before we looked at it, pencils or M & Ms?" (Representational change question.) "When (name of a playmate who has not witnessed the change of contents) sees this bag all closed up will he know what's really in the bag, yes or no?" (Ignorance question.) "What will (name) think is in the bag, M & Ms or pencils?" On such "deceptive box" tasks, the oblique and wordy reference to the new contents might have confused the children. For instance, they could have jumped from the mention of "really" in the ignorance question to the thought that "There really are pencils in the bag and that the playmate will understand this information once it is shared", and interpreted the ignorance and false belief questions to mean, "What will the playmate see when he looks inside?"

REPRESENTATION RECONSIDERED

Whereas a number of investigators have claimed that the 3-year-old has a conceptual deficit in "knowing how" appearance and reality may be discrepant and in "knowing how" beliefs can lead to behaviour with undesired or mistaken outcomes, enough reservations in this controversial area persist to suggest otherwise. The problem may be rather one of "knowing when" to employ the knowledge about representing objects and viewpoints that already exists.

Even at an age of 18–20 months, children appear to appreciate the nature of mental states in their language acquisition and imitative behaviour. In acquiring words for objects, they are guided by a speaker's referential intent (Baldwin, 1993; Macnamara, 1982, 1986), and they infer the intentions of a human model by producing target acts that the model has failed to execute (Meltzoff, 1995). Moreover, children are non-egocentric in that they shift perspectives in early communication. For example, deaf children acquiring sign languages must learn a mirror-image transformation in order to use the signs for "you" and "me". According to Petitto (1986), these children do not first egocentrically sign "me" for "you" in confusing another's perspective for their own. The errors that are made derive from an overgeneralisation of abstract uses of language. For example, a child may sign "you" for "me", treating "you" as a pronoun with a stable referent, the self.

Nevertheless, although preschoolers can be credited with a substantial capacity for representing objects and viewpoints, a major difficulty in research on the ability to judge and remember mental states, perspectives, and behaviour must be acknowledged. Higgins (1981, p. 133) is one researcher who has alleged that many of these tasks do not actually require inferential skills. He has maintained that "judgements involve role-taking when there is an inference about a target's viewpoint (or response) under circumstances where the judge's own viewpoint is salient and different from the target's". The tasks used by researchers examining the development of perspective taking and a theory of mind do not necessary require children to inhibit or control their own responses in subjugating them to the viewpoints of others. In some "perspective-taking" situations, children attach labels to targets and no inference may be necessary. They judge thoughts, emotions, and feelings as if they themselves were in the situations and not someone else whose viewpoint actually differs. Nevertheless, as have been shown by recent studies that have focused on conversational influences in children's understanding, many children can interrelate and represent different points of view and the false beliefs of others. Thus, contrary to a Piagetian analysis in judging the perspectives of others, an increase with age in performance is probably due to accumulated social knowledge.

For example, Higgins, Feldman, and Ruble (1980) examined the ability of children and adults to predict the preferences of peers and non-peers with regard to snacks, meals, and activities. The responses of 4- to 5-year-olds were similar to those of 8- and 9-year-olds or adults. Preschoolers did not egocentrically choose their own preferences for peers and non-peers alike. However, the 4- and 5-year-olds were less accurate in specifying non-peers' preferences. Higgins and his colleagues suggest that the preschoolers lack "social category" knowledge about the category of persons whose preferences are to be predicted. They do not know enough about 8- and 9-year-olds or adults to answer questions; neither do they have a prototypical 8- or 9-year-old or grown-up to use as a reference point in making accurate predictions about activity preferences. The unreliability of children's responses on many role-taking tasks may simply be due to their unfamiliarity with a domain of knowledge rather than the absence of a capacity for understanding.

Although role-taking in the sense of Higgins' stringent definition is difficult to establish in children, the extent to which adults use this ability and control one's own viewpoint is also unclear. There is the story of a man who moans to an acquaintance, "My son was in a car accident last week and we don't know whether he'll ever recover." The acquaintance says, "That is terrible. But it could be worse." The man continues, "My daughter has cancer of the pancreas and doesn't have long to live." The acquaintance says, "That's terrible. But it could be worse." The man retorts, "What do you mean it could be worse?" The acquaintance replies, "It could happen to me!"

Many conversations between adults subtly take this form. While children may disguise their own viewpoints less frequently, they can often represent the perspectives of others. In this respect, they may not necessarily be disadvantaged when compared with adults.

5 Memory and Suggestibility

BREAKING THE MOULD: CHILDREN'S ABILITY TO ANSWER QUESTIONS ABOUT LIES AND MISTAKES

An important aspect of a theory of mind that follows from a consideration of conversational influences on children's responses concerns the critical distinction between a lie and mistake. Children's understanding of what it means to lie has significant implications for both their relationships with others and for their status in legal proceedings in determining whether they can accurately remember and report events. Correct responses on tasks devised to test their understanding would amount to a challenge to the position of Piaget (1932) who maintained that young children regard all false statements as lies and have little or no understanding of lying as deceptive statements intended to mislead others. Although by the age of 5 to 7 years, children are aware of a shade of difference between lies and mistakes in distinguishing between those statements that are intentionally false and those that are not, Piaget maintained that they often use the term "lie" to characterise both kinds of statement.

One example comes from Piaget's (1932, p. 141) report of an interview with a 7-year-old named Chap:

Interviewer: What is a lie?
Chap: What isn't true, what they say that they haven't done.
Interviewer: Guess how old I am.
Chap: Twenty.

Interviewer: No, I'm thirty. Was that a lie you told me?
Chap: I didn't do it on purpose.
Interviewer: I know. But is it a lie all the same, or not?
Chap: Yes, it is all the same, because I didn't say how old you really were.
Interviewer: Is it a lie?
Chap: Yes, because I didn't speak the truth.
Interviewer: Ought you to be punished?
Chap: No.
Interviewer: Was it naughty or not naughty?
Chap: Not so very naughty.
Interviewer: Why?
Chap: Because I spoke the truth afterwards!

On this basis, Piaget (1932, p. 141) claimed that young children "define a lie in a purely objective manner, as an affirmation that does not conform with fact". Yet in a manner similar to research on their knowledge of the distinction between appearance and reality and their understanding of false beliefs, young children may not share the scientific purpose for an experimenter's questioning about lies and mistakes. As Ekman (1985, p. 25) has pointed out, the *Oxford English Dictionary* states, "In modern use, the word [lie] is normally a violent expression of moral reprobation, which in polite conversation tends to be avoided." Should children's answers instead reflect their own local concerns, they might after all reason, why would an adult go to the trouble to raise the question of lying in a hypothetical protagonist's behaviour unless the implication was to use this information in answering the test questions? or "Why would a grown-up ask me about lying unless he thought that lying had occurred?" Indeed, for young children, the "objective" value of an outcome such as in the implication that a lie has been perpetrated may sometimes be so compelling that it outweighs considerations of intentionality in their moral judgements (Yuill, 1984). If so, preschoolers may be prepared to respond in a manner that seems to indicate that they regard all false statements as lies. Particularly in a setting in which the purpose and relevance of the questioning is not readily apparent, they may infer that an adult would not ask about lying unless he or she thought that lying had taken place and be prompted to reply that lying had indeed occurred.

This analysis serves to reinterpret the findings of Wimmer, Gruber, and Perner (1985) who examined the effects produced by the order in which the children were asked questions. They gave 4- and 5-year-olds stories in which a protagonist was said to have the intention of truthfully communicating information based on a false belief about the location of an object to a listener. Half the children who recognised that the character held a false belief were first asked a "lexical" question concerning the applicability of the term, "lie": "Did (name of speaker) lie to (name of listener) or did he not lie to him?" This question was followed by a "moral reward" question, "What would you give to (name of speaker), a gold star because he was nice to (name of listener) or a black point because he was nasty to him?" For the other half, the moral reward question was presented before the lexical one. Out of 29 children who first said in reply to the lexical question that the protagonist had lied, only 3 switched to evaluating his or her moral behaviour positively; however, 22 out of 34 switched from having first evaluated an actor's moral behaviour positively to saying in reply to the lexical question that the actor had lied. In fact, the suggestion of lying may have been so powerful that it undermined the viability of a mistake as the implicit alternative which was unstated in the lexical question, leading Wimmer et al.'s children to reverse their initial positive assessment of an actor's behaviour.

Similarly, in other research of Strichartz and Burton (1990), adults and children aged 3 to 11 years were required to answer a triple-barrelled test question, "Was (the central story character) telling the truth, something else, or a lie?" The younger children aged 3–5 often disregarded beliefs and intentions in judging all false statements as lies. However, even if the children could keep in mind three possibilities in the question, children who do not recognise that the purpose of the stories is to determine their knowledge about truth, lies, and mistakes may view the situation in terms of their own local concerns. They may regard the purpose as simply to determine whether a child's statement was correct and interpret the test question as simply, "Was (the character) right?"

Consistent with this view, Bussey (1992) presented children as young as 4 years with stories about characters who committed misdeeds and then either lied or told the truth about their actions. She found that 4-year-olds distinguished lies from truthful confessions at a level that was above chance, though they were less accurate and less confident of their judgements than were 7-year-olds, who scored almost perfectly. Although Bussey's results did not address the issue of children's ability to distinguish a mistake from a lie, this work suggests that young children are capable of comprehending stories about deception when motives and behaviours are straightforward and described in simple terms.

All of these studies point to the need for a fresh investigation. As shown in Chapter Three, young children possess an early sensitivity to food and contamination and a knowledge that substances that appear fresh may in reality be inedible. Therefore, Candida Peterson and I (Siegal & Peterson, 1996) examined the extent to which young children distinguish mistakes from lies in this domain where they were asked questions in the form, "Did the protagonist lie or make a mistake?" rather than "Did he (or she) lie?" or "Did he (or she) lie or not lie?" By providing "mistake" as an alternative to "lie", we sought to counter the strong moral connotation of the term "lie" that can be interpreted to imply that a questioner suspects that lying has occurred and enable children to indicate that a false statement was not morally reprehensible. Thus their understanding of the purpose of the questioning (i.e. to determine the basis for how a substance could be wrongly regarded as edible) would be facilitated. In contrast to previous research, our hypothesis was that, in the domain of food safety, they would be likely to recognise whether a false statement was a lie or a mistake.

Children aged 3 to 5 years were presented with two teddy bears: one who had seen that bread which appeared edible was in reality contaminated with mould and another bear who had not seen the contaminant (see Fig. 5.1). Both of the bears were described as having told an uninformed friend that the bread was OK to eat. When asked to identify a bear as lying or mistaken, many children of all ages responded correctly that the bear who had seen the mould lied and that the bear who had not seen the mould made a mistake. These findings were replicated in a second experiment in which children often recognised that the bear who told a lie had secret information that the mistaken bear lacked.

In a third experiment, we sought to determine the extent to which children's performance is specific to the domain of food and safety. Children aged 3 and 5 years were given problems in four conditions: (1) FS = food/safety, (2) FSI = food/safety-irrelevant, (3) FIS = food-irrelevant/safety, and (4) FISI = food-irrelevant/safety-irrelevant. In the FS condition, an experimenter showed each child individually a slice of mouldy bread and pointed to two teddy bears, one who was an onlooker and the other who had his back turned away. The experimenter said, "Here's a slice of mouldy bread. Is it OK or not OK to eat?" (All the children said that it was not OK, demonstrating that they understood the context of questions about food avoidance.) "Let's put some Vegemite over the mould so we can't see it." She then asked the child two questions: (1) "This bear didn't see the mould on the bread. He told a friend [at this point, the experimenter produced a stuffed animal toy] that it was OK to eat. Did the bear lie or make a mistake?" (2) "This bear did see the mould on the bread. He told a friend [at this point, the experimenter produced another stuffed animal toy] that it was OK to eat. Did the bear make a mistake or lie?" The orders of the questions and the

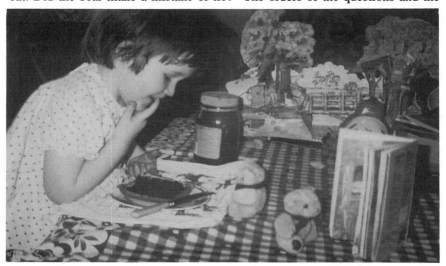

FIG. 5.1   A child in an experiment on the ability to distinguish mistakes from lies involving the two bears.

alternatives (mistake or lie) were alternated across the children in three other formats. The wording for the FSI, FIS, and FISI conditions was similar and involved bears incorrectly stating respectively that there was white bread in a bag when in reality there was brown bread, that it was safe to go into a cubbyhouse when in reality a snake was inside, and that a cubbyhouse was open when in reality it was locked. These conditions were judged on the basis of pilot work with parents and preschool teachers to be familiar to 3-year-olds.

Only in the FS condition was performance by 3-year-olds above the 25% correct performance that would be expected by chance; it significantly exceeded that in each of the other three conditions (see Fig. 5.2). In either age group, the children's answers were not significantly related to their own ratings of the familiarity and danger associated with the stimuli in the conditions. The responses in our Experiment 4 served to rule out the possibility that the children might have prejudged the naughtiness of the onlooker bear by evaluating him as naughtier even before he had been shown to have uttered a false statement. By comparison, in our Experiment 5, when repeatedly asked, "Was that a lie or not?" rather than "Was that a lie or mistake?" both bears were judged as having lied as has been reported in previous studies.

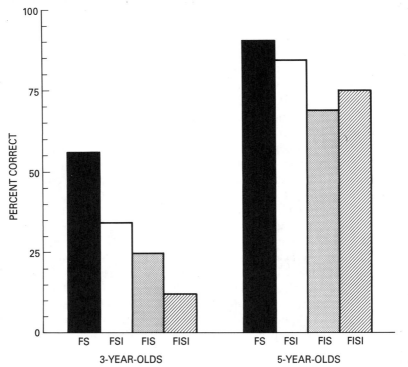

FIG. 5.2 Percentages of 3- and 5-year-olds correctly distinguishing mistakes from lies in conditions relevant to both food and safety (FS), food but not safety (FSI), safety but not food (FIS), and neither food nor safety (FISI) (from Siegal & Peterson, 1996).

Contrary to the Piagetian position, when offered the alternative "mistake", very few children regarded all false statements as lies in responding that both bears had lied. Rather, our research suggests that a rudimentary recognition of lies and mistakes occurs early in the domain of food and safety. The term "lie" in questioning conveys the implication that the speaker presupposes that lying is liable to have occurred. If not counteracted by a viable alternative such as "mistake", children who are inexperienced in the scientific purposes of conversation in experiments are likely to assent to this implication. They state that even the bear who had not seen the contaminant has lied although they have implicitly judged that this perpetrator lacks the knowledge to deceive deliberately and is not as naughty as the onlooker bear.

Additional research may show that problems relevant to food and safety may not invariantly serve to facilitate performance by means of highlighting the relevance of the task purpose and requirements. Nevertheless, in contrast to food-irrelevant danger stimuli such as snakes (Davey, 1995), a preparedness to adapt intelligent behaviour to food safety is in accord with examples from studies of animal learning as well as the rapid human avoidance learning from foods paired with nausea (Revusky & Garcia, 1970; Rozin, 1976a). In this regard, the disgust reaction that occurs from contact with contaminants merits attention as it may lie at the roots of early moral cognition. According to the "ethics of divinity" that predominates in many cultures, the self is seen as a spiritual entity that strives to attain purity and sanctity and to avoid pollution (Haidt, Koller, & Dias, 1993; Shweder, Mahapatra, & Miller, 1987). Even in early childhood, a perpetrator who enacts a deception that exposes individuals to contaminants and jeopardises their purity and sanctity is liable to be the recipient of moral condemnation.

Further research is needed to investigate the extent to which children transfer their understanding to other contexts, can distinguish between white lies and mistakes using terms that vary in their cultural appropriateness, and can match a reaction to a lie and mistake to an angry and neutral face respectively using techniques devised by Ekman (1985, 1994) and Izard (1993). In the latter instance, we have found that, when asked to choose between a neutral and disapproving face, preschoolers generally match a neutral face to represent the reaction of a witness to an honest mistake (Siegal & Peterson, in preparation). Thus mistakes are not regarded as simply "little lies" that, though not as naughty as straight lies, still merit disapproval. On the contrary, mistakes are viewed in an adult sense as escaping disapproval and meriting exoneration. In this connection, it is noteworthy that there are situations in which even some adults define exaggerations, guesses, and memory lapses as lies, which serves to discount the size of the gap envisioned by Piaget in the moral understanding of adults and children (Peterson, 1995; Peterson, Peterson, & Seeto, 1983).

CHILDREN'S TESTIMONY

What of the applied side to such research? For example, can children use their knowledge to provide accurate testimony? Piaget (1932, pp. 160–163) claimed that, although children do not actually lie in the sense of attempting to deceive others, they can make unreliable witnesses because they tend to distort reality and the truth in accordance with their desires. Yet this reassessment of children's ability to identify appearance and reality, the false beliefs of others, and lies and mistakes points to the need to re-examine the extent to which children's memories are vulnerable to false suggestions from others. If children often require conversational enrichment in certain knowledge domains to follow the purpose and relevance of experimenters' questions, they might also need such enrichment to enable them to gain an awareness of the information that is appropriate to report on questions about their memory for events and to ignore misleading information.

According to Gudjonsson (1986, p. 195), suggestibility can be defined as the extent to which persons "come to accept and subsequently incorporate post-event information" into their recollections of memory. In elaborating upon this definition, Ceci, Huffman, Smith, and Loftus (1994, p. 390) have drawn a distinction between "memory-based suggestibility" in which misleading information genuinely alters memory traces and "socially-based suggestibility" in which the contents of memory are "deferred" to children's beliefs about what the interviewer wants them to report.

In an extensive discussion of previous studies, Ceci and Bruck (1993, pp. 432–433) have criticised the position that a central or core action in a story or event that involves the child is likely to diminish or even eliminate suggestibility compared with actions that are peripheral (Goodman, Rudy, Bottoms, & Aman, 1990). They claim that many studies do demonstrate genuine "memory-based" suggestibility because children can be misled to provide false reports about critical events that they personally experience. Thus their failure on memory tests does not only reflect a difficulty in retrieving information (a retrieval deficiency) that has been stored in the original memory trace but a disruption of the original trace itself (a storage failure deficiency).

However, there can be a discrepancy between what adults and children find as central and peripheral issues (Johnson & Foley, 1984; Nelson, 1993a, 1993b). Even in experiments that deal with child abuse issues, children may retain original details which they do not disclose because of the conversational implications inherent in the format of questioning. These implications convey to children that to respond correctly in experimental settings requires the recognition of what is central to answering the experimenter's questions rather than what is central to the original story details. For example, preschoolers have been asked questions about the personally involving details concerning fictitious events such as, "Did he touch your private parts?" or "How many times did he spank you?" Yet they may answer such questions incorrectly, not because the fictitious events have been stored in their memories, but because the questions themselves imply that these events had taken place. A rationale is needed for children to comprehend the purpose of this line of questioning. Otherwise, those who are inexperienced in the scientific purpose of conversations within experimental settings might reason, "Why would a grown-up ask me these questions unless he thought that these events had happened?" It is notable that adults as well as children are not always completely in agreement as to what constitutes the central, personally involving features of child abuse and that, historically, legal definitions of child abuse have varied within and between cultures (Eekelaar, 1984; Wald, Carlsmith, Leiderman, & Smith, 1983). Even if children in a particular culture do understand that the purpose of question is to determine whether serious abuse had taken place, they may fail to report abuse or recant their story as the consequences of telling may appear to be worse than the consequences of further victimisation (Berliner & Barbieri, 1984).

As this discrepancy in perceptions of core and peripheral events can jeopardise the common grounding underlying conversations between children and adults who are seeking to determine what children remember, it has important consequences for what is reported as remembered. As Bartlett (1932, p. 213) vividly observed long ago:

> remembering is not the re-excitation of innumerable fixed, lifeless and fragmentary traces. It is an imaginative reconstruction, or construction, built out of the relation of our attitude towards a whole active mass of organized past reactions or experience, and to a little outstanding detail which commonly appears in image or in language form.

When adult or child listeners hear pieces of information that are semantically related, their comprehension and memory reflects a construction of ideas that depends on their knowledge and perception of their environment (Bransford, Barclay, & Franks, 1972; Bransford & Franks, 1971; Bruner, 1991; Nelson, Fivush, Hudson, & Lucariello, 1983).

Nevertheless, it has often been maintained without reference to children's conversational awareness and issues of common grounding and constructive memory, that preschoolers' memories are genuinely more vulnerable than those of older children and adults and that they are more likely to incorporate misleading information in their performance on memory tasks (Ceci & Bruck, 1993).

A series of four studies carried out by Ceci, Ross, and Toglia (1987) surely stands to date as the most extensive demonstration of suggestibility in young children. In a first experiment designed to test the hypothesis that preschoolers' memory is more vulnerable than that of older children to the effects of misleading information, Ceci et al. read children who were aged 3–12 years a story about a girl named Loren and her first day at school. In the original story, the children were told that Loren had a stomach ache from eating her eggs too fast at breakfast. The story was accompanied by pictures which illustrated the main events. On the following day, the children were met individually, usually by a different experimenter, who presented them with what Ceci et al. termed as either "biased" or "unbiased" information. In the biased condition, the children were provided with information that was inconsistent with the original story details for how and why Loren was sick. They were asked if they remembered a story about Loren who had a headache because she ate her cereal too fast. In the unbiased condition, the children were simply asked if they remembered a story about Loren who was sick from eating her breakfast too fast. Two days after the initial exposure to the story, the children were forced to choose between the original and the biased information in a recognition test in which pictures of the original details (e.g. stomach ache) were paired with pictures of the biased information (e.g. headache). There were no significant age differences in the unbiased condition with most children in all age groups accurately identifying the original information. By contrast, in the biased condition, preschoolers performed significantly worse than the older children. The biased information (e.g. in the form of a headache) appeared to intrude into children's recognition memory, apparently demonstrating their vulnerability to suggestion.

Subsequent experiments using different stories indicated that preschoolers' suggestibility was reduced but not eliminated when a 7-year-old child provided the biased information instead of an adult who may exert a "prestige effect" on responses. To rule out the possibility that both the original and biased information may have coexisted equally in the children's memories but that the biased information may have been chosen because it had been more recently introduced by a second experimenter, a modified recognition procedure was also employed in which the choice was between original and new information that was provided for the first time during the recognition memory test (McCloskey & Zaragoza, 1985). In this instance, suggestibility was also reduced but not eliminated.

The results reported by Ceci et al. are in line with the position of other investigators (e.g. Loftus & Davies, 1984; Yarmey, 1984) concerning the vulnerability of preschoolers' memories to suggestion as compared with the memories of older children and adults. Still, Ceci et al. (1987, p. 47) carefully note that aspects of their research may have been conducive to producing distortion in the children. They proceed to caution that such evidence indicates only that the memories of young children "can be distorted by postevent suggestions, not that they inevitably will be".

Given that memory is a construction of ideas that is influenced by the knowledge and experience that individuals bring to the task, one possibility is that children may have perceived experimenters in the biased conditions of Ceci et al.'s research to portray details of the original story such as those concerning Loren's temporary illness (in setting aside the Gricean quality rule) to be unimportant or irrelevant because they themselves did not bother to get them right. Under these conditions, the children may have been prompted to regard the original story details as trivial. Instead of disclosing what they know on tests of their recognition memory, they may have interpreted the biased information in the conversation with the second experimenter to mean that a biased or altogether different alternative was an acceptable, or even a preferred, test choice when compared with the original story details. In their limited conversational experience, young children are apt to be not very proficient at sorting between the relevant and irrelevant details of messages. In comparison, older children and adults are more likely to share the experimenter's scientific purpose that biased information might be presented in order to test for the accuracy of memory for the original stimuli. They are more likely to block the implication in the biased conditions that the original story details are unimportant or irrelevant and to choose the original stimuli on the recognition tests. In studies where the aim is to retain the relevance of these details by making these the focus of conversation, children should be more likely to avoid the effects of suggestibility and to display their original memory of the story details.

According to Kasher (1991), an important property of conversational implicatures is that they are cancellable and can be "countermanded" (e.g. The statement "John read the book and intended to see the movie" implies a causal relationship which is cancelled by the expanded statement "John read the book and intended to see the movie, but not necessarily in this order.") In research on children's conditional reasoning, Rumain, Connell, and Braine (1983) demonstrated that many children perform well on such reasoning tasks if the implications that convey a biconditional interpretation are "countermanded" through information that expands on the premises. In these studies, children could reason logically to the extent that differences between the performance of children and adults were mostly non-significant.

In this regard, Morton, Hammersley, and Bekerian (1985) have proposed a "headed records" model designed for retrieving answers to explicit questions. This model concerns the retrieval of individual memory records or "memory units" that are assumed to be stored independently of each other. Each experienced event is stored as a record in a folder with a heading that functions as an "access key". Records are attached to headers are searched by consulting the headers with a set of information called a "description". When a match has been found between a description and a heading, the associated record can be retrieved and evaluated. Morton et al. show that a strategic component is necessary to form an effective description of the information needed to gain access to the appropriate record. The processes required for forming descriptions involve the use of components such as temporal modifiers and environmental cues, in other words, time or place. Should two headings match a description, the more recent will be chosen unless a description can be created that discriminates between the alternatives. To formulate such a description spontaneously can be problematic for young children. They are required to learn that access to strategic components will result in a appropriate description that will lead to the retrieval of the desired record (Morton, 1990; Morton et al., 1985).

According to Morton et al.'s analysis, the results of research on memory distortion (e.g. Loftus, Miller, & Burns, 1978) can be reinterpreted in terms of interference which prevents the formation of descriptions that match with the headers of memory records. Asking subjects to recognise original and misleading information out of the order in which they have been exposed to such information is liable to interfere with matches of descriptions to the relevant header which may be more remote in time. It impedes their performance on tests of recognition memory even though their memory for the original event has not disappeared but exists in a separate, unretrieved record. This memory can now be retrieved when temporal order is restored.

To investigate children's ability to remember event details when the questions are temporally specific, Peter Newcombe and I (Newcombe & Siegal, 1996) presented 120 4- and 5-year-olds with a short story about a little girl, Karen, who was excited about her first day at school. Following Ceci et al.'s method, the critical two details of the story referred to what Karen ate too quickly for breakfast (e.g. cereal) and her ensuing sickness (e.g. a stomach ache). The next day, a second experimenter introduced either biased information that was discrepant with the original details (e.g. eggs, headache) or unbiased information about the story. A control group did not receive any information at all. In the test phase one week later, the children were asked to recall the details of Karen's breakfast and illness by pointing to one of three choices that represented original, biased, and novel items. Two test questions were asked in either a specific format that ignored the relevance of the biased information and eliminated the need for children to make sense of this departure from the quality rule (i.e. "Do you remember how Karen was sick when you heard her story for the first time?") or a general, non-specific format ("Do you remember how Karen was sick when you heard her story?"). The control group were asked only the questions in the non-specific format.

As hypothesised, few children provided evidence of suggestibility when the questioning was specific. In the terminology of Morton et al.'s model, providing children with temporally specific cues in questions enabled them to create a description that enabled retrieval of the headed record of the original information that was more remote in time. For those children presented with the biased information, the specific questions significantly improved response recognition from 67% to 90%—a figure that did not differ from the 92% success rate achieved by the unbiased group. This pattern of responses was replicated in subsequent research in which children were presented with two items, either original and biased or original and novel, as recognition choices. Thus the children's memory of the original details could not have merely signified their willingness to refrain from choosing the biased information since, when provided with a choice between original and novel alternatives, they still chose the original.

Further research is needed to determine whether preschoolers display evidence of suggestibility regardless of question format over a longer time interval. However, findings that children are better able to recall the original details of stories and to disregard information that is inconsistent with the original details if provided with specific questions support the position that memories for the original details of events and misleading information coexist (Morton et al., 1985). For whichever reason that adults' memory is distorted following exposure to misleading information (for a discussion, see Loftus, Feldman, & Dashiell, 1995), children who are exposed to misinformation in the stories presented by Ceci et al. may not be aware that the purpose and relevance of the test questions are to determine whether they can remember the original story details. Compared with adults, they need to be given specific cues to retrieve the relevant information. Considerable research has now demonstrated that preschoolers are more likely to recall events that have a logical temporal sequence toward achieving an end result such as making a collage or Playdough model than to recall a sequence that does not have this logical structure (Fivush, Kuebli, & Clubb, 1992). Thus young children often recall details accurately if provided with support in the form of specific temporal cues in questions and structured contexts (Fivush, 1993).

SUGGESTIBILITY RECONSIDERED

Despite the substantial research to date, it cannot be concluded that children *as a rule* are more suggestible than adults according to their definition of genuine, memory-based suggestibility. Rather, when considered in terms of conversational processes that can influence children's answers to an investigator's questions, the potential for socially based suggestibility is widespread. It can occur even when there is a strong knowledge base and the events are salient and central but children do not share the purpose and relevance of questioning. In attempts to use Ceci et al.'s (1987) procedure to investigate suggestibility following exposure to misleading information or in related suggestibility research when care has been taken to ensure that there is an equally strong knowledge base and the events are indeed salient, young children are for the most part no less suggestible than older children and adults (e.g. Duncan, Whitney, & Kunen, 1982; Flin, Boon, Knox, & Bull, 1992; Howe, 1991; Marin, Holmes, Guth, & Kovac, 1979; Toglia, Hembrooke, Ceci, & Ross, 1992; Zaragoza, 1991).

To be sure, Ceci et al. (1994) present evidence consistent with the hypothesis that young children's suggestibility is memory based and actually does distort their memory to a greater degree than older children and adults rather than existing as an artifact of their beliefs about what the investigator wants them to report. Two groups of children aged 3–4 and 5–6 years were given lists of events that either really occurred as reported by parents or were fictitiously generated by the experimenter. The children were told to try to recollect whether these events had happened on 7–10 separate occasions that were each separated by an interval of approximately 7–10 days. Both groups of children nearly always correctly recalled the real events. However, on the initial interview the younger children assented to 44% of the false events as opposed to 25% by the older ones. Comparable numbers for the two groups on the final interview were 32% and 36% respectively. Videotaped interviews of these false assents were often rated as convincing by professionals. Ceci et al. (1994) interpret these results to demonstrate that children, particularly when young, can be easily implanted with false memories. They contend that young children are more likely than older ones to suffer from "source memory errors" in which a memory derived from one source is misattributed to another source and subjects do believe that they saw or heard what was suggested to them (Johnson, Hashtroudi, & Lindsay, 1993; Lindsay, 1990).

Yet as we have noted, children as young as 3 years have been shown to be very adept in distinguishing real from pretend objects and events in a simplified testing procedure where they are asked to sort items into those that are real (can be seen, touched, and acted upon) and those that are not (Leslie, 1994; Wellman & Estes, 1986). Although preschoolers resist, at least in the short term, incorporating mothers' commentaries on events into their own autobiographical memories (Fivush, Hamond, Harsch, Singer, & Wolf, 1991), they may be particularly submissive with unfamiliar adults in testing settings and are unlikely to ask questions spontaneously with the aim of clarifying the procedure (Fivush, 1993). Thus the suggestibility shown in the Ceci et al. (1994) study may be socially based rather than memory based and reflect considerable gratuitous concurrence, given the high rate of assenting to any event in a list occurring regardless of whether it was real or not and the particularly low rate of denials by young children. Moreover, despite rating children's false assents as convincing, professionals themselves are vulnerable to stereotypes of children as naive and innocent and their judgements may be marked by a selective over-reliance on what they perceive to be supportive evidence (Faust & Ziskin, 1988; Leippe & Romanczyk, 1989).

Even if children often commit source attribution errors as a result of memory-based suggestibility, there may remain some coexistence of memories for the original story details and the inconsistent or misleading information. Children may tacitly remember that they have heard or seen both, despite not recognising which memory should be matched to the original details and which to the misleading information. Their recognition is facilitated where there are temporal modifiers in questions which serve to enhance the accessibility of the source or records of the original items through undermining the relevance of the misleading information to choices on memory recognition tasks. Nevertheless, there remains a need for studies of the acceptance of information in children and adults; these may demonstrate how new memories are created, especially when there are no prior memories to be retrieved (Loftus & Hoffman, 1989).

Both children and adults may produce suggestible responses in order to sustain a game, for reasons of personal gain, and to avoid embarrassment, especially when under stress (Ceci & Bruck, 1993, pp. 425–429). Compared to adults, young children's recollections of events are often far less complete and depend more on the time since the events occurred and on the format of the memory task and its relevance to previous knowledge and experience (Durkin, 1994; Poole & White, 1993). Yet at least over relatively short periods of time such as weeks or months, the accuracy of the details that they do report often approaches that of adults (Fivush, 1993; List, 1986). At the same time, young children's reports are vulnerable in that children are motivated to comply to the demands of adults who are perceived as powerful, authority figures. They are more likely than older children and adults to accede to a style of well-intentioned, leading questioning that appears to offer no polite option for denial (e.g. "He was wearing a raincoat, wasn't he?"). In striving to co-operate in unfamiliar experimental procedures when they do not share the purpose for violations of conversational rules, they may be prompted to produce apparently suggestible responses on test questions that, in some circumstances, may not reflect the degree to which they are able to retain the original memories of events. Children's lack of relevant prior knowledge and their failure to utilise strategic memory skills spontaneously such as employing temporal modifiers and environmental cues contributes to their inability to organise disparate events into a cohesive whole or to relate one set of events to another. On recognition memory tests, they require explicit questioning that does not depart from the maxims or rules of conversation and is specific to time or place such as, "Do you remember how Karen was sick when you heard the story *for the first time?*"

Nevertheless, these results are not without substantial limitations. The children in our investigation were presented with a single short picture story and questioned in familiar environments (e.g. their preschools) over a relatively short period of time. They were neither questioned repeatedly over a lengthy period (Cassel, Roebers, & Bjorklund, 1996; Poole & White, 1993) nor faced with an arousing or stressful situation (Peters, 1991). Neither did they actively participate in the event (Baker-Ward, Hess, & Flannagan, 1990; Rudy & Goodman, 1991) nor were the experimenters influential and significant persons in the children's lives (Ceci, Leichtman, Putnick, & Nightingale, 1993). They were also not interrogated to ascertain the extent to which they would accept biased information in a situation where there are no prior memories to be retrieved (Loftus & Hoffman, 1989). All amount to complex factors that can influence what children report on memory tests, and are frequently present when children are questioned in legal settings. The application of research findings to date on children's suggestibility to courtroom testimony is controversial and far from straightforward (Davies, 1993; McGough, 1994; Spencer & Flin, 1990), and a confident appraisal of children's memory and suggestibility over a longer term awaits further extensive research.

Bearing such limitations in mind, our results suggest that preschoolers' memory may not necessarily be impaired when questioners are concerned to ensure that children do not have to follow the conversational implications of questions. When children are questioned in a manner sensitive to their conversational experience, they may exhibit a greater resistance to suggestibility than has often been maintained.

In this connection, it is noteworthy that in a court of law, children's testimony has been used to corroborate adults' attributions of blame (Goodman, Golding, & Haith, 1984). It may be a popular misconception that children's memory is necessarily more susceptible to distortion than that of adults. Johnson and Foley (1984) have pointed out that, while children may have difficulty recalling the details of adult conversations and may produce less detailed courtroom evidence than adults, they may be able to recognise who did what. They may be as proficient as adults in describing a sequence of events and where these took place. Moreover, although children's imagination and lack of experience with strategies for recall may interfere with the reliability of their testimony, they may be without the prejudices that mar the reports of adults. To illustrate, Johnson and Foley have used an example from the work of Allport and Postman (1947). Adults and children viewed a picture of a subway scene. The adults often reported that a black man was holding a razor in an aggressive way. But in reality, it was a white man. If children remembered that a man was holding a razor, they never confused who it was.

6 Understanding Persons

If a parent asks a child, "What did you learn in school today?", the child will often say, "Not much." The reply will also often be "not much" to "Did the teacher read to you?" or "Did you learn more about counting?" But if the question is, "Who got into trouble today?" or "What happened at lunch with your friends?" a wealth of information is obtained. For example, a child may volunteer that "Kate's mom bought her a beautiful dress" or "Jill can skip up to 50" or "A boy was sent to the principal" or "I got into a fight with Jim", accompanied by a vivid description of the incident. Concerns about friendship, popularity, and sex-appropriate behaviour are highly relevant and can predominate in the minds of very young children. Their understanding is revealed when children are questioned in a manner that focuses on these concerns.

THE STAGE APPROACH TO CHILDREN'S CONCEPTS OF FRIENDSHIP

Psychologists in the Piagetian tradition have often explained children's understanding of friendship in terms of conceptual limitations. Following Piaget's clinical method, Selman (1980, p. 106) asked children questions such as: What kinds of things do good friends sometimes fight or disagree about? What are some good ways to settle fights or disagreements with a friend? Can friends have arguments and still be friends?

Selman's interview probed for children's understanding of several issues: why and how friendships are made, how friends resolve problems, how friendships break up, and the nature of trust and jealousy in friendships. Without attaching precise age ranges, Selman proposed on the basis of children's answers that their concepts of friendship develop with increasing age through five stages or levels, from 5 years (predominantly Level 0) to late adolescence and adulthood (predominantly Levels 3 and 4):

Level 0: Momentary friendships and physical solutions to conflicts.
Level 1: One-way friendships and unrelated solutions to conflicts.
Level 2: Bilateral friendships and co-operative solutions to conflicts.
Level 3: Stability of friendships and mutual solutions to conflicts.
Level 4: Autonomous interdependence and symbolic action as a resolution to conflicts.

Selman characterised early friendships at Level 0 in terms similar to those which have been used to interpret preschoolers' lack of success on standard conservation and perspective-taking tasks. Children are said to reason about conflict between friends without reflecting on the psychological effects of a particular strategy for resolution upon either party's feelings or motives. They avoid conflict by separating physically or by moving on to another activity. This level is marked by egocentrism, momentary friendships, and an inability to conceptualise differences in perspective between the self and others.

At Level 1, children view conflicts as problems that are caused by the actions of one party and felt by the other alone. Since they can only conceive of a disagreement as caused by one party, an apology or separation is enough to repair a conflict.

At Level 2, they view conflicts as caused by some external event. The assumption is that a conflict can be resolved independently of a relationship between friends so long as each person is satisfied. At Level 3, there is the understanding that a conflict may originate from the relationship itself. Both sides must accept a mutual resolution that would be satisfactory if the participants changed places. For example, adolescents may claim that, "if you just settle up after a fight that is no good. You gotta really feel that you'd be happy the way things went if you were in your friend's shoes. You can just settle up with someone who is not a friend, but that's not what friendship is really about" (Selman, 1980, p. 111).

Finally, at Level 4, individuals balance personal autonomy with the "close-knit mutuality" of friendship. Relations can be "symbolically" repaired by respecting the independence of the other person and keeping channels of communication open when there are conflicts.

Selman formulated these five levels based on interviews with 91 individuals aged from 3 to 34 years. He concluded that concepts of friendship can be analysed according to Piagetian criteria and maintained that interview responses can be described as a "structural whole", a general orientation towards friendship at each level. In addition, he contended that the levels form an invariant sequence in that no individual skips a level or regresses. For Selman, preschoolers' friendships are unstable owing to their basis in physical characteristics and the transitory nature of their play. Young children are egocentric in their peer relations and, with age, they come to understand the viewpoint of others.

The scope of Selman's research is impressive. However, it is mainly dependent on an interview methodology in which children are asked to respond to direct questions about hypothetical (and possibly irrelevant) stories of friends. The use of this methodology provides evidence to justify the acceptance of a first theoretical leap that young children are conceptually limited as shown by their performance on Piagetian tasks presented in formats where, at least sometimes, they may have misinterpreted the purpose and meaning of the language used by the experimenter. It also serves to justify the acceptance of a second leap that children's friendships are limited by an inherent egocentrism in their ability to take the role of others. My position is that both these leaps rest on questionable premises.

When children are asked questions about the actual relationships and situations that are relevant to their everyday concerns, evidence emerges that many preschoolers have stable reciprocal friendships and that these are not necessarily tied to physical characteristics. For example, Gershman and Hayes (1983) asked 37 children (mean age 50 months; range 34–61 months) to name a real child at their preschool as "someone you like more than anyone else" and to give justifications for their choices. Out of the 37, 22 (or 11 pairs) could be identified as reciprocal friends through their mutual choices. In observations of their behaviour at preschool, friends spent between 60 and 70% of their time with each other in free play. In a later phase of the study, the children were again asked to name their best friend after a 4–6 month interval. Contrary to Selman's proposal of a Level 0 in which preschoolers' concepts of friendship can be characterised by momentary and physical attributes, most of those children who were initially involved in reciprocal friendships remained stable in that category. Similar studies (e.g. Denham & Holt, 1993; Ladd, Price, & Hart, 1988) have shown that there is substantial consistency over time in preschoolers' ratings of the children that they like and dislike and in the co-operative or prosocial behaviour of preschoolers who are preferred as playmates.

In other work, Furman and Bierman (1983) compared methods of studying friendship in children aged 4 to 7 years. Friendship conceptions were measured in three ways: on an open-ended interview, on a picture recognition task, and on a forced-choice rating task. The interview consisted of four questions: (1) "What is a friend?" (2) "A friend is someone who . . . ?" (3) "Why do people need to have friends?" and (4) "Tell me what you do with friends?" In the picture recognition task, different activities were shown in pictures and the children were asked to say whether these would promote friendship. The pictures represented five potential bases for friendship: (1) affection (for example, love each other, care for each other); (2) support (help and share with each other); (3) common activities (play and make things together); (4) propinquity (are together a lot, sit by each other); and (5) physical characteristics (wear blue hats, have black hair). Finally, in the forced-choice rating task, the children were shown the pictures again in pairs and were asked to select the activity that it was more important for friends to do.

Significant age differences for both sexes in conceptions of friendship were found only in one specific area. Consistent with Selman's approach, children aged 4 and 5 years were more likely than 6- and 7-year-olds to mention physical characteristics, particularly in their answers to the open-ended interview questions.

However, even on the interview, 63% of the younger children mentioned affection as an aspect of friendship and 53% mentioned support. Moreover, although the children in Furman and Bierman's sample had been enrolled at day-care centres, length of attendance was left unspecified in their research report. Those children who mentioned the more abstract features of friendship may have been day-care veterans who had been provided with the opportunity for intensive peer interaction. Whereas the newly enrolled might identify wearing similar hats as a sign of friendship, this type of choice does not amount to evidence for a conceptual limitation in young children's peer relations. There are occasions when a reliance on physical characteristics is a sensible strategy to enter a group. In fact, it can be employed by adults in new situations such as first-time attendance at a professional conference. The same may apply in the case of preschool novices meeting other children for the first time. In any case, as Furman and Bierman point out, apart from the role of physical characteristics in the formation of friendships, ideas about affection and support have not yet been shown to be necessary or sufficient conditions for children to infer that a friendship is present.

In a further study, McGuire and Weisz (1982) examined the relationship between children's social behaviour and their popularity and friendships. The participants in their study were 293 fourth and fifth graders in rural North Carolina. The children listed their five best friends in order of preference on a questionnaire. Popularity was simply defined in terms of the number of nominations received by each child. Friendship, defined as "chumship", was measured by stable, mutual, best-friend choices; children were assigned membership in a chum group if they had scores above the mean for their sex and grade on a Chumship Checklist, including items such as "Tell each other things you wouldn't tell anyone else" and "Sleep over at each other's house."

In addition, the children were given measures of perspective-taking such as those described in the last chapter, together with measures of "altruism", involving observations of incidents during lunch and recess. Children with chums had higher levels of perspective-taking and observed altruism than did children without chums. Generally, popularity scores did not correlate with perspective-taking or altruism. Nor did perspective-taking itself relate to altruism.

This study is notable in that the authors distinguish between friendship and popularity. From our school years, we know many popular individuals who would have been at times chosen by virtually everyone as persons with whom we would have most liked to spend our time. However, these disgustingly popular persons would not necessarily be regarded as close, intimate friends by anyone in particular. By contrast, even though an unpopular child can have a close friend, children without friends and children who are unpopular tend to be one and the same. The friendless are neglected or even outwardly rejected by their peers. Not surprisingly, they may be less altruistic, and less likely to share and co-operate.

REJECTED AND NON-REJECTED CHILDREN

Selman's clinical interview is based on a Piagetian approach. It is tied into Piaget's theory of cognitive development and proposes that there are serious restrictions in young children's concepts of friendships and capacity for understanding persons. But as we have seen in Chapters Four and Five, children have at least some ability to take the role of the other and to infer others' mental states. Yet under direct or prolonged questioning in hypothetical situations, which can lay aside, for example, the quantity and relevance rules, they may be doing little more than responding to please (or even displease) a well-meaning interviewer.

Let us not be misled by the apparent lack of depth in young children's concepts of friendship as many appear to be able to use their insight into mental states in judging the emotions and behaviour of others in contexts that influence friendship. For example, in a study of 2- and 3-year-olds, Denham (1986) correlated cognitive and "affective" measures of perspective-taking with observers' ratings of children's social responsiveness and concern for others. The correlations were moderate and inconsistent across measures and were based on small numbers of children. But the important point is that performance on both types of perspective-taking measures was significantly above chance. On the cognitive perspective-taking task, puppets enacted stories in which one puppet had arrived late and lacked privileged information about how the late-arriving puppet would respond in the situation. The children were able to show how the puppet who lacked the information would behave (i.e. by searching in the wrong place for his or her mate). On the affective task, children could indicate how a puppet would feel in a particular story situation (e.g. happy or sad to come to day care, afraid or pleased to see a doctor). After having heard a story, they could affix the appropriate label on the puppet's face from a choice of "happy, sad, angry, and afraid". Their answers were frequently opposite to those which mothers had reported that the children themselves would feel in the same situations. This early understanding of emotions is in keeping with an understanding of what others see in cognitive perspective-taking tasks. Similarly, many young children also have the insight that people may express an emotion which does not correspond to what they really feel (Harris, Donnelly, Gaz, & Pitt-Watson, 1986).

The ability of preschoolers to understand emotional situations is associated with their likeability. In an extensive study carried out in Virginia, Denham, McKinley, Couchoud, and Holt (1990) asked 3- and 4-year-olds to indicate their responses to story situations where a puppet displayed various happy, sad, angry or fearful responses to a particular stimulus (e.g. having a nightmare). The children were asked to affix the face that best described how the puppet would feel. In order to increase the difficulty of the task and ensure that children did not simply attribute their own feelings to the puppet, the expressed response of the puppet in certain stories was the opposite to the mothers' report of the subjects' own emotional reactions to similar situations. The study also involved teachers' ratings of each child's prosocial behaviour, including helping, and peer ratings of each child's likeability. To measure likeability, peers were asked to sort photographs of each classmate into one of three boxes on which drawings of positive, neutral, and negative faces were affixed to represent a child who was liked "a lot", "kinda" liked, or not liked, respectively.

Many of the children displayed an ability to represent the feelings of the puppets accurately. Their performance was significantly related to their likeability, which in turn was significantly related to ratings of their prosocial behaviour. This latter finding was replicated in a subsequent 12-month longitudinal study that attempted to examine whether likeability is a cause or consequence of preschoolers' social behaviour (Denham & Holt, 1993). Although prosocial behaviour was not found to follow ratings of likeability over and above the previous prosocial behaviour already displayed by children, likeability was associated with their concurrent prosocial behaviour.

Therefore, since preschoolers are not necessarily constrained by an inability to share perspectives and to have insight into others' mental states, it is appropriate to examine the relationship between their knowledge about others and status among peers. Children who are rejected may have different knowledge and beliefs about others than those who have friends or who are popular. In their case, this knowledge may fail short of matching their capacity for understanding. Without the knowledge to develop the skills for dealing effectively with social situations, they may have difficulties in peer relations and in following teachers' directions (Coie & Krehbiel, 1984, p. 1466).

In this respect, a key aspect of children's friendships consists of the skill to anticipate and evaluate the consequences of behaviour that lead to acceptance in the peer group (Dodge, 1985). According to Turiel's (1983) account, to anticipate and evaluate consequences involves the ability to distinguish between different types of transgressions. By the age of 4 to 5 years, children can distinguish between violations of "social" conventions, which are arbitrarily defined with reference to a particular setting, and violations of moral prohibitions that are intrinsically wrong irrespective of the setting (Smetana, 1981, 1985). For instance, they are likely to regard transgressions such as injuring another child as morally wrong even if no punishment or prohibition existed. Violations such as not placing a toy in a designated spot or calling a teacher by the first name are likely to be regarded as transgressions tied to arbitrary settings. Outside these contexts, these acts would be permissible.

Importantly, in keeping with conversational rules, questions about different types of transgression are likely to be perceived as clear, sincere, and relevant to children's concerns. As demonstrated in a variety of studies, preschoolers distinguish between the gravity of these two types of violation in commenting on actual behaviour (Nucci & Nucci, 1982; Nucci & Turiel, 1978; Peery, 1979). For example, children who have witnessed social transgressions respond permissively to questions such as "What if there wasn't a rule in the school about (the observed act), would it be all right to do it then?" and seldom react at all. But they frequently react to moral transgressions by expressions of emotion, injury, or loss. This distinction demonstrates that they possess concepts of right and wrong; they do not adhere simply to a doctrine that all transgressions are equally serious and punishable.

In earlier work (Siegal & Storey, 1985), we showed that day-care veterans who had been enrolled in child-care centres for at least 18 months more clearly distinguished between moral and social transgressions than did a group of newly enrolled children with similar verbal intelligence scores. Compared to the newly enrolled, veterans judged social violations to be less naughty and worthy of punishment. However, as the relationship between children's ideas about transgressions and their acceptance or rejection by other children is unclear, we attempted to explore this issue (Sanderson & Siegal, 1988). The preschoolers in our study were classified in five peer status groups: controversial, popular, average, neglected, and rejected.

It has often been noted (Coie, Dodge, & Coppotelli, 1982; Coie & Kupersmidt, 1983; Dodge, Coie, & Brakke, 1982; French & Waas, 1985; Hartup, 1983; Hymel, 1983; Ladd, 1983) that popular children are received positively by their peers while the rejected are rebuffed in reaction to inappropriate approach behaviours. Controversial children produce high rates of prosocial and aggressive behaviour. They are skilled at eliciting both highly positive and negative reactions from others. Neglected children display low rates of behaviour and can be inept with peers, though the interaction they do show frequently resembles that of others.

On this basis, we hypothesised that controversial and popular children, with their superior social skills, would have the most highly developed knowledge and would distinguish most clearly between social and moral transgressions. By contrast, since unpopular preschoolers are more likely to transgress (Furman & Masters, 1980) and rejected children possess fewer social skills than their popular and controversial peers (Dodge, 1983), we predicted that the distinction between the gravity of social and moral transgressions should be unclear in this group.

The children in our study were 102 4- and 5-year-olds (51 boys and 51 girls) in full-time attendance for a mean of 19½ months at five child-care centres located in middle-class districts. Their ages ranged from 48 months to 68 months with a mean of 53 months. The centres provided continuous care for children between the ages of 2 and 5 years.

Each child was seen individually by a female experimenter during a session lasting approximately 10 to 15 minutes. He or she was given instances of moral and social transgressions followed by a peer nomination task to determine his or her status among others.

Questions About Transgressions. The children were presented with the same six items that we used in a previous study (Siegal & Storey, 1985, Study Two). The three moral transgressions involved: (1) a child hitting another; (2) a child not sharing toys with another child; and (3) a child not helping another who had tripped on the playground. Social transgressions were: (4) a child not putting toys away in the toy box; (5) a child not sitting at story time; and (6) a child eating ice-cream with a fork. The items were presented to the children in a random order.

Four questions were asked on each of the six items. The first question concerned judgements of naughtiness. The child was shown a cardboard sheet with four faces: a happy face (verbally labelled "OK"), a slight frown ("a little bit bad"), a larger frown ("very bad"), and a big scowl ("very, very bad"). Before the questioning, each child demonstrated proficiency in using the scale.

The first question involved a description of the relevant transgression. The children were asked to choose the face from a 4-point scale of naughtiness "that tells me about it". Responses were scored from 1 for "OK" to 4 for "very, very, bad". For the second question, they were asked if the transgressor should be punished. They were then required to indicate whether this should be a little or a lot. Responses were scored on a 0 to 2 scale, with 0 for no punishment, 1 for a little, and 2 for a lot. Question 3 dealt with the "contingency" of transgression. The children were asked whether it would be all right to commit the transgression if the perpetrator did not get into trouble. For question 4 on the "relativity" of the transgression, they were asked if each of the six transgressions would be permissible at home or in another child-care centre. Responses on questions 3 and 4 were scored as "yes" or "no".

Peer Status Measures. Before the start of testing, all the children were photographed in small groups of four to six, with girls and boys represented in roughly equal proportions in each photograph. The children were shown the photographs of their child-care group. The experimenter pointed to the pictures and named each child successively. She then requested the children to look at all photographs and to nominate the three peers with whom they most liked to play and the three with whom they least liked to play.

Peer status was classified by the "binomial probability" method used in an earlier study of fifth graders by Newcomb and Bukowski (1984). The number of nominations each child received from his or her peers on both the like most (LM) and like least (LL) questions was used to calculate social impact scores. These consisted of the total number of nominations the child received on both categories (LM + LL). There were five nominating groups, one from each child-care centre; their sizes were 12, 13, 22, 23, and 29. Rare scores on both the LM and LL questions ranged from 4 and above for the smallest nominating group of 12, to 6 and above for the largest nominating group. A "rare" score on the social impact dimension was identified as consisting of 2 nominations or less.

Using this method, the preschoolers were classified into controversial, popular, average, neglected, and rejected groups consisting of 8, 16, 54, 13, and 11 children respectively. Popular children had a rare LM score plus a score below the mean on LL. Controversial children were identified by a rare score on either one, or both, of the LM or LL dimensions. If the rare score occurred on only one category, then the other score was above the mean. Rejected status was assigned to children with a rare LL score, plus an LM score that was below the mean. Those who were classified as neglected had a lower social impact score than would be expected by chance alone. The average group obtained social impact scores at a chance level and did not have rare LL or LM scores.

Peer status had a significant effect only on the amount of punishment due to the perpetrators of transgressions (question 2, see Fig. 6.1), possibly because children regard punishment to be more immediately related to anticipating and evaluating the consequences of behaviour than issues of naughtiness, contingency, and relativity. The four non-rejected groups (controversial, popular, average, and neglected) rated moral transgressions as deserving more punishment then social ones. As predicted, rejected children (who were enrolled for the same length of time as the non-rejected) did not discriminate between the punishment due to moral and social transgressions.

Except for the item on hitting, the rejected prescribed little punishment for transgressions. In particular, compared to other peers, they tended to regard "not sharing" to be less worthy of punishment. Although the responses on this single item did not differ significantly from those of the other groups, the tendency is consistent with the results of studies indicating that unpopularity is associated with children's lack of reciprocity in sharing rewards (Enright, Enright, & Lapsley, 1981; Enright & Sutterfield, 1980). The rejected may not anticipate the consequences of a refusal to share or they may expect that sharing will not result in a positive outcome in peer relations (Sobol & Earn, 1985; Sobol, Earn, Bennett, & Humphries, 1983). Possibly, the parents of the rejected do not critically differentiate between their children's transgressions. A lack of clarity in childrearing methods may promote the inappropriate or aggressive approach

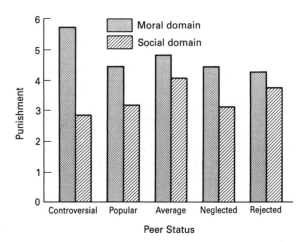

FIG. 6.1   Peer status and punishment assigned to the perpetrators of transgressions (from Sanderson & Siegal, 1988). Scores ranged from 0 to a possible maximum of 6. All status groups, except the rejected, rated violations of moral rules to be significantly worthier of punishment than violations of social conventional transgressions.

behaviour that is characteristic of rejected children (see Chapter Seven for a further discussion).

Unlike the rejected group, the neglected children differentiated between the punishment due to social and moral transgressions. The scores of the neglected and average groups were similar. Studies using older children (e.g. French & Waas, 1985) have found that the behaviour of the neglected resembles that of average ones. The distinction between the rejected and neglected groups is an important one and merits more attention (see Asher & Dodge, 1986; Asher & Wheeler, 1985; Rubin & Mills, 1988). Some children may be neglected by others, not because they feel rejected, but because they choose to be alone.

The controversial group most clearly distinguished between the punishment due to moral and social transgressions. They assigned more punishment to the moral transgressions than did the popular and rejected children and, compared to the average group, they rated social transgressions as meriting less punishment. Although the numbers of controversial children were few, their finely tuned distinction between types of transgression concurs with the observation that the behaviour of controversials is highly skilled. While the behaviour of controversial children may often meet with negative reactions from peers and reprimands from adults, controversials may engage in even more prosocial behaviour than do popular peers (Dodge, 1983). Their peer interaction may be both more extensive and intensive than that of other children, including those who are popular. The peer status of controversials may be a reflection of high rates of attention seeking or "manipulation", supported by a sophistication in their knowledge about the punishment due to different transgressions.

In this way, concepts of transgressions appear to be related to both the quality and quantity of peer experience. Contrary to stages derived from Selman's interview technique, the majority of young children do display a capacity to form more than transitory friendships in their responses on tasks in which they do not have to have extensive conversational experience in interpreting and answering questions in experiments. This is confirmed by a moderate degree of stability in peer nominations over periods of two weeks or more. Preschoolers have not only been found to place emphasis on affection and support in their friendships; often they have the skill to evaluate the consequences of social behaviours that are ordinarily unacceptable to either adults or other children. A lack of knowledge about persons, rather than a conceptual limitation, may underscore rejection in early childhood.

Nevertheless, this initial study had definite limitations. Our results were based on small numbers of boys and girls, especially in the groups of non-average children. Further, contrary to prediction, the responses of popular and average children were not significantly different. Distinctions between different types of transgressions may be an important but insufficient condition for peer acceptance.

CULTURE AND KNOWLEDGE

What is the influence of culture on children's responses to questions about transgressions? To answer this question, Nisan (1987) compared the judgements of three groups of schoolchildren in a study carried out in Israel: secular middle-class Jews from a large city, secular Jews from kibbutzim, and Moslem Arabs from a traditional village. Forty children were in each group; half were 6- and 7-year-olds and half were 10- and 11-year-olds. The children were asked to evaluate behaviours such as taking a toy belonging to another child and calling a teacher by the first name in a country where these behaviours were either prohibited or permitted. Then they were asked to say what the law should be. Compared to the two groups of Jewish children, the traditional Arab group, regardless of age, evaluated both moral and social transgressions more seriously. The great majority of the traditional Arab children maintained that all the transgressions, whether moral or social, should be prohibited by law.

Nisan attributed his results to differences in social norms that are grounded in a general cultural outlook. Turiel, Nucci, and Smetana (1988) have disputed this interpretation. They take issue with the familiarity of the behaviours that Nisan presented to the children and with the nature of the questions and the scoring system used in this study. But what if culture does limit the distinction made? How might peer status be affected? As Nisan (1988) has maintained, even a culturally determined analysis leaves room for children's cognition. The more complex the situation, the more amenable it will be to the influence of both culture and knowledge on their ideas about transgressions. This process and its outcome may be subtle. Even seemingly minute differences in the orientations of children may be significant influences on their friendship and popularity.

For example, the belief in consistency between attitudes and behaviour in collectivist societies such as Japan is not as strong as that in individualist Western societies such as Australia (Kashima, Siegal, Tanaka, & Kashima, 1992); Japanese adults are more likely than Australians to attribute behaviour to the constraints of situations rather than to individual mental states. Thus, compared to their Japanese counterparts, Western children may be more likely to identify occasions where it is wrong to act inconsistently to one's expressed attitude even if one did not get into trouble or nobody cared. In a collective society such as Japan, such violations might be judged less severely; there may be a normative understanding that inconsistency can reflect group solidarity and pressure.

In Japan, as well, individual speakers show deference to preserve the ranking of the group; they seek to humble themselves and to exalt the addressee (Matsumoto, 1988). This norm of group solidarity may be the focus of cultural differences in distinctions between social and moral transgressions. Compared to their Western counterparts, Japanese children may regard peers as wrong not to display the trappings of group solidarity at school (for example, to refuse to join in singing the school anthem) even if they did not get into trouble or nobody cared. If children construe this norm as a moral prohibition, they may reject those who transgress.

Would cross-cultural differences in ideas about transgressions invalidate the position that the social–moral distinction is theoretically useful? Turiel (1989) has pointed out that in many instances overlaps between categories are present and the numbers of marginal cases are large. Yet the categories are still retained. Many books, for example, are a mixture of fiction and non-fiction, but bibliophiles do not discard these terms in categorising books. Similarly, cases exist such as wearing a bikini to the funeral of a parent—a transgression which would have both social conventional overtones in style of dress and moral overtones in showing respect for the dead person and mourners. What does matter is that there should be prototypical instances of categories. For example, near unanimity exists that rape and unprovoked killing are moral transgressions.

Distinctions between social conventional and moral transgressions are not of course the only ones that can be made. There are transgressions that can be judged to be morally wrong but have neither a harmful intent nor a harmful consequence to the well-being of others. These could involve actions that evoke a sense of disgust such as the breaking of a promise to visit a mother's grave or eating a family dog after it had been killed in a car accident (Haidt et al. 1993). Like adults, children have a strong disgust reaction. Although only some may say that such disgusting actions should be stopped and punished, nearly all are liable to regard such actions as wrong and, as seen in Chapter Three, disgust in the domain of food and contamination may prompt an early recognition of deception through distinguishing mistakes from lies. In this respect, the disgust reactions of many young children may be no different than those of adults in eliciting moral condemnation, though differences may persist between those who are rejected and non-rejected by their peers.

HOSTILITY AND HUMOUR REPUTATION

Naturally, there are other aspects of popularity and friendship besides ideas about transgressions. For example, peer relations can be influenced by children's physical attractiveness, motor skills, and, especially, their reputation as humorists. McGhee (1979) has hypothesised that interaction has an important role to play in humour development, with significant others such as parents who model and reinforce the use of humour. The child learns that humour is not only pleasurable in its own right, but that it also engenders positive responses in others. Interestingly, a study by McGhee and Lloyd (1982) points to a similar process occurring in peer relations. The authors report that the most significant predictor of humour development in preschoolers was the amount of their engagement in social play. According to McGhee and Lloyd, the social sharing and reinforcement inherent in social play served to strengthen humour initiation and responsiveness. In an investigation of the relation between humour and peer status in fifth graders (Nugent, 1994), popular children as compared to their rejected counterparts regarded humour as an effective social strategy for handling conflict, particularly as an effective means of stopping fighting among peers. .

Rejected children may substitute hostility for humour. Dodge and Somberg (1987) divided classes of third-, fourth-, and fifth-grade boys into adjusted/non-aggressive and rejected/aggressive groups. In contrast to the adjusted group, the rejected boys had social preference scores below zero and were rated low on social competence and high on aggression by their peers. The children were shown a set of video-recorded incidents involving a pair of boys in a play activity. The intention of the *provocateur* in the incidents was portrayed as hostile, accidental, prosocial, or ambiguous. The children were asked to interpret the boy's intention and to indicate how they would respond if the provocation had actually happened to them.

The rejected unjustifiably attributed hostility to the actions of boys with accidental or ambiguous intentions and were more likely than their non-aggressive peers to indicate retaliation in cases of accidental provocation. Similarly, in a recent study by Sanderson (1996), rejected, aggressive preschoolers were significantly more likely than non-rejected children to attribute hostile intentions to others and to indicate that they would never choose to forget when confronted with hostile provocations. A tendency to overattribute hostile motives in others is of course not limited to children. Adults can do the same, particularly when faced with an unfamiliar culture. For example, tourists during the 1987 coup in Fiji were heard to misinterpret the native greeting "bula, bula" (hello, hello) as "Put your hands up and give us your wallet."

Just as hostile attributions may produce rejection in children, humorous attributions may be associated with popularity. Masten (1986) investigated the relation of children's "peer reputation" with humour appreciation, comprehension, and production. Fifth-graders were asked to assess the funniness of cartoons on a 5-point scale ranging from 1 (not funny at all) to 5 (very, very funny) while, unknown to the subject, an experimenter rated their "mirth" reactions to each cartoon. The children also explained the humour portrayed in the cartoons and produced titles or captions to make a cartoon funnier. After controlling for the effects of IQ, humour appreciation (funniness and mirth) and production were related to a dimension of peer reputation; humourless children were regarded by their peers as withdrawn, shy, or unhappy.

Even though humour may sometimes be more a consequence rather than a cause of peer status, rejected children may believe that they are ineffective in using humour in peer relations. Unlike many of the neglected, they may feel alone; yet they may lack knowledge about the strategies and purposes of humour in making friends. To cope with threatening situations, they may substitute hostility for humour.

Some rejected children may not be able to gain peer acceptance through physical attractiveness or abilities. The cultivation of a humour reputation is presumably an easier route. It is one that may be influenced by parents and teachers in the light of evidence, from studies in which experimenters have not set aside conversational rules, that children ordinarily are capable of concepts of friendship that go beyond mere physical characteristics.

GENDER CONCEPTS

Children's peer relations are closely connected to their sex-role preferences. They are very concerned about how their appearance and behaviour conforms to sex-role conventions and stereotypes. From at least 2 years of age, they have knowledge of sex-role stereotypes and the appropriateness of games and clothes for boys and girls (Weinraub, Clemens, Sockloft, Etheridge, Gracely, & Myers, 1984).

According to Kohlberg (1966; Kohlberg & Ullian, 1974), children's sex-role development is influenced by an understanding of gender concepts. (Another account that focuses on the different treatment boys and girls receive from parents is discussed in the next chapter.) Of special importance is the establishment of a stable concept of gender identity. This concept involves the stable and constant categorisation of the self despite superficial opposite-sex transformations in features such as dress.

Kohlberg, like Selman, was inspired by Piagetian theory and methodology. He contended that, since young children centre on the perceptual appearances rather than the invariant features of a transformation, they base their judgements of gender on changes in games and clothes. Thus the concept of gender identity is derived from conservation abilities. Once children have achieved a stable concept of gender, they know that, for example, a boy will remain a boy even if he wears girls' clothing or plays girls' games. In efforts to live up to a self-definition as a boy or girl, children seek out sex-appropriate activities.

In tests of Kohlberg's account, Slaby and Frey's (1975) interview has been widely used (for example, Ruble, Balaban, & Cooper, 1981; Smetana & Letourneau, 1984). The measure consists of 14 questions and counterquestions: 9 questions on children's knowledge of their "gender identity" (e.g. "Are you a girl or boy?"), 2 questions on gender stability (e.g. "When you were a little baby were you a boy or a girl?" "When you grow up will you be a mummy or daddy?"), and 3 questions on "gender consistency" (e.g. "If you wore (opposite sex of subject) clothes would you be a boy or a girl?" "If you played (opposite sex of the subject) games, would you be a girl or a boy?") The counterquestions were designed to probe the certainty of the children's original responses (e.g. "If you played (opposite sex of subject) games, would you be a (opposite sex of subject's first response)?"). Children seem to find the identity questions (given first) easier than the stability questions (given second). The consistency questions (given last) are most difficult.

However, support for a relationship between sex-typed behaviour and gender constancy remains inconclusive (Huston, 1983; Martin & Halverson, 1981; 1983). Contrary to the quantity and relevance rules, children may perceive gender-constancy questions to be pointless or have answers that are obvious. Since they do not share the experimenter's purpose to test children's knowledge of gender concepts, their answers might be influenced by the context and order in which the questions are asked. As on conservation tasks, at least some may be switching their responses in an effort to satisfy the experimenter.

In fact, gender constancy has been shown to be closely related to performance on conservation tasks (Marcus & Overton, 1978). The sequence of questions and counterquestions in the gender-constancy interview, while not identical, are very similar in nature and maybe perceived as redundant and to violate the quantity rule. In the traditional conservation experiment, post-transformation questions are more difficult to answer than pretransformation ones, just as questions on gender consistency are more difficult than those on identity and stability. The repetition of items may provoke children, who are uncertain in the first place, to change their answers. Alternatively, when seen from the child's point of view, the questions may seem sillier and sillier and demand even sillier answers. According to this analysis, repetition should result in a lack of gender constancy on the more "difficult" or silly consistency items. If children are given the consistency items first, they should provide more gender constant responses.

In a study we carried out (Siegal & Robinson, 1987), the interview questions were posed in a reversed order. We hypothesised that more gender-constant answers would be given when the interview questions were asked in a reversed order than in the usual order. In addition, to supplement the responses on the consistency items with justifications, children were asked to give causal attributions for the presence or absence of gender consistency in the responses of others their own age. If the absence of consistency reflects a willingness to satisfy demand characteristics of the interview, this type of response should produce "external" attributions expressed in terms of a desire to please an adult.

The participants in the study were 30 boys and 30 girls whose ages ranged from 42 to 54 months with a mean of 47.9 months. The children attended kindergartens and preschools located in middle-class areas. The experimenter was a female undergraduate student in her early 20s.

The study consisted of two parts in which each child was seen individually. Half the children received one part first (i.e. the gender constancy interview in the traditional or reversed order) and the other part second (i.e. the attribution measures); the sequence was switched for the remainder.

In the first part, the experimenter gave the interview questions in a reversed order to 15 boys and 15 girls. First, she asked the gender consistency questions on retaining gender while wearing the clothes and playing the games of the opposite sex, together with the counterquestions (although the purpose of counterquestions may remain obscure to young children). Then the gender-stability questions and counterquestions were followed by the gender-identity ones. In the latter case, as in the Slaby and Frey study, dolls and photographs served as props. The remaining children received the gender constancy interview in the traditional order with the questions on identity asked first, stability second, and consistency third. Responses were scored following the criteria used by Slaby and Frey. A child was credited with gender constancy on a question only if both the question and the counterquestion were answered correctly.

In the second part, the experimenter gave the children four stories on gender consistency: two dealt with games and two with clothes. The story characters were the same sex as the subjects and the order of story presentation was counterbalanced across subjects. For one of the stories involving games and one involving clothes, the story character made a gender-constant response; in the others, he or she gave a response that indicated a lack of gender constancy.

After hearing each story, the subjects were asked to attribute the story character's response to an "internal" source (i.e. his or her own beliefs) or to an "external" source (i.e. pretending to please the grown-up questioner). To control for recency effects in the children's attributions, the order of the internal and external alternatives was varied systematically across the stories as shown in parentheses. For example:

Gender Constancy Present.   A grown-up asked a little boy called John who was 4 years' old whether he would be a boy or a girl if he wore girls' clothes. John said that he would still be a boy if he wore girls' clothes. Do you think that John really thought that he would still be a boy if he wore girls' clothes or was John just pretending to please the grown-up? (Do you think John was just pretending to please the grown-up, or did John really think that he would still be a boy if he wore girls' clothes?)

Gender Constancy Absent.   A grown-up asked a little girl called Michelle who was 4 years' old whether she would be a boy or a girl if she played boys' games. Michelle said that she would be a boy if she played boys' games. Do you think that Michelle was just pretending to please the grown-up, or did Michelle really think that she would be a boy if she played boys' games? (Do you think that Michelle really thought that she would be a boy if she played boys' games, or was Michelle just pretending in order to please the grown-up?)

All of the children were correct on the gender identity and stability interview questions. As predicted, the order in which the questions were asked had a significant effect on the children's responses to gender consistency. Of the 30 children in the reversed order condition, 23 out of 30 (76.7%) gave gender-constant responses on both items involving clothes and games compared to only 10 of the 30 children in the traditional order condition. Far more external attributions were given when the story character was described as lacking gender constancy than when gender constancy was present in the character's responses.

Several limitations of our study should be noted. The age range was rather restricted in comparison to previous work; younger children may not have responded to the interview items in the same way, Additionally, the reversed order procedure may have overestimated knowledge of gender consistency and, in the absence of additional information on the children's sex-role attitudes and behaviours, the possibility of "pseudoconstancy" (correct answers based on some incorrect source) in the children's responses must be recognised. The choice of attribution for the responses of other children in stories can be interpreted to supplement the pattern of responses on the interview items; alternatively, the interview responses may be independent of attributions since it is possible for children to maintain that peers hold genuine or false beliefs in gender consistency (or its absence) irrespective of their own beliefs.

Nevertheless, while these qualifications remain, our hypothesis that the lack of gender constancy shown by children in the traditional interview format is influenced by the context in which the questions are posed was supported. Through prolonged questioning on the topic of gender that can contravene the quantity and relevance rules, at least some children may change their responses in an effort to be silly, cute, or attractive instead of correct. This scenario is illustrated in Fig. 6.2. As Bem (1989, p. 650) has observed, questions in the

FIG. 6.2   A possible context of lack of gender constancy.

original Slaby and Frey gender constancy measure such as "If you wore (opposite-sex) clothes, would you be a boy or girl?" might be interpreted by children to mean, "Would you look like a girl or a boy?" or "Would you be pretending to be a girl or a boy?"

Susan Gelman and her co-workers (Gelman, Collman, & Maccoby, 1986) have reported a study which strengthens our conclusion that young children often do not rely on perceptual appearances when judging gender. In their study,

4-year-olds were told, for example, that boys have "andro" in their blood and girls have "estro" in theirs. Then they were shown pictures that conflicted with these properties, such as a boy who looked like a girl. The preschoolers were asked to infer whether the boy or girl had andro or estro. While they performed poorly on a traditional gender-constancy task, the preschoolers correctly ignored perceptual information in specifying the properties of the children in the pictures. They had less success at using properties such as andro to classify gender in perceptually discrepant cases but, as Gelman and her colleagues note, similar difficulties may plague adults.

Thus preschoolers' judgements of gender may be guided by a theory that is based on the reality defined by biological differences between boys and girls. Cultural reinforcement for sex-typed imitation and toy preferences in children as young as 2 years may draw preschoolers' attention to these biological differences and contribute to their knowledge of gender constancy and sex-role stereotypes (Bauer, 1993; Perry, White, & Perry, 1984).

Although considerable research on children's knowledge about persons has been generated from Piaget's approach, much of this work has consisted of interview studies in which questioners have been inadvertently prone to infringe conversational rules. More recent experiments are attuned to the need to pose questions that are relevant, non-redundant, and avoid ambiguity. These have illustrated that young children can have meaningful peer relations and concepts of friendship and gender identity.

7 Authority and Academic Skills

The experiments discussed so far have shown that many children at least as young as 4 or 5 years of age are at times often equipped to identify causal relations between objects and to distinguish between appearance and reality. Contrary to the broad Piagetian thesis that young children are egocentric, they have at least some understanding of mental states and false beliefs. They can often report differences between knowing and pretending and have an understanding of friendship and gender identity. To explain differences between these results and those of Piaget and his followers, I have developed the theme that experimenters' departures from conversational rules can account for children's lack of success on many cognitive tasks.

If young children are often able to detect causality, to represent objects and viewpoints, and to understand persons, why do so many ultimately have difficulty in acquiring academic skills at school and, more generally, in following the directions of adults? My hypothesis is that, in part, children have an implicit theory of child care and parental authority which is often not recognised by adults whose own theory of what children know is close to that of Piaget. Yet, as the influential Russian psychologist Vygotsky (1978) emphasised, children's potential for learning and understanding can be defined by the difference between what they can achieve on their own individually and what they can achieve with assistance from others upon whom they depend for caregiving.[1]

---

[1] See Cole (1985) and Valsiner and van der Veer (1993), for a discussion of the various senses in which this difference—often termed the "zone of proximal development"—has been used in research on instructing children's academic skills.

The belief that children are unable to understand abstract concepts can serve to undermine the quality of parental involvement in promoting children's academic potential. This involvement may fall short of what children are capable and place obstacles in the way of adult–child communication, even though conversational understanding is central to parent–child relations (Grusec & Goodnow, 1994, p. 10). Should adults believe that children cannot understand simple instructions about a concept, they may decide that to talk to children is a waste of time. In Grice's (1975, p. 49) terminology, they may "opt out" of the co-operative principle altogether and express messages such as "I cannot say more; my lips are sealed." To elicit children's compliance, they may resort to coercive or rote techniques without a verbal rationale and avoid challenging instruction in academic skills.

However, given that children have a theory of the legitimate uses of adult authority, they often evaluate adults' verbal inputs positively. They have negative perceptions of adults' passivity, permissiveness, or coercion that, in part, may contribute to non-compliance and have adversive consequences for their academic progress and concern for others.

Experiments have now cast a favourable light on an adult conversational involvement which uses reasoning to ensure that children follow directions. It is now known that children can and do advance in reading and number skills through an early individualised instruction that takes care to build upon their capabilities. In the light of the evidence which undermines the idea of a basic conceptual limitation in early childhood, consideration must be given to parent–child relations and their effect on success at school.

KNOWLEDGE OF RATIONALES

A central aspect of children's development is learning to follow adult instructions and standards for behaviour in the absence of external surveillance. Should children be unable to understand the rationale underlying directions in conversation, a parent might feel warranted in using other, more coercive tactics to ensure that they complete a task or behave with concern for others. In exasperation, some parents may decide that directing reasoning and explanations to children is not worthwhile at all. To what extent, then, can children understand the rationales underlying adults' behaviours?

In his discussion of causal attribution, Kelley (1973) noted cases in which adults may regard multiple causes as sufficient to produce behaviour. When both intrinsic (voluntary) and extrinsic (external) causes are present, they can use a "discounting" strategy in recognising that external factors can pressure an individual to behave against his or her will. In explaining this behaviour, they may discount the importance of intrinsic causes.

Can young children use this strategy to recognise behaviour that has been performed without coercion? Piaget (1932) would suggest that they do not. He proposed that they do not distinguish between different sorts of transgression and have a unilateral respect for adult authority. They believe that the consequences of an act should determine the degree of naughtiness and punishment irrespective of the perpetrator's intentions. As described in Chapter Three, according to Piaget, children also believe that mishaps can result in immanent justice. They think that adults are so powerful that misfortune such as illness will inevitably befall those who are disobedient.

Researchers applying Kelley's ideas to children have sought to demonstrate, on the basis of Piaget's position, that they have little or no appreciation of the legitimate uses of authority. According to this analysis, young children cannot use a discounting strategy in reasoning about the causes of behaviour and do not discriminate between a voluntary and forced compliance to an adult request. For example, Karniol and Ross (1976) asked children and adults to judge characters in stories presented in pairs. In one story, a child would play with a particular toy without any (extrinsic) suggestions from an adult. In the other, the child would play with a toy following an adult directive to do so. The task was to say which child really wanted to play with the toy. In contrast to older children and adults, kindergarten children showed no clear preference for one story character over the other.

Some years ago, it could be speculated that children's responses in this sort of study might be influenced by methodological problems, including difficulties related to the story content and the desire to give acceptable answers to the experimenter (Siegal, 1982, pp. 114–116). In view of the research reviewed in Chapter Three on children's understanding of others' mental states, it is hard to avoid the conclusion that this concern is a valid one, especially in light of research that has re-examined children's causal attributions for the helping of story characters. In a key study carried out by Dix and Grusec (1983), participants at four age levels (5–6 years, 8–9 years, 11–13 years, and adults who were parents of children aged 5 to 13 years) heard six stories representing different strategies used by parents to elicit helping behaviour on the part of children: power assertion (threats of punishment with or without reasoning); modelling (with or without reasoning); and spontaneous helping (with or without reasoning). For example:

> One day, Mom, Carolyn, and little Mike were putting on their winter clothes. They were going to play in the snow. Little Mike couldn't get his boots on. He got mad and said, "I can't do it." Mom said, "It's alright, Mike. Those boots are hard to put on, especially for someone as small as you. You just need help (reasoning statement). I'll help you. Stick your leg out straight. I'll try to pull your boot up." A moment later little Mike was having trouble with the other boot. Carolyn did what Mom did before. Carolyn said, "Here, Mike, let me help you. You hold your leg straight. I'll pull your boot" (modelling).

For each story, the subjects were asked to indicate whether Carolyn (and the other central story characters) helped willingly or to conform with the wishes of an adult. Therefore, either an internal or external causal attribution could be given. In response to the stories, even 5- and 6-year-olds discriminated between causes attributable to different parental strategies. They gave external attributions for power assertion and internal attributions for modelling and spontaneous helping. Similar results have been reported in other studies (Dalenberg, Bierman, & Furman, 1984).

CHILDREN'S THEORY OF LEGITIMATE ADULT AUTHORITY

Thus, consistent with the research on the understanding of physical and psychological causality discussed in Chapter Three, young children have at least some capacity to understand the rationales underlying adults' instructions. They can use a discounting strategy to distinguish between a compliance that is intrinsically, rather than extrinsically, motivated. Can they go a step further? Can they distinguish between behaviour that ought to be regulated by authority as opposed to that which ought to be left to a child's own devices?

Recall that many preschoolers are able to distinguish between social and moral transgressions. They evaluate the punishment due to social transgressions as tied to specific contexts whereas they view moral transgressions as naughty and worthy of punishment regardless of context. According to Weston and Turiel (1980) and Tisak (1986; Tisak & Tisak, 1990), children advocate that the use of adult authority should be limited to prohibit violations of moral transgressions. It should not be used to interfere in situations concerning social transgressions or personal choices that do not necessarily affect others' welfare.

Weston and Turiel (1980) presented four hypothetical situations to a group of children aged 4–11 years. Each situation contrasted schools in which a given act was permitted or prohibited by school policy. The situations were: (1) a child removes his or her clothes on the school playground after getting too warm from playing; (2) a child hits and pushes another child out of a swing after discovering that all the swings on the playground are occupied; (3) a child goes outside to play, leaving some toys on the floor after playing with them; and (4) a child refuses to share his or her snack with another child visiting the school who asked for some crackers because there were none remaining in the box.

Within a particular school setting, the children were asked to evaluate the policies and the behaviour of the culprit in the situation. They also predicted and evaluated the intervention (or non-intervention) of a teacher in the context of different school policies.

Regardless of age, children generally felt that a teacher would reprimand a child who hit another even in a school where hitting did not contravene policy. They viewed a permissive school policy positively in the cases of undressing, leaving toys on the floor, and refusing to share, but they evaluated negatively a policy that permitted hitting. However, young children responded that the action of a child who hit in a permissive school was all right while the older children said that hitting was wrong.

To interpret this finding, Weston and Turiel referred to age-related differences in causal attributions. They suggested that, until the age of 8 or 9 years, children view extrinsic situational factors as the main constraints on behaviour. Therefore they do not negatively evaluate the behaviour of a child when that behaviour is permitted by school policy. However, given the results reported by Dix and Grusec, Weston and Turiel may be underestimating the capacity of younger children to infer the causes of behaviour. Indeed, young children may be more likely than older ones to offer what they perceive to be the answer desired by the questioner when asked by an adult about a child who acted within the bounds of school rules. Such answers may not reflect their genuine convictions. In any event, there were no age differences in predictions of teachers' behaviour.

A study by Tisak (1986) supports young children's ability to delimit the bounds of authority. The method was quite similar to that of Weston and Turiel except that it dealt with conceptions of parental authority rather than teachers' authority in schools. Children aged 6 to 11 years were given hypothetical situations with three themes: (1) taking another child's toy (stealing); (2) leaving dishes on the table after eating (family chores); and (3) playing with a forbidden friend. In each instance, they were asked whether there should be an obligation to follow the instructions of a parental authority and whether a child should respond to another child's transgression in the absence of an explicit requirement to do so. Even the youngest children drew boundaries around the jurisdiction of parents. For example, they indicated a stronger likelihood of responding to another's transgression in the case of stealing than in the cases of neglecting chores and, especially, choosing prohibited friends. Children of all ages maintained the greater legitimacy of parental rule making for stealing than for regulating chores or choosing friends. Similar results were reported in a follow-up study (Tisak & Tisak, 1990) in which children maintained a greater legitimacy for parental rule making with regard to both moral events (stealing and hitting others) and prudential events which could affect one's health and welfare (leaving the house without telling anyone and running across the street without looking) than for personal acts (not dressing neatly and playing with older children).

Therefore, children can at times distinguish between the gravity of different types of transgressions and there are areas in which they prefer that behaviour should be left unregulated such as dress, hairstyles, friendship choices, and toy preferences. Even preschoolers can often identify acts that are voluntary and those that are constrained by extrinsic forces. Not only can young children recognise the legitimacy of attempts to regulate behaviour but they may expect authorities to be fair in investigating alternative explanations for a mishap

(Gold, Darley, Hilton, & Zanna, 1984). Moreover, even though young children appear to have difficulty conceiving of someone in a supervisory role who lacks the knowledge to deal with problem behaviour, adult status by itself does not confer an advantage in perceived legitimacy of intervention. Children commonly perceive the intervention of knowledgeable peers entrusted as supervisors to be as legitimate as that of adults (Laupa, 1991).

What then are the consequences of children's perceptions of parental control for their voluntary acceptance of adults' instructions? We might surmise that methods to elicit compliance should aim to promote internal attributions. The more subtle the methods of persuasion, the less children will attribute their behaviour to extrinsic forces. Reasoning should be more effective than techniques which assert the power of the parent.

Yet considerable controversy persists over the role of the parent. For those who place emphasis on the importance of attributions in behaviour (see, for example, Lepper, 1983; Lepper & Gilovich, 1981; Lewis, 1981), children's following of instructions in the absence of external surveillance is promoted by the least and most subtle pressure that is sufficient to obtain compliance. Alternatively, for researchers such as Baumrind (1983), "salient" techniques of "firm control" are most effective, and these often must be moderately severe to be effective.

Both positions converge, though, to emphasise the importance of children's perceptions and evaluations of authority. As an advocate of an attributional approach, Lewis (1981, p. 562) has suggested that from the child's point of view "rules may not be imposed or enforced at all but distilled from the child's own social interactions." Children's sense of voluntary compliance—their "internalisation" of adult standards for behaviour—may be essential in following directions. To support the use of parental firm control, Baumrind (1983, p. 141) has maintained:

> the use of reasoning accompanied by power-assertion should be more effective with young children than reasoning alone: with young children a display of power captures their attention and clarifies in their minds that compliance is required, whereas the use of reason without a display of power often signals to the child that the parent is indecisive about requiring compliance.

A mother may feel compelled to use more power assertive methods should she believe that children had been naughty even though they understood the nature of their misbehaviour and had the capability to avoid this misbehaviour (Dix, Ruble, & Zambarano, 1989).

FATHERS AND MOTHERS, SONS AND DAUGHTERS

Neither Lewis nor Baumrind deal specifically with differences in the socialisation roles of the mother and father. Often they group both together in referring to parents. All the same, our work suggests that differences in the treatment of sons and daughters by mothers and fathers can provide an explanation for differences in children's perceptions of parental control techniques and resulting compliance.

In one study (Siegal & Cowen, 1984), we gave children in preschool to grade 12 stories where a child disobeyed a mother, including cases of simple disobedience and physical or psychological harm to others (for example, laughing at a crippled person who crosses a road and skipping inside a room causing a lamp to fall and break). An experimenter read each story and listed the child-rearing techniques used by four mothers. She asked the children to consider each mother in turn and told them to indicate how right each of the mothers was to do as she did. The techniques fell into the broad categories defined by Hoffman (1970): (1) induction in which the mother was described to the subjects as reasoning with the culprit and pointing out the harmful consequences of the transgression for the self and others; (2) power assertion in which she was described as physically punishing the culprit (a salient method of control); and (3) love withdrawal in which she was described as telling the culprit that she would not have anything more to do with the child for the time being. In addition, a fourth type of mother was described as choosing not to intervene, believing that the child would learn independently. The inclusion of permissiveness as a discipline technique allowed comparisons to be made between evaluations of non-intervention and different forms of intervention. At all ages, children generally expressed strong approval for induction backed by milder approval for physical punishment. The nature of the situation was a strong influence on their evaluations, with children appreciating the mother's flexibility.

Yet in a follow-up study on evaluations of fathers' behaviours using the same methodology and similar age groups (Siegal & Barclay, 1985), young children aged 5 and 6 years showed no clear preferences for the same techniques as used by fathers, and their ratings of fathers were not strongly determined by the situation. Physical punishment often received approval compared to induction. Moreover, in contrast to the study of perceptions of mothers, boys and girls differed in their ratings. Boys in general rated fathers more favourably than did girls, particularly in their use of physical punishment in situations of simple disobedience and physical harm to the self. Girls rated fathers' use of induction more highly than boys in the simple disobedience situation.

A qualification to these studies is that the children were asked to consider hypothetical rather than real parents. However, the results fit well with the observations of Lynn (1959, 1962) and Block (1983) that, compared to the father, the mother is generally more visible in child rearing. Since mothers ordinarily have a greater day-to-day involvement with children, they are likely to be seen by both boys and girls as more sensitive than fathers to individual situations. Girls are provided with a model for sex-appropriate behaviour, and they may be more likely to advocate the use of induction and to reject the use of physical punishment. As fathers are comparatively unavailable as sources of induction, reasoning, and sensitivity, boys are left more on their own to search for the appropriate model.

Girls' willingness to follow adults' directions may be promoted by their self-perceptions of gentleness and physical weakness (Ullian, 1984) and by mothers' frequent mention of states of feeling in conversations with daughters at an early age. In this connection, the conversational interactions between parents and children can differ for sons and daughters. Dunn, Bretherton, and Munn (1987) studied communication about feelings between mothers and their children aged 18 and 24 months. The frequency of the mother's reference to feeling states when the target child was 18 months predicted the frequency of that child's own references to feeling states at 24 months. Moreover, mothers of girls were significantly more likely to initiate conversations about feelings than were mothers of boys. When their child was 24 months' old, girls' mothers initiated 3.26 conversations per hour about feeling states whereas boys' mothers initiated only 1.61 conversations. Yet boys and girls did not themselves differ in the rates in which they initiated conversations about feeling states. This pattern would seem to suggest that mothers are more concerned about ensuring that a consideration of feelings is present in girls than in boys.

Later research by Dunn and her co-workers (Dunn, Brown, & Beardsall, 1991; Dunn, Brown, Slomkowski, Tesla, & Youngblader, 1991) has not always reproduced a comparative advantage for girls in the amount of messages about feelings that are offered by mothers. Nevertheless, consistent with the notion that girls are encouraged to think more about feelings than boys, girls by the age of 40 months have been found to be significantly more likely than boys to identify the feelings of characters in stories as happy, sad, angry, and afraid. In this sense, mothers may be speaking less than is necessary for boys to realise their potential in their understanding of emotion. Denham, Zoller, and Couchoud (1994) report that mothers' negative emotional responsiveness is associated with a lack of emotional understanding in boys and not girls. They suggest that girls are "automatically" socialised by maternal and societal expectations about emotion; these expectations are lacking for boys and so they are likely to be more influenced by the specific child-rearing strategies of the mother.

In the absence of the extensive day-to-day interaction that marks the mother–child relationship, father–child evaluations may be more likely to be influenced by mutual sex-typing and less communication about emotions, particularly between fathers and their sons. For example, fathers of sons have been reported to be more biased in their child-rearing expectations than are fathers of daughters in agreeing with statements such as, "It is more acceptable for girls than for boys to cry (excluding major injuries)" (Turner & Gervai, 1995).

Boys' and girls' differential evaluations of the father's behaviour are consistent with his different treatment of boys and girls. In their review of the research on sex differences, Maccoby and Jacklin (1974, p. 348) report that they were handicapped by a lack of information on the father. But in agreement with the differential socialisation theory of Johnson (1963, 1975), they speculated that "fathers may differentiate between the sexes to a much greater degree than mothers". Since then considerable research has indicated that fathers, more than mothers, do differentiate between boys and girls (e.g. Bronstein, 1984; Langlois & Downs, 1980; Tauber, 1979). Although some studies have used multiple measures of parent–child interaction and often only a few of these have revealed differences related to the sex of the parent, results that are significant provide general support for a pattern of differential behaviour that is specific to the father (Siegal, 1987). In particular, the father gives more positive and negative reinforcement to boys than girls, is more punitive, and uses more firm control techniques. Though there are studies in which no differences at all have been found in parents' treatment of boys and girls, differences restricted specifically to the mother when comparisons are made of mothers and fathers have been virtually non-existent.

For girls, given the greater day-to-day involvement of the mother, a harmonious, peaceful environment in which subtle control can be used may often be effective in promoting an acceptance of adults' instructions. But for boys, the affective atmosphere of the home may preclude the use of subtle control. Owing to the father's and son's orientations towards the use of power assertion and the father's differential treatment, the boy may respond more positively to a parental authority that is made salient through firm discipline techniques. To achieve self-control, the boy may seek to bring himself in line with environmental forces. He may associate and identify vicariously with powerful others such as the father (see Rothbaum, Weisz, & Snyder, 1982, pp. 20–21). With greater paternal involvement and a father–son relation as close as that which ordinarily exists between the mother and daughter, subtle control techniques may be effective and appropriate for sons as well. In this respect, fathers may opt into the co-operative principle and initiate conversations with sons about feelings and rationales for following directions.

Conflict between the mother and father can exacerbate these difficulties in communication with children. For example, Kerig, Cowan, and Cowan (1993) observed conversations between children aged between $3\frac{1}{2}$ and 4 years and their parents. Each child was observed participating during 10 minutes of un-structured play separately with the mother and father in which the purpose was for the pair to "make a world together" using a sand tray and miniature objects. These observations included recording positive messages such as, "What a nice game" and "This going to be great" and negative messages such as, "Never mind" and "Oh, you don't know." Fathers who demonstrated evidence of poor marital adjustment showed the most negativity to daughters while mothers tended to reciprocate the negative expressions of their sons. In such circumstances, the troubled father–daughter relationship may be marked by authoritarian parenting; hence the absence of conversational understanding can be associated with negative attributes such as severe procrastination in daughters (Ferrari & Olivette, 1994).

Another aspect of conflict between parents that can influence communication with children is in the area of household work (Bowes & Goodnow, 1996). For example, fathers and mothers may disagree on the appropriate household chores for boys with fathers insisting that their sons do only stereotypical male jobs such as car washing but with mothers directing their sons to do female jobs such as cleaning the bathtub. Such discrepancies in messages from parents can at times create stress in boys, lower their sense of competence, and strain their relationships with parents (McHale, Bartko, Crouter, & Perry-Jenkins, 1990).

AUTHORITY AND CONVERSATIONAL UNDERSTANDING IN YOUNG CHILDREN

In her continually growing programme of research, Dunn (1994) has shown that parent–child relations may provide a special focus for the conversational transmission of knowledge of mental states. According to these studies, the children of parents who engage in "causal talk" about events that involve mental states are more likely to perform well on false belief tasks, discussed in Chapter Four, that require children to share the conversational implications of questions. Such causal talk must implicitly be based on the principle of "temporal priority" that causes must precede effects and thus are liable to highlight the temporal modifiers necessary to retrieve items in memory. Dunn also notes that performance on false belief tasks is related to shared humor which relies on conversational inferences as well as children's ability to demonstrate "connectedness" in communication through taking into account what others say and mean in their own messages. In support of these observations, parents' displays of emotional attachment and understanding have been shown to promote young children's friendships and their relations with others (Cassidy, Parke, Butkovsky, & Braungart, 1992; Finnie & Russell, 1988; Youngblade & Belsky, 1992).

It is often said that the younger the child, the more hopelessly ineffective is the use of reason as a way to make children comply with instructions and to behave well. However, bearing in mind Baumrind's (1983) contention that young children need clear messages that are backed up by displays of parental power such as the threat to withdraw privileges, reason seems every bit as important as techniques of power assertion in creating a responsive, compliant child. Even 2-year-olds may react well to reasoning in the form of guidance if this is paired with messages of firm control that include directives offering no choice or holding out the prospect of a reward which is conditional upon the child's compliance.

For example, in research conducted at the National Institute of Health in Washington, DC, Leon Kuczynski, Kochanska, Radke-Yarrow, and Girnius-

Brown (1987) observed mothers and children aged from 15 to 44 months who came for a visit to a suite of rooms in a laboratory apartment. A total of 90 minutes of interaction between the mother and child were videotaped through one-way mirrors in six contexts: arrival at the apartment, lunch including preparation and clean-up, mother engaged in a telephone conversation, free time, mother's rest period, and story time. From the videotapes, trained coders categorised the forms of the mother's control and her child's responses. There were significant associations between the type of maternal strategy and the type of child response. Unclear commands were associated with a lack of compliance and passive non-compliance whereas both unclear and direct commands were associated with direct defiance. By contrast, explanations and indirect commands on the part of the parent were associated with the use of negotiation on the part of the child.

In a similar study, Crockenberg and Litman (1990) observed mothers and their 2-year-olds in two situations. In one situation, each mother was recorded instructing her child to pick up toys in a playroom and to place these in a large basket. In the other situation, recordings were made of conversations between the mother and her child during preparation for meal time. The mother's behaviour was classified in clusters that included negative control, control, and guidance. Negative control was defined to involve anger, annoyance, criticism, non-empathic behaviour, criticisms, threats, spanking, or slapping. Control was defined to consist of stating a directive with no choice or providing a reward contingent upon compliance. Guidance consisted of attempts to direct the child's behaviour positively, including asking if the child needs help, persuading, and explaining. When mothers used control and guidance, their children were more likely to comply than when mothers used any other technique including control alone. By contrast, during preparation for meal time, children were most likely to demonstrate defiance by expressing anger or aggression in opposition to the mother when she used techniques of negative control alone without control or guidance. Although reasoning with very young children may not seem effective immediately, over a longer term of weeks it serves to facilitate compliance and spontaneous helpfulness. It provides a rationale for children to interpret parents' messages about good and bad behaviour as these are intended.

The key to talking to children in a manner that legitimates authority about right and wrong may be seen in terms of effective transmission of messages concerning others' welfare. How good are parents at this? Often parents are so frustrated in dealing with children's impolite requests or demands that their responses consist of reactions such as "What's the magic word? I beg your pardon. The maid is on strike today. Who is your servant? I must be going deaf?" or even "Were you born in a tent?" In these instances, children are addressed as if they were adults. Such messages depart from the quantity and manner rules in that adults say less than is necessary for effective communication and what they do say is framed in an unclear, ambiguous manner. And it is hardly surprising that preschoolers have little understanding unless this is followed up by more explicit or "direct" instructions as in this example given by Becker and Goodnow (1991):

Child: I want doll clothes. You can make me five or four clothes.
Mother: I beg your pardon.
Child: What?
Mother: Are you ordering me to do it?
Child: Mmm, I don't know, Momma.
Mother: Can't you say *"Mommy would you please make me some?"* Don't order me on how many to make. That's not very nice.
Child: Mommy, please can you make me some?

Yet often explicit, direct instructions that would facilitate communication with children do not follow indirect ones. Few parents have the patience to always recast the nature of their language to meet the child's conversational world. Indirect instruction that requires an understanding of conversational implications may be easier for the adult as it is the customary, efficient mode of communication in the adult world. Parents may require a break from the monotony of tailoring their messages to suit children and may feel the need to relate to others as an adult.

PARENTAL INVOLVEMENT

To promote academic skills and concern for others, parents may often use subtle techniques that avoid power assertion. In his many writings, Sigel (1981, 1993) has called for parents to use "distancing behaviours" to encourage learning in children. These are behaviours that place demands on the child to separate himself or herself from the ongoing field of observable events through representations in space and time. The child is required to "anticipate outcomes, recall events, and attend to transformations of objects or phenomena". Through high-distancing strategies, parents can lead the child to gain insight into the mental states of others. Opportunities are provided to plan and to evaluate the consequences of actions. Distancing that gives rise to preschoolers' "delay of gratification" in the form of planning and waiting for rewards is associated with children's later academic success (Mischel & Rodriguez, 1993; Mischel, Shoda, & Rodriguez, 1989).

For school-aged children, the quality of parental involvement can provide a continual basis for encouragement to do well on academic subjects. Grolnick and Ryan (1989) interviewed mothers and fathers of 48 children in grades 3 to 6 in a rural elementary school in upstate New York to identify a group of "autonomy-promoting" parents (particularly mothers) who used reasoning and empathy in setting limits. These parents were more likely to have children who were judged by their teachers to be successful at school. Compared to children of parents who used power assertive techniques such as physical punishment, children of autonomy-promoting parents were rated as displaying fewer learning difficulties and behaviour problems. Grolnick and Ryan suggest that parental support for autonomy promoted children's acceptance of classroom rules.

In follow-up research, Grolnick and Slowiaczek (1994) studied a sample of 300 11- to 14-year-olds. Bearing in mind that their data were correlational and parental behaviour might be seen as a consequence rather than an antecedent of children's academic success, Grolnick and Slowiaczek found that parents' perceived involvement was significantly associated with children's perceptions of their competence at school and their actual school performance.

Apart from the use of autonomy-promoting techniques of control, parents' attitudes and beliefs about development may influence children. A parent who has accurate expectations about children's capabilities may be best equipped to promote not only their compliance and responsiveness to others' interests and feelings but their success at school. One of the most important aims for children is to instil an intrinsic motivation to pursue reading, mathematics, and other school subjects voluntarily.

Scott Miller (1986) sought to test the hypothesis that the mother's knowledge of the child enables her to create an "optimally challenging" environment. First-graders were given either traditional Piagetian measures (such as conservation of number and length) or items from the Stanford–Binet test of intelligence (such as naming five days of the week). Their mothers were shown these tasks and were asked questions about the probable responses, both for their own child and for children in general. Mothers more commonly overestimated than under-estimated their children's performance. The most accurate mothers had the most successful children. These mothers may have provided the most stimulating environments. Miller's results were largely replicated in a later study involving the mothers and fathers of children in second and fifth grade in which there was considerable similarity between the estimates of parents (Miller, Manhal, & Mee, 1991). Yet it may be the case that all mothers are optimistic in praising their children's performance so that mothers who happen to have an intelligent child will be scored as more accurate than those who do not.

The extensive work of Stevenson and his colleagues (Stevenson, Chen, & Lee, 1993; Stevenson, Lee, & Stigler, 1986) is compatible with the interpretation of unjustified optimism among mothers of children who are not high achievers. They carried out a comparison of the factors underlying the mathematics achievement of American, Taiwanese, and Japanese school children from Minneapolis, Taipei, and Sendai. The cognitive abilities of the three groups appeared to be similar in the early primary school years. Yet by grade 5, the Japanese and Taiwanese far outstripped the Americans in mathematics. Parents in Japan and Taiwan indicated a greater concern with homework. For example, the percentage of parents who bought their fifth-graders workbooks in mathematics was 58% in Japan, 56% in Taiwan, but only 28% in the United States. Only 63% of the American fifth-graders had desks at home compared to 98% of the Japanese and 95% of the Taiwanese.

But despite the superiority of their children's performance at mathematics, Japanese and Taiwanese parents often expressed dissatisfaction with the quality of education received by the children. By contrast, the American parents were often very satisfied and could even be termed to have an attitude of complacency and overoptimism. Whereas Japanese and, to a lesser extent, Taiwanese parents focused on effort as a factor contributing to academic success, American parents were more likely to rate ability as a key factor. The belief in success through hard work was more apparent in Japan and Taiwan. Western commentators often mention the stressful nature of the Japanese education system with a serious, intense emphasis on the importance of academic success. Even so, there were no cross-cultural differences that appeared to disadvantage Japanese and Taiwanese children as shown by ratings of their happiness at school. If anything, American children reported the greater stress.

Such results might be attributed to a systematic bias in response scales in which Asian students and their parents are more likely to display their interdependence and modesty by avoiding extreme points on rating scales concerning the factors perceived to underlie school success. However, this possibility has been ruled out as any differences in using response scales appear to be small and cannot account for such large cross-cultural differences in group means (Chen, Lee, & Stevenson, 1995). Thus, on the basis of their extensive investigation, Stevenson and his colleagues conclude by advocating an increased involvement in reading, mathematics, and other elementary school subjects by American parents. They also maintain that through a process of acculturation, Chinese-American students apparently come to lag significantly behind their Japanese and Taiwanese counterparts in mathematics achievement, although they retain a significant lead over Caucasian-Americans (Chen & Stevenson, 1995).

However, parental involvement and an emphasis on effort rather than innate ability as the source of achievement is liable to be far from the whole story in so complex a problem as that of children's school success. Miller, Smith, Zhu, and Zhang (1995) point out that the base-10 structure of names for numbers is more salient in Asian languages such as Chinese than in English. For example, the Chinese term for the number 11 is translated as "ten-one" in contrast to the English word "eleven", which has no clear relation to either 10 or 1. Thus Chinese preschoolers are favoured in their learning to count and significantly outperform Americans. As counting is the basis for later mathematical competence, Chinese children may acquire a head start in mathematics which magnifies their advantage over English-speaking children during the school years.

Even within a culture, differences between groups of children may be rooted in the preschool years and widen with increasing age. In a very important though speculative article, Stanovich (1986) has attempted to explain the acquisition of academic skills such as literacy in terms of "Matthew effects". He maintains that the process of learning to read can be viewed in terms of effects in which the rich get richer and the poor get poorer. He paints a scenario in which children's knowledge of the alphabet and their ability to "decode" correspondences between letters and sounds leads to successful reading experiences. Increased vocabulary in turn leads to children's acquisition of a vocabulary of readable words which in turn produces further successful reading experiences and fluency in comprehension.

The outcome is a series of bidirectional or reciprocal effects in which successes in reading and reading experiences are mutual determinants of each other. During this process, children's reading experience can lead to an association with literate peers that in turn increases vocabulary and comprehension. Stanovich has argued that young children who have difficulty in distinguishing sounds and in matching sounds to letters will later become more and more disadvantaged compared to children who have performed well on these ground-floor prerequisites for reading. He calls for a "surgical strike" around the preschool period to diagnose and remediate reading problems.

Although the notion of Matthew effects may seem appealing as a framework for efforts at intervention, the precise nature of bidirectional forces in academic skills is exceedingly difficult to locate. Let us consider a somewhat different scenario. In a disordered home environment, parents do not equip children with a knowledge of moral and social transgressions. Children's behaviour leads to rejection by literate and numerate peers and poor motivation and concentration at school. Their poor academic performance in turn leads to a further lack of acceptance by peers who do well. In a New Zealand longitudinal study of boys' reading skills (McGee, Williams, Share, Anderson, & Silva, 1986), a strong association was found between reading disability and behaviour problems. The relation between difficulties at school and aggression has been confirmed in a recent American study (Wentzel & Asher, 1995). One interpretation of such results is that academic difficulties such as reading disability exacerbate problem behaviour that already exists at school entry. Coie and Krehbiel (1984) have suggested that behaviour problems may be reduced by involving children on tasks that enhance the acquisition of basic reading and writing skills. The ground floor in acquiring literacy is still during the early childhood period; but it calls for a broader form of intervention that enlists both the home and school environment and individual attention from adults as conducive to transmitting academic skills. There are now a variety of studies on instructing children in this manner.

INDIVIDUALISED INSTRUCTION IN READING AND NUMBER: SOME EXAMPLES

Hewison and Tizard (1980) showed how children's reading can benefit from an increased parental involvement. They examined home background factors and reading ability and found a strong relationship between mothers' self-reports of hearing the child read (referred to as "coaching") and reading achievement in 7- and 8-year-olds. In a sample of 70 British children with average IQ test scores, 24 of the 32 good readers studied by Hewison and Tizard had coaching mothers as opposed to only 8 of 38 poor readers.

Hearing children read involves training in language skills. Work by Bryant and Bradley (1983), also in Britain, and by Content, Kolinsky, Morais, and Bertelson (1986) in Belgium has shown how 4- and 5-year-olds can be trained to have an awareness of language in matching sounds to letters. The children seen by Bryant and Bradley later performed well on standardised reading tests compared to others who did not receive this training in early childhood. Furthermore, Goswami (1986, 1992, pp. 122–131) has reported that children who are learning to read can often be prompted to use analogies in "decoding" new words. For example, they can use the word "beak" to read, "peak", and "rail" to read "pail". In this respect, research carried out in Australian schools has shown that children's success when they first learn how to read can be enhanced still further should they have a foundation of alphabetic knowledge (Bowey, 1994; Byrne & Fielding-Barnsley, 1989, 1990).

Young children's representation abilities can also be used to promote links between what they already know and the symbols and regularities they are expected to acquire in the area of mathematics. As the following four examples illustrate, instructing children to use forms of representation may be a means to draw out their implicit knowledge about number. First, Fuson (1986a, 1986b) has reported that the learning of addition and subtraction can be facilitated by "counting-on" strategies in which children's attention is drawn to finger patterns as a form of representing sums and differences. Second, Hudson (1983) has shown that 4- and 5-year-olds can solve subtraction tasks that involve comparisons between sets using pretend items such as birds and worms, dogs and bones, butterflies and objects. If shown five birds and two worms and asked how many birds won't get a worm, children will respond with the correct answer. Third, Resnick and Ford (1981, pp. 210–213) have described how symbols may assist school-aged children to add and subtract using rows of blocks arranged in "tens" and "units" columns. For example, to subtract 47 from 85, the 85 is first represented as 8 ten-bars in the tens column and 5 ones-cubes in the units column. To arrive at the correct answer (38), the experimenter induces the child to notice that there are not enough ones-cubes in the units column to remove 7. The child is then trained to "borrow" a ten-bar from the tens column to the units column, separate the bar into ones-cubes, remove 7 of the cubes as part of subtracting 47, write down the remaining number of cubes in the units column, then remove 4 more ten-bars from the tens column, and count and write down the number of bars remaining to complete the problem.

Fourth, Cummins et al. (1988) have proposed that, rather than the absence of a capacity for representation, primary schoolers' difficulties with "word arithmetic problems" can be attributed to their misunderstanding of the uses of words such as "some" and linguistic forms such as "How many more Xs than Ys?" and "How many Xs do they have altogether?" It has been argued (Willis & Fuson, 1988) that such difficulties can be approached through having children (for example, second-graders) use schematic drawings to represent the various types of addition and subtraction problems: operations involving comparisons between quantities, changes to quantities resulting in a story character possessing more or less, and putting together quantities possessed by story characters. For example, a large box can be placed over two small boxes containing the numbers possessed by two characters to represent and clarify the meaning of a "put-together" problem.

To instruct children on number problems that primarily involve counting and placing objects in a one-to-one correspondence often involves the need to invoke a relevant context. But children appear to have special difficulties on problems that involve a knowledge of the relation between parts and wholes such as ratios, proportions and fractions (Bryant, 1995; Gelman, 1991) as, at a wide variety of ages, children very frequently have difficulty in accepting the possibility of numbers between integers. Fractions in particular appear to be avoided with the result that many cannot identify $\frac{1}{3}$ an $\frac{1}{4}$ or translate between common and decimal fractions (Hiebert & Wearne, 1986). They often do not connect the idea of a fraction as part of a whole with the operation of division and do not recognise how it is possible that a number can be divided by a larger one (Hart, 1981; Kerslake, 1986).

Explanations for difficulties with fractions have often been attributed to an inability to conceive of numbers as anything more than the consecutive integers (1, 2, 3, 4, 5, etc.) that are used for counting. Some children may know how many pieces will result when an object such as a piece of string is cut (Miller, 1984) and they may have an intuitive knowledge of how wholes can be decomposed into parts (Lampert, 1986). Yet they do not grasp the possibility of a systematic representation of fractions as numbers. In the absence of a "mental model", they may overgeneralise their use of counting numbers in a way which provides a formidable obstacle to accommodating their theory of number to accept fractions as those numbers which fill in the gaps between the integers.

Despite considerable training on fraction problems, many children regard fractions as if these were whole numbers. For example, Rochel Gelman (1991) reports a series of studies in which children in kindergarten and grades 1 and 2 were asked to place parts of circles ($\frac{1}{2}$, $\frac{1}{3}$, $\frac{1}{4}$) on a number line marked by whole circles representing 1, 2, and 3. Instead of ordering the parts of circles between whole ones, the children often placed a $\frac{1}{2}$ circle on top of the whole circle '1' and $1\frac{1}{2}$ on top of the '2'. Although children who could read the numerical representations or "numbergraphs" of fractions did better, many ignored the inversion sign in responding that $\frac{1}{4}$ is more than $\frac{1}{2}$.

Geary (1995) goes so far to claim that such mathematical abilities are "biologically secondary" in that these are culture-specific and require extensive practice and drill. Unlike "biologically primary" skills such as the counting of discrete quantities that occur in all cultures and appear inherently enjoyable to children, abilities requiring an understanding of part–whole relations involve the use of spatial representations that need to be explicitly taught and practised. It is desirable that this endeavour be made enjoyable, although enjoyment is not easily compatible with practice and drill.

In this respect, there are no easy answers. However, an approach that has been advocated as effective by Japanese educators is still worthy of note (Ginbayashi, 1984; Kobayashi, 1988; see also Hatano & Inagaki, 1991). For example, to train children's knowledge of part–whole relations, an instructor first focuses on continuous quantity in which the unit and numeral value has not been determined a priori in contrast to discrete quantities that possess countable units. To convey the critical notion that the instructor is referring to continuity, a water supply metaphor is commonly used in which children are shown litre containers of water that are partly filled, completely filled, or overfilled. From observations in Japanese classrooms, this is a powerful metaphor for the measurement of continuous quantity. Having witnessed the relation between water supply and measurement, the children then construct their own rulers out of tiles and make comparisons of quantity first using their own particular unit of constructed tiles, and then the universal unit of metres in which they are prompted to conceive of part–whole relations. To consolidate and enrich their understanding, each individual child in the class provides the others with a verbal demonstration of their knowledge and its point.

In Vygotsky's terms, this method may aid children to achieve what they are capable of through conveying the cultural use of part–whole relations in measurement. Gelman and Lee (1995, p. 41) refer to such a process as a form of "cognitive mentorship" in which the mentor explicitly instructs the student what, how, and why the task is to be learned. In this connection, the effectiveness of instruction in the area of mathematics may be enhanced by research on children's abilities to use analogies and to represent objects spatially (Goswami, 1992; Siegal, 1993).

AUTHORITY AS COMPLACENCY?

This brief description of examples illustrates how adults' involvement in early individualised instruction could play a key role in the development of literacy and numeracy. Interestingly, of all the subjects taught in school, mathematics is least dependent on the understanding of natural language. Even so, a focus by parents and teachers can capitalise on children's capacity for representation in order to clarify the meaning and purpose of language required for success on number, as well as on reading, tasks. Indeed, through exposure to instruction, children are initiated into the conversational world of adults. Extended instructions and increasingly specific questions encourage children to delay their interpretation of messages and prompt them to gain insight into how initial messages can be vague in conveying more than one meaning (Lloyd, Camaioni, & Ercolari, 1995; Robinson & Whittaker, 1986). Through engaging in tasks that require literacy and numeracy, children are required to construct inferences that explain why states and events are mentioned in the text (Graesser, Singer, & Trabasso, 1994; Markman, 1981; Olson, 1980).

However, guidance is hardly provided by an authority that amounts to complacency. While much more remains to be known about the consequences of parents' attitudes and beliefs for children (for an exposition of possible implications, see Bowes & Goodnow, 1996; Goodnow, 1988; Miller, 1988; Miller et al., 1991), the persistence of a complacent ideology demands a re-examination of the issue of education for young children. There are those who worry that demonstrations of the early benefits of teaching will result in formal schooling for 4-year-olds, depriving children of a time for childhood (Zigler, 1987). Yet there is no reason why instruction cannot be imparted informally to children within a warm, enjoyable family atmosphere. At 4 years of age, an austere formal schooling environment would hardly seem necessary—only a commitment by parents and preschool and daycare workers. As it stands now, in many cases, our underestimation of what parents can do in early childhood may be accompanied by an overestimation of what schools are doing, and will do, to meet children's needs. Gelman and Lee (1995, p. 29) remark that "... the longer we wait to introduce the novel, the better the chance that established knowledge systems will 'misinterpret' what is presented, often unwittingly".

It is notable that Piaget's theory is an ideal servant to this complacent approach. At times, his disinterest in applying developmental psychology to education surfaced in statements such as "it is impossible to deduce good pedagogy from psychology" and "it is better for a child to find and invent his own solutions rather than being taught" (Smith, 1985, p. 183). By virtue of his experimental results, Piaget (1972, p. 49) termed the issue of how to speed up developmental processes in order to move children into a more advanced stage as the "American dilemma". This approach is certainly in line with the brash proposition that potential genius can be discovered very early and accelerated. However, an uncritical acceptance of Piaget's position can distract educators from legitimate concerns about children's potential.

As Resnick and Ford (1981, p. 189) have exclaimed, the conception of matching instruction to the children's readiness as shown by their performance on Piagetian tasks is "virtually a counsel of despair for education, because it implies that there is little for teachers to do except to await certain developments". A more optimistic "neo-Piagetian" interpretation of "matching" is to give children problems that are moderately challenging for their present capability but are not so difficult as to be incomprehensible. Still, educators have often used Piaget to derive guidelines for schooling on the basis of a notion of developmental readiness. For example, it has been stated that, before children attain the age at which they attend primary school, they "lack a firm foundation of judgement or reasoning". As a consequence, before teaching academic skills such as reading, they should have achieved "readiness" and "prerequisite skills" (Furth & Wachs, 1974, pp. 42–43). The interpretation of Piaget's negative message for education flies in the face of the accumulating wealth of evidence on young children's capacity for understanding and the effectiveness of instruction during the preschool and early primary school years.

8 Models of Knowledge

CONVERSATIONAL RULES FOR KNOWING CHILDREN

Much of the knowledge of children which appears in textbooks on child development has been derived from their responses in interviews with adults. Nevertheless, interviews often involve prolonged or other forms of unconventional questioning methods where children can perceive that conversational rules have been violated. Not enough recognition has been accorded to the shortcomings of these types of study. Instead of a conceptual limitation, their incorrect responses may reflect uncertainty, a misinterpretation of the meaning or purpose of the question, a desire to give attention-seeking answers, or simply a wish to end the conversation.

We must remember that children are speaking to interrogators who are physically much larger and more powerful and that conversations between children (usually 3 to 4 feet high) and adults (usually 5 to 6 feet high) reflect differences in stature. The ratio is similar to that between average-sized adults and 8-foot giants. Even adult speakers are influenced by the physical characteristics of their listeners. With a more limited experience of the social world and personalities of adults, children may appear to be highly suggestible in an interview setting. They may fear the unsuspecting adult who nevertheless approaches the interview with gentleness and sincerity. In judging that an adult speaker has said enough to communicate effectively, children nevertheless may concede that their interpretation of an ambiguous message could be incorrect (Robinson & Whittaker, 1986).

Moreover, children recognise that adults ordinarily have more knowledge than they do. As Freeman, Sinha, and Condliffe (1981) have pointed out, this recognition adds to the imbalance of power that is implicit in conversations between children and adults. If knowledge creates power, a situation of confrontation may develop in which children can feel obliged by using extraneous information provided by adults to give a response. The result may be an answer to a question different from the one that the experimenter had intended.

The power relations in conversations between adults and children are like the relations between powerful and submissive groups of adults. For example, anthropologists and linguists have observed differences in the conversations of white and Aboriginal Australians (Eades, 1982). They have found considerable "gratuitous concurrence" among Aborigines who attempt to accommodate to the requests of white Australians. To respond, Aborigines rein nods, muffle sounds, and use silence as "Marcel Marceau" strategies (Liberman, 1981). In order not to offend the questioner, the answer often approximates a "Might be!"

Moreover, there are many cultures where the turntaking that is so much a part of the conversation of speakers in Western cultures actually becomes an obstacle to effective communication. In his investigation of the Dowayo culture in the Cameroons, Barley (1983, p. 67) writes:

> To begin with I was distressed to find that I couldn't extract more than ten words from Dowayos at a stretch. When I asked them to describe something to me, a ceremony, or an animal, they would produce one or two sentences and then stop. I would have to ask further questions to get more information. One day, after two months of fruitless endeavor, the reason struck me. Whereas in the West we learn not to interrupt when somebody else is talking, this does not hold in much of Africa . . . When listening to someone else talking, a Dowayo stares gravely at the floor, rocks backwards and forwards and murmurs, 'Yes', 'It is so', 'Good', every five seconds or so. Failure to do so leads to the speaker rapidly drying up. As soon as I adopted this expedient, my interviews were quite transformed.

Barley chronicles how both age and co-vocalisation are prerequisites for many conversational exchanges among the Dowayo. Young adults are excluded from the presence of conversations between powerful, learned elders and, within the community of elderly conversationalists, the addresses "old man" and "grandfather" are liberally employed as terms of respect.

When adults from non-Western cultures are questioned to determine their understanding of Western logic, they may import their own local concerns rather than the scientific concerns of the investigator. For example, when given a syllogism such as "All Kpelle men are rice farmers. Mr Smith is not a rice farmer. Is he a Kpelle man?" a Kpelle might well reply, "I don't know the man in person . . . Since I do not know him I cannot answer that question" (Scribner, 1977, p. 490).

Similarly, in specialised settings where well-meaning investigators question children for the scientific purpose of determining what they know, conversations are apt to have some of the characteristics of the relations between powerful and submissive groups of adults who vary in age and cultural background. Ordinarily, as Clark (1992, pp. 3–6) observes, speakers engaged in the co-operative activity of conversation accumulate information through readily identifying what can be assumed to be given as common grounding and the new, additional information that the listener does not previously know. They thus adhere to a "new-given contract" about the co-operative use of new and given information. Yet children who recognise that an adult ordinarily has more knowledge and more power than they do may not identify the novel component in the conversation initiated by the adult questioner and view this to be a breach of the contract. Should they not share an adult speaker's purpose of eliciting knowledge that he or she already possesses, they may be reluctant to accede to such requests and remain silent, or they may respond curtly and switch their answers under repeated questioning in an effort to placate the investigator and bring the conversation to an end, or they may simply attempt to assent to what they believe has been asked in every question. Dias and Harris (1988) demonstrate that Western children aged between 4 and 6 years respond to syllogisms in a manner that resembles the Kpelle unless efforts are made to present problems in which the premises run contrary to their own experience in the context of make-believe play situations.

In this respect, ethnographic research has shown that the methods used by adults to instruct children as to how, when, where, and with whom to converse vary across regions and cultures (Heath, 1983; Ochs, 1983; Schieffelin, 1983, 1986, 1990). The resulting differences in conversational patterns and routines pose a challenge for studies of cognitive development in situations that are located outside middle-class urban settings in Western countries. Schieffelin (1983) reports that children in the Kaluli culture of New Guinea are not regarded as significant communicators until they produce the "hard speech" of adults who refrain from using simplified language or baby talk in language socialisation. To achieve the objective of arming children with speech habits that are well-formed and socially appropriate, Kaluli mothers directly instruct children on what to say in conversation by providing model utterances followed by the imperative "Say like that." Similarly, Rogoff and Mistry (1990) give the example of Mayan culture in which it is inappropriate for children to speak freely to adults. When tested for their ability to recall a story, Mayan children fidget, avoid eye content and often barely speak. To continue at all, they require considerable prompting and commonly qualify their messages with the word *cha* ("So I have been told") in order to show that they are not claiming a possession of greater knowledge than adults.

In any culture, once children do reply, they may import their own relevance. They may interpret questions in a manner different than those intended by speaker (Beal & Belgrad, 1990; Bonitatibus, 1988; Donaldson, 1978; Hughes & Grieve, 1983; Siegal & Peterson, 1994). Even Western children can be like the Kpelle and the Maya in their responses. For instance, Labov (1972, pp. 201–240) has documented the effects of the social situation on African-American children's responses to adults' questions about their daily activities and has shown that the more asymmetrical the power relationship, the less willing are children to offer answers freely. Similarly, African-American children from inner-city areas may provide an apparently poor level of performance on forms of conservation tasks. They may furnish responses aimed to meet what they perceive to be the experimenter's needs and interpret "why" questions as a signal to change answers (Goodnow, 1984). This type of response may seem satisfactory to children who do not, or choose not to, understand the intent of the questioner. But it frustrates attempts at drawing out what children do know.

The potential for a clash of conversational worlds underscores the complexity of the task involved in establishing what children know through using techniques that require a conversational knowledge that children have have not yet acquired. Thus in the case of children and their competence in conversation, a paradox arises. On many occasions, young children communicate well with others. However, in specialised settings such as in testing situations, communication between children and adults who are both conversationally competent within their own worlds of experience and social interaction may be impaired simply because they do not share the interpretation of each other's conversational contribution. In order to overcome this obstacle, investigators need to talk to children in an explicit manner that does not set aside the Gricean maxims and does not require them to follow the conversational implications of questions.

There is defence for interviewing children with questions that one would ask adolescents or adults. Leahy (1983), for example, has maintained that interviewing allows researchers to examine the structure and quality of children's justifications for their opinions. It may also reveal unexpected responses that would not be discovered using different methodologies. Yet, as Leahy concedes, interviews are only a start and other techniques must be found to validate interview results.

But even though results from experiments which have used alternative methodologies have very often yielded contradictory results, interviewing continues to be used as a sole or primary source of knowledge about children. Many questions that require children to make judgements about their world inadvertently violate the rules of ordinary conversation that a speaker's messages should be sincere, informative, relevant, and non-redundant, and use linguistic forms that are clear and unambiguous in meaning. If listeners are inexperienced in the world of adult conversation, they may respond, for example, as if the speaker really meant that the properties of the objects to be compared, such as colour, are relevant to the correct answer. We cannot assume that children share the experimenter's definition of the attributes relevant to the task.

In sorting persons or objects into groups, young children typically rely on their own experiences. For example, Chi (1985) has described a study of a 5-year-old girl who was asked to sort the names of her classmates into groups. The groupings turned out to correspond to the seating order in the classroom. The girl was asked in a second study to sort and then to recall the names in alphabetical order with a list of the alphabet as a pointer. So long as the names were those of her classmates, she could easily retrieve a cluster of names beginning with the same letter. When asked to sort and recall names that did not represent classmates, but were none the less familiar, her recall was poor.

Children may need to connect their representation of their environment to the use of a new strategy. If knowledge is represented in a specific, familiar domain, even young children may be able to use concepts to sort things into organised taxonomies. Chi has reported the case of a 4-year-old who was an expert in his knowledge of dinosaurs. In his field, he was able to produce on request the names of 46 dinosaurs. A set of 40 was then chosen for further testing. Using the frequency of inclusion in the boy's nine dinosaur texts and his mother's judgement of his knowledge, the dinosaurs were divided into better known and lesser known groups. The boy could easily sort the 20 better known dinosaurs by food habits (meat-eaters and plant-eaters) and could categorise the dinosaurs further according to type of locomotion (e.g. two-legged, four-legged, or flying). These dimensions were more salient for the better known than for the lesser known groups, and guided the quick and exhaustive sorting behaviour of the expert boy.

Chi's findings once more clash with the position that young children are at a stage in which they suffer from a basic conceptual limitation. If a task is set in a relevant, co-operative, and informative atmosphere that abides by conversational rules, they will be more likely to demonstrate what they know.

Where the results of prolonged or unconventional questioning in interviews reveal a failure to understand, we often are left with the possibility that children are interpreting questions in ways different than those intended by the experimenter. As Hughes and Grieve (1983) have shown, young children will seek to answer even the most bizarre questions. They will strain to make sense out of questions such as "Is milk bigger than water?" and "Is red heavier than yellow?" by importing a context of relevance into their replies: for example, "Yes, because there is more milk than water when you pour them into bottles" and "Yes, because red is darker than yellow." Similarly, adults can seek to answer questions that imply answers which are contrary to elementary logic. For example, Winer, Hemphill, and Craig (1988) had third-graders, sixth-graders, and college students respond to misleading questions such as "When do you weigh the most? When you are walking or running?" Regardless of age, the majority selected one of the two incorrect choices rather than the logically correct response of rejecting the question and indicating that the weight remains the same.

Good experimental designs will avoid the possibility that children will use strategies of silence or gratuitous compliance. To reduce the difficulties inherent in interview studies and assist children to demonstrate the depth of their understanding, attractive, experimental contexts are often required in which they can produce and evaluate the rightness, truthfulness, and sincerity of responses in conversations.

HOW MUCH UNDERSTANDING IS THERE?

Very young children can often represent the invariant properties of number and length in conservation experiments and have insight into causal relations and the mental states of others. To what extent do they understand abstract concepts? The short answer to this question, which was raised at the start of this book, is that children have a good deal more knowledge than they were credited with by Piaget. If so, in what sense are they fundamentally different from adult thinkers?

In an ambitious attempt to address the issue, Carey (1985a, 1985b) has argued that the major differences are in "domain-specific" knowledge. Children are novices and adults are experts in specific knowledge domains. Compared to adults, they simply know less about the world of number, peers, and so on. Consequently, children and adults hold different theories of the world. Once children identify, practise, and know when to use skills that permit problems to be solved, their theories become more adult-like.

Part of this process is "metaconceptual" or "metacognitive". Young children may not know when they should apply the knowledge that they already have or can have. They may not identify a need to acquire and use symbols to represent numbers, letters, and names. Another part is "metalinguistic". For example, children can understand messages guided by conversational rules better than messages that involve implications which depart from convention. It is difficult to see how children can accomplish metaconceptual tasks without first overcoming the metalinguistic problem of sharing the purpose and meaning of the experimenter.

To define competence in children's problem solving, Gelman, Meck, and Merkin (1986) have made a threefold distinction. First, there is a "conceptual-competence" that characterises knowledge in specific domains such as counting. Second, there is a "utilisation-competence" that involves the ability to determine the relevant features of the task and correctly interpret instructions. For example, on a counting task the child must appreciate that some displays have a clear beginning at the top or bottom where counters are arranged in rows while other displays in which counters are arranged in circles have no clear beginning. To avoid double-counting, the child must take note of this feature. Third, we have a "planning" or "procedural competence". This is the ability to select goals and strategies—for example, to co-ordinate the use of words for counting to tag each object to be counted only once with the goal of finding the correct cardinal number.

Knowing the goal to be achieved and knowing how to achieve it is different from knowing the correct solution. As Karmiloff-Smith (1986) points out, we can usefully examine knowledge in terms of that which is consciously accessible and that which can be implicitly represented in behaviour. Although each of these terms have connotations with different levels of awareness, knowledge that is consciously accessible has at times been called "explicit" or "declarative knowledge" (or roughly, in Gelman's terms, "conceptual knowledge") and implicit knowledge has at times been referred to as "procedural knowledge". For example, in communication tasks, young children can implicitly identify linguistic forms such as sentences by responding correctly when they are asked to repeat the last sentence that they heard in a story. However, if asked directly and explicitly to say whether linguistic forms such as the articles "a" and "the" are words, they may not be able to reply explicitly. Similarly, children may have a substantial implicit knowledge of the AR distinction before possessing a conscious access to a dual representational code that is necessary to respond to AR questions across a wide range of knowledge domains. Moreover, although they may not be able to state that 6 minus 4 equals 2 in their arithmetic, they will be likely to state the answer to a problem such as "There are 6 boys and 4 biscuits. How many boys will not have a biscuit?" They may also have an implicit knowledge of proportions or fractions such as ½ and ¼ without consciously accessing these symbols. Thus, if an experimenter has the goal of examining the early capacity for representation through direct questioning about a remote or not clearly relevant matter, some children—even in non-redundant, single-task conditions—are liable to misinterpret the task requirements. Without knowing what to do, they are unlikely to demonstrate what they know. Since they may not consciously access their knowledge, they may represent appearance when asked to report reality or incorrectly represent whole numbers where fractions are required.

By contrast, children may demonstrate a procedural or implicit knowledge if the experimenter examines their understanding as a means to obtain a clear-cut goal such as the detection of pretence in familiar situations or the procurement of food and the avoidance of illness. Even many 2-year-olds, for example, may implicitly demonstrate knowledge of the distinction between appearance and reality by labelling as inedible food that appears safe but is contaminated in reality. Certainly, we would feel more secure in these circumstances if they could display a convincing explicit knowledge by spontaneously telling us that "Even if a drink looks OK it may have had a bug in it. So the drink may be contaminated." But to recognise that their knowledge in a domain may be mainly of the implicit sort is very different from embracing the conclusion that they have little or no understanding at all.

Yet experimenters can often seek explicit, declarative knowledge from children using methods which require still further explicit knowledge. In communication with adults, young children may initially operate under a "mental model" that does not represent departures from conversational rules. As Johnson-Laird (1983) has proposed, in making inferences listeners typically imagine a state of affairs based on the meaning of the premises. They then formulate an informative conclusion that corresponds to this state, and search for alternative models to test the validity of the conclusion. For young children, their experience in communication with adults often takes the form of the simple model: A (adult) wants B (information) which can be found by asking C (child). The inference is simply that in questioning C (and C having co-operatively conveyed B to A), A has obtained the goal of knowing B.

But, for example, what if this mental model is disturbed by prolonged questioning on very similar tasks that sets aside the quantity rule that a speaker should speak no more than is required to communicate effectively? Children may not construct an alternative model based on the correct state of affairs: A wants to be sure that C knows about B and for this reason A uses redundant and prolonged techniques of questioning. Instead, they may operate on the basis of premises such as A believes that B can be found from C if C would change his or her mind, or that A was looking for a different B in the first place. Therefore, even if some children have an explicit or declarative understanding of a problem such as the knowledge that milk in a blue glass is white in reality and blue in appearance, it may not be conveyed in response to techniques that require the construction of an alternative model of the task and the experimenter's intentions.

According to Johnson-Laird (1983, pp. 126–145), we can distinguish between implicit and explicit inferential ability in interpreting discourse. Implicit inferences are based on a single or default mental model that processes information rapidly. Explicit inferences are required when the default model does not work and alternative models must be sought. Although young children are inexperienced in meeting this requirement, very often the strong claim is made that they are conceptually limited, that they have little or no understanding of features of the physical and mental world, and that instruction in academic skills should be postponed until they attain a requisite stage of development. The use of unconventional or unfamiliar language that requires the explicit construction of alternative mental models may not only conceal an implicit knowledge of a problem but an explicit one as well.

The consequences of children's inexperience in constructing models of the experimenter's intent are serious, and can mislead adults to tap into a fraction of their understanding. As I noted in Chapter Two, there are at least five possible explanations for their lack of success on many of the tasks that have been commonly used to characterise their inadequacies under prolonged, repeated, or other forms of questioning that set aside conversational rules where an answer may be perceived to be obvious or unobtainable.

1. *"Switching under uncertainty"*. Children who are uncertain of the answer in the first place may be induced to change their responses. For example, young

children very often are inclined to conserve. But, as in many matters, they can be less certain of the answer than older more experienced individuals. Under repeated questioning that is liable to stray from the quantity rule, they can be more easily led to comply with the suggestion that their first response may have been in error.

2. *Insincerity*. Children may be certain of the answer. However, they may respond incorrectly in an effort to end a conversation with a well-meaning experimenter who apparently does not accept their answers and to return to activities that are more attractive. For example, on conservation or AR tasks, children may be unwilling to repeat a correct response for an experimenter who has heard it before. If alternative activities are present, they may respond incorrectly just so that they can return to these.

3. *The overattractive task*. Children again may be certain of the answer. However, contrary to the quantity and relevance rules, they may perceive the questions to be silly or to have obvious answers which require "cute" responses instead of correct ones. As in the case of adults' constant interest in gender-related matters, their answers to well-meaning questions about their gender concepts probably provide the ideal example. If alternative activities are unavailable, they may respond to attract the attention of adult questioners and to prolong the experiment. As in some perspective-taking or false belief tasks, if asked to consider two alternatives, only one of which is visible, they may simply choose the one that is more visible and salient without carefully attending to the question. When pitted against a visible alternative, the child's perception of the viability of the invisible alternative is liable to be undermined.

4. *Trust in the experimenter*. Young children in the presence of adults are inclined not to be very bold. They are encouraged to defer to the directions and judgements of adults, particularly, for example, in health-related matters. Therefore, although at least some are knowledgeable about the invisible basis of contamination, they are not likely to question the motives of a grown-up who wants to test their knowledge about contaminants and have no grounds to assume that, contrary to the quality rule, they would be offered unsafe substances to eat or drink.

5. *Word use*. In particular domains of knowledge, children may not share adults' use of words or certain linguistic forms that are liable to infringe the manner rule to avoid ambiguity and obscurity. For example, they may interpret the word "same" to mean the "exact same" in size or dimension, or "number" to mean only whole numbers rather than fractions in referring to parts of circles, or "altogether" in word arithmetic problems to indicate "each". As Wertsch (1985) points out, how children define the meaning of words is central to Vygotsky's (1962, 1978) notions of the nature of development in that, at first, children may relate the use of words that refer to scientific and mathematical concepts in a way that is close to their own experience. To enable children to solve problems

eventually on their own, the challenge for the adult is to find a context and mode of communication with children that bridges the disparity between children's and culturally appropriate definitions of the tasks that involve these concepts.

Questionable questioning techniques may be employed whenever due regard is not given to (1) the implicit nature of much of children's early knowledge and (2) their implicit reliance on a default model of communication compatible with Grice's co-operative principle and the rules or maxims for conversation (quantity, quality, relevance, and manner) which prescribe that a speaker should be sincere, informative, unambiguous, and say no more or no less than is required to elicit an answer.

Children's explicit inferential ability in interpreting discourse and the explicit knowledge of a subject matter warrants attention in itself and cannot be reduced to stages of memory development. In order to understand the meaning and purpose of the language used by an experimenter and to represent simultaneously different characteristics of a problem, children may remember to consider alternative mental models. Yet they may not realise which kind of model to construct and select.

For example, in two experiments on children's logical reasoning (Johnson-Laird, Oakhill, & Bull, 1986), 9- to 12-year-olds were given problems for which no alternative mental models could refute the validity of a conclusion and problems for which alternative mental models exist. For example, premises that require only one mental model to be constructed are "All the artists are beekeepers. All the beekeepers are chemists." No model exists to refute the conclusion: "All the artists are chemists." Children are significantly better at solving this sort of problem compared to one with premises such as: "Some of the artists are beekeepers. Some of the beekeepers are chemists." Although one model suggests the conclusion, "Some of the artists are chemists", explicit consideration needs to be given to an alternative that exists to refute it: "None of the artists are chemists." As predicted, the children's success at drawing valid conclusions from the premises was dependent on the number of mental models to be considered. However, the prediction that performance would be related to a measure of memory load (involving the transformation of sets of two and three letters to a designated later place in the alphabet) was not supported.

One may level the criticism that this sort of experiment is "ecologically invalid" because it uses premises that do not reflect everyday experiences and reasoning strategies. If this is so, how would the use of logic have come about in the first place? Moreover, as Johnson-Laird and his colleagues note, it is ironic to use a logical form of argument to criticise research on the use of logic. Their results highlight first, how mental models can guide effective problem solving and, second, that more than memory is involved in the use of models.

In fact, even very young children can be instructed to use models if the goal of the problem is made explicit and the context is made attractive. To examine the ability to transfer solutions across problems, Brown, Kane, and Echols (1986, p. 107) read 3- to 5-year-olds a prototype problem about a Genie:

> A magic Genie lived for many years in a field behind a wall. His home was a very pretty bottle where he lived happily and collected a fine set of jewels. But one day an envious witch put a spell on the Genie. He was stuck to the spot, he couldn't move his feet, all his magic powers were gone. If he could move his home to the other side of the wall, he would be out of reach of the spell and his magic would come back. He had found an even prettier larger bottle on the other side, but he has a problem. How can he get his jewels across the high wall into the new bottle without breaking them and without moving his feet. The Genie has all these treasures to help him (glue, string, tape, etc.). Can you think of any way the Genie can get his jewels into the new bottle?

Children in a "recall" condition were asked to tell all they could remember about the story. Children in an "explicit goal structure" condition were given prompts to emphasise the abstract structure common to the Genie and subsequent transfer tasks: "Who has a problem? What did the Genie want to do? What is stopping the Genie? How did the Genie get his jewels across?" Compared to the recall group, those who were required to attend to the goal transferred their understanding across problems. In addition to their memory for story details, the knowledge of a common model contributed to their ability to transfer solutions.

In a more recent investigation of preschoolers' abilities to map relations across problems (Goswami, 1995), 3- and 4-year-olds were read a short version of the story of Goldilocks and the Three Bears. Then they were told to choose from a first set of three cups a Daddy Bear size cup, a Mummy Bear size cup, and a Baby Bear size cup. Once the children had done this, they were asked to choose the same cup in other sets of three in which the cups differed in size from the original set. As in the case of the research on preschoolers' ability to distinguish mistake from lies, the use of bears was often successful in producing good performance. In choosing from these new sets, most children regardless of age were able to ignore the absolute size of the cup they had chosen from the original set and to display the abstract ability of choosing the cup that was the same relative size. In follow-up studies, many of the same children, particularly the 4-year-olds, could also choose portions of pizza and chocolate for the three bears according to their relative size, as well as attributes such as mirrors that varied in height.

Once again, an explanation that rests upon the notion of a conceptual limitation in children's development does not fit their performance in experiments. To realise the skills that need to be employed in problem solving, children at times require prompting. If the goal is explicit and attractive, they will be more likely to access their knowledge as a means to achieve an end. If the goal is explicit, attractive, and familiar, they may do so even without prompting.

If the means is incidental to achieving some relevant purpose, they will be more likely to know what is to be done and to know when and how to use their knowledge.

THE CHILD IN SOCIETY

Whichever way one looks at it, children are active producers of their environment. This was recognised by Piaget and is a significant advance over the behaviourist account, current in the first part of this century, that development is mainly the result of conditioning and reinforcement. Furthermore, it must be recognised that a major purpose of Piaget's work was to specific criteria for identifying the structure of thinking and reasoning and children (Chapman, 1988). In devising measures of the development of these cognitive structures, he has made an invaluable contribution in demonstrating the usefulness of experiments with children. As pointed out in a recent spirited defense of Piaget's work (Lourenço & Machado, 1996), showing that an abstract conceptual knowledge is present in children younger than those originally studied by Piaget does not automatically invalidate his theory, for Piaget's interest was to identify a developmental sequence in which the child constructs a representation of reality in the physical and mental world.

However, Piaget interpreted his often astonishing results to support the existence of a basic, pervasive conceptual limitation in early child development. Age differences in conservation answers, for example, were seen as mainly due to differences in the schema or functional architecture required to use concepts such as invariance. In adapting to the environment, he claimed that children later come to share the same logic or capacity for representation as adults. Despite many neo-Piagetians working in this tradition and the theoretical leaps taken by investigators of social development and education, recent experiments have challenged his analysis of children's knowledge. If we would have to deliver a verdict at this point in time, it would be that Piaget's developmental psychology frequently consists of a series of false negative results: His research methods have generated studies that have too often underestimated children's knowledge.

To be sure, followers of Piaget often contend that (1) such accounts are guilty of the "converse, false-positive error" in "ascribing to children operational competences that, on further analyses, turn out to be only preoperational" (Lourenço & Machado, 1996, p. 146) and that (2) "Piaget did not argue for evidence of cognitive incompetence in children but for the lack of evidence for a cognitive competence" (Lourenço & Machado, 1996, p. 148). Yet to display what he regarded as their authentic competence, Piaget required even very young children to provide sophisticated justifications for their responses. He often credited children with competence in their operations only if they explicitly used logical necessity to justify their solution to a problem. For example, to credit children with the ability to conserve number, they not only have to recognise that two rows of buttons have the same number as before despite the fact that one has been lengthened and the other shortened but to provide the explanation that the number *must* be the same as nothing has been added or taken away (e.g. by responding to the experimenter, "You haven't added or taken away any buttons so there are still as many as before.") This requirement goes far beyond the normal facility that conversationally inexperienced children (or, for that matter, adults in many cases involving intercultural communication or communication between superiors and subordinates) can often exhibit. Not only does it assume that children recognise the purpose and relevance of the adults' questions, but it also assumes that children can boldly portray the strength of their beliefs in providing an explanation that they know the adult already knows—one that involves spontaneously evaluating the inscrutable actions of the experimenter.

To carry out a deeper exploration of justifications such as that advocated by Lourenço and Machado requires techniques that avoid the need for children to share the conversational implications of an experimenter's questions and to be confronted with the sole responsibility of ensuring that their answers to direct questions are correct. As shown in this book, if children are given the opportunity in a manner that invites collaboration in conversation with the experimenter to choose and evaluate justifications for correct and incorrect answers on a task, they often respond in a sophisticated manner. Thus insofar as false positive errors permeate studies of cognitive development, these can sometimes be seen in well-meaning investigators' acceptance that children understand the conversational implications of questions about what they know.

Conversational exchanges often take place between speakers who are empowered in having knowledge of the relevance and purposes of their questions and listeners who do not. Conversational influences create pressure for yet-to-be-empowered children to come back with answers that fulfil what they perceive as the submissive role of someone who is striving to gain knowledge from a superior questioner. Thus in conservation of number experiments, children may be led, particularly following repeated questioning, to assume that they are to pick a longer row as having more or else an adult would not have gone to the trouble to ask whether that row had more. Similarly, in experiments on children's ability to distinguish a mistake from a lie, they may reason that an adult may not have gone to the trouble of asking, "Was that a lie or not?" unless he or she believed lying had occurred and assent to this implication even in the case of a mistake. In experiments on children's understanding of contamination, they may be led to assume that they are to say that an apparently inedible substance could not in fact be bad to eat in deferring to a belief that the questions of a well-meaning experimenter would not mask a deception. They may also seek to complement an experimenter on appearance–reality tasks by claiming that he or she has changed the nature of an object not only in its appearance but in reality.

Young children are notoriously unwilling to abandon their traditional social role as a submissive learner whose task is to comply by absorbing information from others. They are particularly inflexible in admitting to justifiable departures from etiquette (Levy, Taylor, & Gelman, 1995) and strive to make sense of information and instructions, no matter how irrelevant these may be. In this light, a systematic re-examination of the evidence requires adults to reorganise theories of development and models of knowledge. When children are studied in relation to their appreciation of conversational rules in specific domains of knowledge and efforts are made to align children's interpretation of the purpose and relevance of questioning with that intended by the experimenter, we soon discover that children come closer to displaying the competence that Piaget advocated. The evidence comes in the form of an early, incipient understanding of abstract concepts such as number, causality, and the identity of persons and objects that is in line with the talent which infants display in representing their environment. No longer can we ascribe to the simple (and perhaps for that reason, enticing) view that the emergence of abstract concepts across domains of knowledge is necessarily tied to some stage where children at last emerge from their limitations.

In this sense, children do not stand apart from adult society. In granting that even preschoolers have an understanding of the physical and mental world, albeit one based on a restricted set of contexts and experiences, we find that an intensive involvement in early childhood is not misplaced. Preschoolers are not limited to superficial physical characteristics and can have friendships and peer relations based on a mutual knowledge of mental states.

The studies of Asian children that were mentioned in Chapter Seven point to the effectiveness of parental involvement in promoting academic skills. Expectations for children vary cross-culturally. In contrast to the Asian situation, the conception of childhood in the West may reflect a complacency that—and I am conscious of a deliberate effort to be provocative here—is "infected" by a parental belief in stages or levels. Yet children's perceptions of parents, parenthood, and society may influence how and when they use their abilities (Siegal, 1985). Parental involvement and children's association with literate and numerate peers contributes to their academic achievement and concern for others. Of course a child's path in society is not determined as a preschooler or even in primary school. But a parental orientation that pays little attention to the active nature of the preschooler's reading and number skills can scarcely be expected to change radically as the child matures.

The challenge here is real and pressing. While we may legislate to prevent child abuse and to ensure that children attend school (though not necessarily to learn), it is more difficult to legislate that parents must give their children practice in identifying sounds and letters and in solving number problems—let alone to be sensitive to conversational rules that facilitate communication. Taxpayers may resist the suggestion that a desk be provided to students, even if they are children from poor families. The autonomy of parents to rear children in the way they see fit is a doctrine that is usually respected in Western society (see Eekelaar, 1984, for a discussion). We can only use techniques of persuasion in publicising the importance of the family context of development.

All the same, most parents are not familiar with issues in child development and research. Many do not consider whether children have the capacity to understand concepts. Nor do they strive for an ideal or detailed conception of the conditions under which children learn. Instead, their dealings with children are often influenced by a personal acquaintance with parent–child relationships. Accordingly, the quality of parental involvement may have its origin in early experiences, possibly in mothers' and fathers' childhood relationships with their own parents (Main, Kaplan, & Cassidy, 1985; Ricks, 1985; Slade, 1987).

A parental involvement that fosters academic skills in early childhood is more likely to be followed by high expectations and demands for the older child than in cases where parents have been comparatively non-involved. The involved parent of a preschooler who, for example, uses word and number games to help the child with reading and arithmetic, will more likely become the involved parent of a primary schooler. Moreover, parenting characteristics may be transmitted across generations so that parents' treatment of their children influences the upbringing of the next generation. In this respect, early experience may indirectly affect later human development.

In what way does a climate of parental involvement require a recognition of differences between parent–child communication and communication between adults? Hockett (1963), a linguist, has listed design features for language and communication that are common to human speech in both adults and young children. Linguistic messages may refer to things and events that are distant in time and space (the design feature of "displacement"). New messages are coined freely and easily (the feature of "openness"). In addition, communication involves the ability to understand what has been termed "prevarication", the notion that linguistic messages can be false and meaningless. In many subject matters, children's knowledge may be more fragile than deep. But according to evidence from experiments, at least by the age of 4 years if not earlier, children have a concept of mental representation together with a capacity to understand false beliefs and to express the past and future. Therefore, they have an ability to use language to formulate and communicate hypotheses. Their conversation is guided by rules which are embedded in their spontaneous language development.

However, since children know less about adults' use of the rules of conversation and less about language generally, they may be more easily misled and their capacity for understanding left unrecognised. They are less likely to share an adult's intentions and goals for communication and the implications of adult conversation. At least to this extent, parent–child communication differs from communication between adults, and recognition ought to be accorded to a particular child's possible inexperience with the use of language, symbols, and departures from the conventional rules of conversation rather than to some unaccountable conceptual limitation. In this sense, conversational rules and children's interpretation of the meaning and purpose of language are a building block for theories of child development, and for a developmental cognitive science that embraces linguistics, philosophy, psychology, and related disciplines.

Children's knowledge of the intent underlying departures from conventional methods of questioning—the conversational implications used by adults—may develop later. With intensive daily experience at home and school, they come to understand when, for example, the quantity rule can be violated deliberately with tact and politeness as a form of implicature for the purpose of obtaining clarification. Indeed, languages in some cultures such as Australian Aboriginal groups are based on this notion, with repeated questioning enshrined in communication patterns (Liberman, 1981; Siegal, 1988b).

Of course there is more to development that the ability to share purposes and meanings in experimental settings. Even if children understand the conversational context of the task and are not misled by unfamiliar language, and would know how and when to apply the solution if they had it, they may still lack the conceptual competence—the logico-mathematical knowledge and principles—to succeed fully. Only a skeletal understanding may be present and experimenters must be wary to steer between two errors: to avoid false negatives in claiming that children do not know when they actually do, and to avoid false positives in claiming that they do know when they actually do not. To ensure that a conceptual limitation in development is deep rather than superficial, it is necessary to rule out explanations for negative results. Ways are required to test the rival hypotheses that children's lack of performance is due to ambiguity in questioning, certain perceptions of the experimenter and task, and unfamiliar language that does not map on to children's theories of the mental and physical world. These methods may include having children offer causal attributions for peers' responses, placing tasks in relevant (e.g. food-related) contexts, and simplifying linguistic forms by pairing numbers with pictures. An approach that focuses on the language of the experiment and the presence of an early implicit knowledge harbours the possibility of discovering more capacity in children's understanding than has often been envisioned.

In line with Helmholtz's notion of unconscious, perceptual inferences, many experiments have now revealed a subtle understanding that is implicit in infants and young children. Similarly, Darwin's emphasis on the diversity of species in adapting to their environment is a forerunner to modern studies on biological constraints that promote learning. In their accolade to Darwin, Rozin and Schull (1988) enumerate four broad categories of "fitness-promoting" activities in biological organisms: sheltering, predator avoidance, nutrient procurement, and parenting. Experiments have supported the notion that constraints towards the learning of these behaviours are present in young children. The early understanding of objects in space, time, and mental states forms a basis for sheltering and predator avoidance. The very early knowledge of the distinction between appearance and reality in the domain of food and contamination surely contributes to the procurement of nutrients. Then there is continuity between generations and the ability of young children to discern and evaluate authority in sustaining patterns of parenting behaviour.

Nevertheless, psychologists and educators are far short of charting the full extent of children's capacity for understanding. To date, it is true, in searching for original states and for mechanisms of change, an impressive depth of understanding has been uncovered. Through experiments, it is known that child development is better characterised by development towards a conscious accessibility of implicit knowledge rather than a simple lack of conceptual knowledge or coherence at different stages. However, important gaps remain— ones that are larger than the outline of development that has been provided up to now. It remains easier to state what should not be included in models of knowledge in young children than what should be. It is easier to state descriptions than to offer explanations of developmental changes.

Studies of children's number and reading, their understanding of health, illness, and safety, their ability to represent viewpoints and causal relations, and their conceptions of authority and friendship are areas for research on development. Only a start has been made and much remains to be done. The task ahead is to negotiate an account of development guided by breadth, depth, and vision. At the same time, it is to promote communication in knowing children.

References

Ackerman, B. P. (1981). When is a question not answered? The understanding of young children of utterances violating or conforming to the rules of conversational sequencing. *Journal of Experimental Child Psychology, 31,* 487–507.

Allport, G. W., & Postman, L. (1947). *The psychology of rumor.* New York: Henry Holt.

Antell, S. E., & Keating, D. P. (1983). Perception of numerical invariance in neonates. *Child Development, 54,* 695–701.

Asch, S. E. (1958). Effects of group pressure upon the modification and distortion of judgments. In E. E. Maccoby, T. M. Newcomb, & E. L. Hartley (Eds.), *Readings in social psychology* (3rd edn.). New York: Henry Holt.

Asher, S. R., & Dodge, K. A. (1986). Identifying children who are rejected by their peers. *Developmental Psychology, 22,* 444–449.

Asher, S. R., & Wheeler, V. A. (1985). Children's loneliness: A comparison of rejected and neglected peer status. *Journal of Consulting and Clinical Psychology, 53,* 500–505.

Au, T. K., & Romo, L.F. (1996). Building a coherent conception of HIV transmission: A new approach to AIDS education. In D. Medin (Ed.), *Psychology of learning and motivation* (vol. 35, pp. 193–241). New York: Academic Press.

Au, T. K., Sidle, A. L., & Rollins, K. B. (1993). Developing an intuitive understanding of conservation and contamination: Invisible particles as a plausible mechanism. *Developmental Psychology, 29,* 286–299.

Baillargeon, R., & Graber, M. (1988). Evidence of location memory in 8-month-old infants in a nonsearch AB task. *Developmental Psychology, 24,* 502–511.

Baillargeon, R., Spelke, E. S., & Wasserman, S. (1985). Object permanence in five-month-old infants. *Cognition, 20,* 191–208.

Baker-Ward, L., Hess, T., & Flannagan, D. (1990). The effects of involvement on children's memory for events. *Cognitive Development, 5,* 55–69.

Baldwin, D. (1993). Early referential understanding: Infants' ability to recognize referential acts for what they are. *Developmental Psychology, 29,* 832–843.

Barley, N. (1983). *The innocent anthropologist: Notes from a mud hut.* Harmondsworth, UK: Penguin.

Bartlett, F. C. (1932). *Remembering.* Cambridge, UK: Cambridge University Press.

Bauer, P. J. (1993). Memory for gender-consistent and gender-inconsistent event sequences by twenty-five-month-old children. *Child Development, 64*, 285–297.

Baumrind, D. (1983). Rejoinder to Lewis's reinterpretation of parental control effects: Are authoritative parents really harmonious? *Psychological Bulletin, 94*, 132–142.

Beal, C., & Belgrad, S. L. (1990). The development of message evaluation skills in young children. *Child Development, 61*, 705–712.

Becker, J. A., & Goodnow, J. J. (1991). "What's the magic word?", "Were you born in a tent?"— The challenge of accounting for parents' use of indirect forms of speech with children. *Quarterly Newsletter of the Laboratory of Comparative Human Cognition, 13*, 55–58.

Bem, S. L. (1989). Genital knowledge and gender constancy in preschool children. *Child Development, 60*, 649–662.

Berger, M. (1985). *Germs make me sick.* New York: Harper & Row.

Berliner, L., & Barbieri, M. K. (1984). Children's testimony. *Journal of Social Issues, 40*, 125–137.

Bertoncini, J., Bijeljac-Babic, R., Jusczyk, P. W., Kennedy, L. J., & Mehler, J. (1988). *Journal of Experimental Psychology: General, 117*, 21–33.

Bibace, R., & Walsh, M. E. (1981). Children's conceptions of illness. In R. Bibace & M. Walsh (Eds.), *New directions for child development: Children's conceptions of health, illness, and bodily functions* (No. 14). San Francisco: Jossey-Bass.

Block, J. H. (1983). Differential premises arising from differential socialization of the sexes: Some conjectures. *Child Development, 54*, 1335–1354.

Bonitatibus, G. (1988). What is said and what is meant in referential communication. In J. W. Astington, P. L. Harris, & D. R. Olson (Eds.), *Developing theories of mind* (pp. 326–338). Cambridge, UK: Cambridge University Press.

Borges, J. L. (1964). *Labyrinths.* New York: New Directions.

Borke, H. (1975). Piaget's mountains revisited: Changes in the egocentric landscape. *Developmental Psychology, 11*, 240–243.

Bos, M. C. (1937). Experimental study of productive collaboration. *Acta Psychologica, 3*, 315–426.

Bowes, J. M., & Goodnow, J. J. (1996). Work for home, school or labor force: The nature and sources of changes in understanding. *Psychological Bulletin, 119*, 300–321.

Bowey, J. A. (1994). Phonological sensitivity in novice readers and nonreaders. *Journal of Experimental Child Psychology, 58*, 134–159.

Braine, M. D. S., & Rumain, B. (1983). Logical reasoning. In P. H. Mussen (Ed.), *Handbook of child psychology* (Vol. 3; pp. 263–340). New York: Wiley.

Brandt, A. M. (1987). *No magic bullet.* New York: Oxford University Press.

Bransford, J. D., Barclay, J. R., & Franks, J. J. (1972). Sentence memory: A constructive versus interpretive approach. *Cognitive Psychology, 3*, 193–209.

Bransford, J. D., & Franks, J. J. (1971). The abstraction of linguistic ideas. *Cognitive Psychology, 2*, 331–350.

Bremner, J. G., & Knowles, L. S. (1984). Piagetian stage IV search errors with an object that is directly accessible both visually and manually. *Perception, 13*, 307–314.

Bretherton, I., & Beeghly, M. (1982). Talking about internal states: The acquisition of an explicit theory of mind. *Developmental Psychology, 18*, 906–921.

Broerse, J., & Elias, G. (1994). Changes in the content and timing of mothers' talk to infants. *British Journal of Developmental Psychology, 12*, 131–145.

Bronstein, P. (1984). Differences in mothers' and fathers' behaviors toward children: A cross-cultural comparison. *Developmental Psychology, 20*, 995–1003.

Brown, A. L., Kane, M. J., & Echols, C. H. (1986). Young children's mental models determine analogical transfer across problems with a common goal structure. *Cognitive Development, 1*, 103–121.

Brown, P., & Levinson, S. C. (1987). *Politeness: Some universals in language usage.* Cambridge, UK: Cambridge University Press.

Brown, R., & Hanlon, C. (1970). Derivational complexity and the order of acquisition in child speech. In J. R. Hayes (Ed.), *Cognition and the development of language* (pp. 155–207). New York: Wiley.

Bruner, J. (1991). The narrative construction of reality. *Critical Inquiry, 18,* 1–21.

Bryant, P. E. (1974). *Perception and understanding in young children.* London: Methuen.

Bryant, P. E. (1985). The distinction between knowing when to do a sum and knowing how to do it. *Educational Psychology, 5,* 207–215.

Bryant, P. E. (1995). Children and arithmetic. *Journal of Child Psychology and Psychiatry, 36,* 3–32.

Bryant, P. E., & Bradley, L. (1983). *Children's reading problems.* Oxford: Blackwell.

Bryant, P. E., Jones, P., Claxton, V., & Perkins, G. M. (1972). Recognition of shapes across modalities by infants. *Nature, 240,* 303–304.

Bryant, P. E., & Kopytynska, H. (1976). Spontaneous measurement by young children. *Nature, 260,* 773.

Bullock, M. (1985). Animism in childhood thinking: A new look at an old question. *Developmental Psychology, 21,* 217–225.

Bussey, K. (1992). Lying and truthfulness: Children's definitions, standards, and evaluative reactions. *Child Development, 63,* 129–137.

Butterworth, G., & Hopkins, B. (1988). Hand–mouth coordination in the new-born baby. *British Journal of Developmental Psychology, 6,* 303–314.

Byrne, B., & Fielding-Barnsley, R. (1989). Phonemic awareness and letter knowledge in the child's acquisition of the alphabetic principle. *Journal of Educational Psychology, 81,* 313–321.

Byrne, B., & Fielding-Barnsley, R. (1990). Acquiring the alphabetic principle: A case for teaching recognition of phoneme identity. *Journal of Educational Psychology, 82,* 805–812.

Carey, S. (1985a). Are children fundamentally different kinds of thinkers and learners than adults? In S. F. Chipman, J. W. Segal, & J. R. Glaser (Eds.), *Thinking and learning skills* (Vol. 2). Hillsdale, NJ: Lawrence Erlbaum Associates Inc.

Carey, S. (1985b). *Conceptual change in childhood.* Cambridge, MA: Bradford Books/MIT Press.

Carey, S. (1994). Does learning a language require the child to reconceptualize the world? *Lingua, 92,* 143–167.

Case, R. (1985). *Intellectual development: Birth to adulthood.* Orlando, FL: Academic Press.

Cassel, W. S., Roebers, C. E. R., & Bjorklund, D. F. (1996). Developmental patterns of eyewitness responses to repeated and increasingly suggestive questions. *Journal of Experimental Child Psychology, 61,* 116–133.

Cassidy, J., Parke, R. D., Butkovsky, L., & Braungart, J. M. (1992). Family–peer connections: The role of emotional expressiveness within the family and children's understanding of emotions. *Child Development, 63,* 603–618.

Ceci, S. J., & Bruck, M. (1993). Suggestibility of the child witness: A historical review and synthesis. *Psychological Bulletin, 113,* 403–439.

Ceci, S. J., Huffman, M. L., Smith, E., & Loftus, E. F. (1994). Repeatedly thinking about a non-event: Source misattributions among preschoolers. *Consciousness and Cognition, 3,* 388–407.

Ceci, S. J., Leichtman, M. D., Putnick, M. E., & Nightingale, N. N. (1993). The suggestibility of children's recollections. In D. Cicchetti & S. Tooth (Eds.), *Child witnesses, child abuse, and public policy* (pp. 117–137). Norwood, NJ: Ablex.

Ceci, S. J., Ross, D. F., & Toglia, M. P. (1987). Suggestibility of children's memory: Psycholegal implications. *Journal of Experimental Psychology: General, 116,* 38–49.

Chapman, M. (1988). *Constructive evolution: Origins and development of Piaget's thought.* Cambridge, UK: Cambridge University Press.

Chen, C., Lee, S.-Y., & Stevenson, H. W. (1995). Response style and cross-cultural comparisons of rating scales among East Asian and North American students. *Psychological Science, 6,* 170–175.

Chen, C., & Stevenson, H. W. (1995). Motivation and mathematics achievement: A comparative study of Asian-American, Caucasian-American, and East Asian high school students. *Child Development*, *66*, 1215–1234.

Chi, M. T. H. (1985). Interactive roles of knowledge and strategies in the development of organized sorting and recall. In S. F. Chipman, J. W. Segal, & R. Glaser (Eds.), *Thinking and learning skills* (Vol. 2). Hillsdale, NJ: Lawrence Erlbaum Associates Inc.

Clark, H. H. (1987). Relevance to what? *Behavioral and Brain Sciences*, *10*, 714–715.

Clark, H. H. (1992). *Arenas of language use*. Chicago, IL: University of Chicago Press.

Clark, H. H., & Brennan, S. E. (1991). Grounding in communication. In L. B. Resnick, J. M. Levine, & S. Behrens (Eds.), *Perspectives on socially shared cognition* (pp. 127–149). Washington, DC: American Psychological Association.

Clements, W. A., & Perner, J. (1994). Implicit understanding of belief. *Cognitive Development*, *9*, 377–395.

Cohen, L. J. (1971). Some remarks on Grice's views about the logical particles of natural language. In Y. Bar-Hillel (Ed.), *Pragmatics of natural language*. Dordrecht, Netherlands: D. Reidel.

Coie, J. D., Dodge, K. A., & Coppotelli, H. (1982). Dimensions and types of social status: A cross-age perspective. *Developmental Psychology*, *18*, 557–570.

Coie, J. D., & Krehbiel, G. (1984). Effects of academic tutoring on the social status of low-achieving, socially rejected children. *Child Development*, *55*, 1465–1478.

Coie, J. D., & Kupersmidt, J. B. (1983). A behavioral analysis of emerging social status in boys' groups. *Child Development*, *54*, 1400–1416.

Cole, M. (1985). The zone of proximal development: Where culture and cognition create each other. In J. V. Wertsch (Ed.), *Culture, communication, and cognition: Vygotskian perspectives* (pp. 146–161). New York: Cambridge University Press.

Content, A., Kolinsky, R., Morais, J., & Bertelson, P. (1986). Phonetic segmentation in prereaders: Effect of corrective information. *Journal of Experimental Child Psychology*, *42*, 49–72.

Cords, M. (1992). Social versus ecological intelligence, *Behavioral and Brain Sciences*, *15*, 151.

Cowan, R., Foster, C., & Al-Zubaidi, A. S. (1993). Encouraging children to count. *British Journal of Developmental Psychology*, *11*, 411–420.

Crockenberg, S., & Litman, C. (1990). Autonomy as competence in 2-year-olds: Maternal correlates of child defiance, compliance, and self-assertion. *Developmental Psychology*, *26*, 961–971.

Cross, T. G. (1977). Mothers' speech adjustments: The contribution of selected child listener variables. In C. Snow & C. A. Ferguson (Eds.), *Talking to children: Language input and acquisition* (pp. 151–188). Cambridge, UK: Cambridge University Press.

Cummins, D. D., Kintsch, W., Reusser, K., & Weimer, R. (1988). The role of understanding in solving word arithmetic problems. *Cognitive Psychology*, *20*, 405–438.

Dahl, R. (1959). *Kiss, kiss*. New York: Knopf.

Dalenberg, C. J., Bierman, K. L., & Furman, W. (1984). A reexamination of developmental changes in causal attributions. *Developmental Psychology*, *20*, 575–583.

Darwin, C. R. (1859). *On the origins of species by means of natural selection, or the preservation of favoured races in the struggle for life*. London: John Murray.

Davey, G. (1995). Preparedness and phobias: Specific evolved associations or a generalized expectancy bias. *Behavioral and Brain Sciences*, *18*, 289–297.

Davies, G. (1993). Children's memory for other people: An integrative review. *Minnesota Symposia on Child Psychology*, *26*, 123–157.

DeCasper, A. J., & Fifer, W. P. (1980). Of human bonding: Newborns prefer their mother's voice. *Science*, *208*, 1174–1176.

DeLoache, J. S. (1987). Rapid change in the symbolic functioning of very young children. *Science*, *238*, 1556–1557.

DeLoache, J. S. (1991). Symbolic functioning in very young children. *Child Development, 62,* 736–752.

Denham, S. A. (1986). Social cognition, prosocial behavior, and emotion in preschoolers: Contextual validation. *Child Development, 57,* 194–201.

Denham, S. A., & Holt, R. W. (1993). Preschoolers' likability as cause or consequence of their social behavior. *Developmental Psychology, 29,* 271–275.

Denham, S. A., McKinley, M., Couchoud, E. A., & Holt, R. (1990). Emotional and behavioural predictors of preschool peer ratings. *Child Development, 61,* 1145–1152.

Denham, S. A., Zoller, D., & Couchoud, E. A. (1994). Socialization of preschoolers' emotional understanding. *Developmental Psychology, 30,* 928–936.

De Villiers, J. G., & De Villiers, P. A. (1978). *Language acquisition.* Cambridge, MA: Harvard University Press.

DeVries, R. (1969). Constancy of generic identity in the years three to six. *Monographs of the Society for Research in Child Development, 34* (Serial No. 127).

Diamond, A. (1985). The development of the ability to use recall to guide action, as indicated by infants' performance on AB. *Child Development, 56,* 868–883.

Dias, M. G., & Harris, P. L. (1988). The effect of make-believe play on deductive reasoning. *British Journal of Developmental Psychology, 6,* 207–221.

Dix, T., & Grusec, J.E. (1983). Parental influence techniques: An attributional analysis. *Child Development, 54,* 645–652.

Dix, T., Ruble, D. N., & Zambarano, R. J. (1989). Mothers' implicit theories of discipline: Child effects, parent effects, and the attribution process. *Child Development, 60,* 1373–1391.

Dodge, K. A. (1983). Behavioral antecedents of peer social status. *Child Development, 54,* 1386–1399.

Dodge, K. A. (1985). A social information processing model of social competence in children. In M. Perlmutter (Ed.), *Minnesota Symposium on Child Psychology* (Vol. 18). Hillsdale, NJ: Lawrence Erlbaum Associates Inc.

Dodge, K. A., Coie, J. D., & Brakke, N. P. (1982). Behavior patterns of socially rejected and neglected preadolescents: The roles of social approach and aggression. *Journal of Abnormal Child Psychology, 10,* 389–410.

Dodge, K. A., & Somberg, D. R. (1987). Hostile attributional biases among aggressive boys are exacerbated under conditions of threat to the self. *Child Development, 58,* 213–224.

Donaldson, M. (1978). *Children's minds.* Glasgow, UK: Fontana.

Donaldson, M. (1982). Conservation: What is the question? *British Journal of Psychology, 73,* 199–207.

Donaldson, M., & Balfour, G. (1968). Less is more: A study of language comprehension in children. *British Journal of Psychology, 59,* 461–471.

Duncan, I. M., Whitney, P., & Kunen, S. (1982). Integration of visual and verbal information in children's memories. *Child Development, 53,* 1215–1223.

Dunn, J. (1994). Changing minds and changing relationships. In C. Lewis & P. Mitchell (Eds.), *Children's early understanding of mind: Origins and development* (pp. 297–310). Hove, UK: Lawrence Erlbaum Associates Ltd.

Dunn, J., Bretherton, I., & Munn, P. (1987). Conversations about feeling states between mothers and their young children. *Developmental Psychology, 23,* 132–139.

Dunn, J., Brown, J., & Beardsall, L. (1991). Family talk about feeling states and children's later understanding of others' emotions. *Developmental Psychology, 27,* 448–455.

Dunn, J., Brown, J., Slomkowski, C., Tesla, C., & Youngblader, L. (1991). Young children's understanding of other people's feelings and beliefs: Individual differences and their antecedents. *Child Development, 62,* 1352–1366.

Durkin, K. (1994). The lure and language of implicit memory: A developmental perspective. In N. Ellis (Ed.), *Implicit and explicit learning of languages* (pp. 523–548). London: Academic Press.

Eades, D. (1982). You gotta know how to talk . . . Information seeking in South-East Queensland Aboriginal Society. *Australian Journal of Linguistics, 2*, 61–82.

Eekelaar, J. (1984). *Family law and social policy* (2nd edn.). London: Weidenfeld & Nicolson.

Eimas, P. D., & Miller, J. L. (1980). Contextual effects in infant speech perception. *Science, 209*, 1140–1141.

Eiser, C. (1985). *The psychology of childhood illness.* New York: Springer-Verlag.

Ekman, P. (1985). *Telling lies.* New York: Norton.

Ekman, P. (1994). Strong evidence for universals in facial expressions: A reply to Russell's mistaken critique. *Psychological Bulletin, 115*, 268–287.

Enright, R. D., Enright, W. F., & Lapsley, D. K. (1981). Distributive justice and social class: A replication. *Developmental Psychology, 17*, 826–832.

Enright, R. D., & Sutterfield, S. J. (1980). An ecological validation of social cognitive development. *Child Development, 51*, 156–161.

Fallon, A. E., Rozin, P., & Pliner, P. (1984). The child's conception of food rejections with special reference to disgust and contamination sensitivity. *Child Development, 55*, 566–575.

Falmagne, R. J. (1990). Language and the acquisition of logical knowledge. In W. F. Overton (Ed.), *Reasoning, necessity and logic: Developmental perspectives* (pp. 111–134). Hillsdale, NJ: Lawrence Erlbaum Associates Inc.

Faust, D., & Ziskin, J. (1988). The expert witness in psychology and psychiatry. *Science, 241*, 31–35.

Ferguson, C. (1977). Baby talk as a simplified register. In C. Snow & C. A. Ferguson (Eds.), *Talking to children: Language input and acquisition* (pp. 209–235). Cambridge, UK: Cambridge University Press.

Ferrari, J. R., & Olivette, M. J. (1994). Parental authority and the development of female dysfunctional procrastination. *Journal of Research in Personality, 28*, 87–100.

Field, T. M., Woodson, R., Greenberg, R., & Cohen, D. (1982). Discrimination and imitation of facial expressions by neonates. *Science, 218*, 179–181.

Finnie, V., & Russell, A. (1988). Preschool children's social status and their mothers' behavior and knowledge in the supervisory role. *Developmental Psychology, 24*, 789–801.

Fivush, R. (1993). Developmental perspectives on autobiographical recall. In G. S. Goodman & B. L. Bottoms (Eds.), *Child witnesses: Understanding and improving testimony* (pp. 1–24). New York: Guilford.

Fivush, R., Hamond, N. R., Harsch, N., Singer, N., & Wolf, A. (1991). Content and consistency in young children's autobiographical recall. *Discourse Processes, 14*, 373–388.

Fivush, R., Kuebli, J., & Clubb, P. A. (1992). The structure of events and event representation: A developmental analysis. *Child Development, 63*, 188–201.

Flavell, J. H. (1993). The development of children's understanding of false belief and the appearance–reality distinction. *International Journal of Psychology, 28*, 595–604.

Flavell, J. H., Everett, B. A., Croft, K., & Flavell, E. R. (1981). Young children's knowledge about visual perception: Further evidence for the Level 1–Level 2 distinction. *Developmental Psychology, 17*, 99–103.

Flavell, J. H., Flavell, E. R., & Green, F. L. (1983). Development of the appearance-reality distinction. *Cognitive Psychology, 15*, 95–120.

Flavell, J. H., Flavell, E. R., & Green, F. L. (1989). Young children's ability to differentiate appearance–reality and Level 2 perspectives in the tactile modality. *Child Development, 60*, 201–213.

Flavell. J. H., Green, F. L., & Flavell, E. R. (1986). Development of the appearance–reality distinction. *Monographs of the Society for Research in Child Development, 51* Serial No. 212.

Flavell, J. H., Green, F. L., Wahl, K. E., & Flavell, E. R. (1987). The effects of question clarification and memory aids on young children's performance on appearance–reality tasks. *Cognitive Development, 2*, 127–144.

Flavell, J. H., & Wohlwill, J. F. (1969). Formal and functional aspects of cognitive development. In D. Elkind & J. H. Flavell (Eds.), *Studies in cognitive development* (pp.67–120). New York: Oxford University Press.

Flin, R., Boon, J., Knox, N., & Bull, R.   (1992). Children's memories following a five month delay. *British Journal of Psychology*, *83*, 323–336.

Fluck, M., & Hewison, Y. (1979). The effect of televised presentation on number conservation in 5-year-olds. *British Journal of Psychology*, *70*, 507–509.

Fodor, J. (1992). A theory of the child's theory of mind. *Cognition*, *44*, 283–296.

Ford, M. E. (1979). The construct validity of egocentrism. *Psychological Bulletin*, *86*, 1169–1188.

Ford, M. E. (1985). Two perspectives on the validation of developmental constructs: Psychometric and theoretical limitation in research on egocentrism. *Psychological Bulletin*, *97*, 497–501.

Freeman, N. H., & Lacohée, H. (1995). Making explicit 3-year-olds' implicit competence with their own false beliefs. *Cognition*, 56, 31–60.

Freeman, N. H., Lloyd, S., & Sinha. C. G. (1980). Infant search tasks reveal early concepts of containment and canonical use of objects. *Cognition*, *8*, 243–262.

Freeman, N. H., & Schreiner, K. (1988). Complementary error-patterns in collective and individuating judgements: Their semantic basis in 6-year-olds. *British Journal of Developmental Psychology*, *6*, 341–350.

Freeman, N. H., Sinha, C. G., & Condliffe, S. G. (1981). Collaboration and confrontation with young children in language comprehension testing. In W. P. Robinson (Ed.), *Communication and development*. London: Academic Press.

French, D. C., & Waas, G. A. (1985). Behavior problems of peer-neglected and peer-rejected elementary-age children: Parent and teacher perspectives.   *Child Development*, *56*, 246–252.

Friedman, W. J. (1990). Children's representations of the pattern of daily activities.   *Child Development*, *61*, 1399–1412.

Friedman, W. J. (1991). The development of children's memory for the time of past events. *Child Development*, *62*, 139–155.

Furman, W., & Bierman. K. L. (1983). Developmental changes in young children's conceptions of friendship. *Child Development*, *54*, 549–556.

Furman, W., & Masters, J. C. (1980). Peer interactions, sociometric status, and resistance to deviations in young children. *Developmental Psychology*, *16*, 229–236.

Furth, H. G., & Wachs, H. (1974). *Thinking goes to school: Piaget's theory in practice*. New York: Oxford University Press.

Fuson, K. (1986a). Roles of representation and verbalization in the teaching of multi-digit addition and subtraction. *European Journal of the Psychology of Education*, *1*, 35–56.

Fuson, K. C. (1986b). Teaching children to subtract by counting up. *Journal for Research in Mathematics Education*, *17*, 172–189.

Gauvain, M., & Greene, J. K. (1994). What do children know about objects?   *Cognitive Development*, *9*, 311–329.

Geary, D. (1995). Reflections on evolution and culture in children's cognition: Implications for mathematical development and instruction. *American Psychologist*, *50*, 24–35.

Gelman, R. (1982). Accessing one-to-one correspondence: Still another paper about conservation. *British Journal of Psychology*, *73*, 209–220.

Gelman, R. (1991). Epigenetic foundations of knowledge structures: Initial and transcendent constructions. In S. Carey & R. Gelman (Eds.), *The epigenesis of mind: Essays on biology and cognition* (pp. 293–322). Hillsdale, NJ: Lawrence Erlbaum Associates Inc.

Gelman, R. (1993). A rational-constructivist account of early learning about numbers and objects. In D. Medin (Ed.), *Psychology of learning and motivation* (Vol. 30; pp. 61–95). New York: Academic Press.

Gelman, R., & Gallistel, C. R. (1978). *The child's understanding of number*. Cambridge, MA: Harvard University Press.

Gelman, R., & Lee, M. G. (1995). *Trends and developments in educational psychology in the United States* (Educational Studies and Documents No. 61). Paris: UNESCO.

Gelman, R., & Meck, E. (1983). Preschoolers' counting: Principles before skill. *Cognition, 13,* 343–359.

Gelman, R., Meck, E., & Merkin, S. (1986). Young children's numerical competence. *Cognitive Development, 1,* 1–29.

Gelman, R., & Shatz, M. (1977). Appropriate speech adjustments: The operation of conversational constraints on talk to two-year-olds. In M. Lewis & L. A. Rosenblum (Eds.), *Interaction, conversation, and the development of language* (pp. 27–61). New York: Wiley.

Gelman, S. A., Collman, P., & Maccoby, E. E. (1986). Inferring properties from categories versus inferring categories from properties: The case of gender. *Child Development, 57,* 396–404.

Gelman, S. A., & Kremer, K. E. (1991). Understanding natural cause: Children's understanding of how objects and their properties originate. *Child Development, 62,* 396–414.

Gershman, E. S., & Hayes, D. S. (1983). Differential stability of reciprocal relationships among preschool children. *Merrill-Palmer Quarterly, 29,* 169–177.

Gibson, E. J., & Walker, A. S. (1984). Development of knowledge of visual-factual affordance of substance. *Child Development, 55,* 453–460.

Ginbayashi, K. (1984). *Principles of mathematics education.* Tokyo: Association of Mathematical Instruction.

Glick, J. (1978). Cognition and social cognition: An introduction. In J. Glick & K. A. Clarke-Stewart (Eds.), *The development of social understanding.* New York: Gardner Press.

Gold, L. J., Darley, J. M., Hilton, J. L., & Zanna, M. P. (1984). Children's perceptions of procedural justice. *Child Development, 55,* 1752–1759.

Goldin-Meadow, S., Alibali, M. W., & Church, R. B. (1993). Transitions in concept acquisition: Using the hand to read the mind. *Psychological Review, 100,* 279–297.

Goodman, G. S., Golding, J. M., & Haith, M. M. (1984). Jurors' reactions to child witnesses. *Journal of Social Issues, 40,* 139–156.

Goodman, G. S., Rudy, L., Bottoms, B., & Aman, C. (1990). Children's concerns and memory: Issues of ecological validity in the study of children's eyewitness testimony. In R. Fivush & J. Hudson (Eds.), *Knowing and remembering in young children* (pp. 249–284). New York: Cambridge University Press.

Goodnow, J. J. (1984). On being judged "intelligent". *International Journal of Psychology, 19,* 391–406.

Goodnow, J. J. (1988). Parents' ideas, actions, and feelings: Methods and models from developmental and social psychology. *Child Development, 59,* 286–320.

Gopnik, A. (1993). How we know our minds: The illusion of first-person knowledge of intentionality. *Behavioral and Brain Sciences, 16,* 1–14.

Gopnik, A., & Slaughter, V. (1991). Young children's understanding of changes in their mental states. *Child Development, 62,* 98–110.

Goswami, U. (1986). Children's use of analogy in learning to read: A developmental study. *Journal of Experimental Child Psychology, 42,* 73–83.

Goswami, U. (1992). *Analogical understanding in young children.* Hove, UK: Lawrence Erlbaum Associates Ltd.

Goswami, U. (1995). Transitive relational mappings in three- and four-year-olds: The analogy of Goldilocks and the Three Bears. *Child Development, 66,* 877–892.

Graesser, A. C., Singer, M., & Trabasso, T. (1994). Constructing inferences during narrative text comprehension. *Psychological Review, 101,* 371–395.

Graumann, C. F. (1995). Commonality, mutuality, reciprocity: A conceptual introduction. In I. Markova, C. F. Graumann, & K. Foppa (Eds.), *Mutualities in dialogue* (pp. 1–24). Cambridge, UK: Cambridge University Press.

Grice, H. P. (1975). Logic and conversation. In P. Cole & J. L. Morgan (Eds.), *Syntax and semantics: Vol. 3. Speech acts* (pp. 41–58). New York: Academic Press.

Grolnick, W. S., & Ryan, R. M. (1989). Parent styles associated with children's school-related adjustment and competence. *Journal of Educational Psychology, 81,* 143–154.

Grolnick, W. S., & Slowiaczek, M. L. (1994). Parents' involvement in children's schooling: A multidimensional conceptualization and motivational model. *Child Development, 65,* 237–252.

Grusec, J. E., & Goodnow, J. J. (1994). Impact of parental discipline methods on the child's internalization of values: A reconceptualization of current points of view. *Developmental Psychology, 30,* 4–19.

Gudjonsson, G. (1986). The relationship between interrogative suggestibility and acquiescence: Empirical findings and theoretical implications. *Personality and Individual Differences, 7,* 195–199.

Haidt, J., Koller, S. H., & Dias, M. G. (1993). Affect, culture, and morality, or is it wrong to eat your dog? *Journal of Personality and Social Psychology, 63,* 613–628.

Halford, G. S., & Boyle, F. M. (1985). Do young children understand conservation of number? *Child Development, 56,* 165–173.

Harner, L. (1975). Yesterday and tomorrow: Development of early understanding of the terms. *Developmental Psychology, 11,* 864–865.

Harris, P. L., Donnelly, K., Gaz, G. R., & Pitt-Watson, R. (1986). Children's understanding of the distinction between real and apparent emotion. *Child Development, 57,* 895–909.

Hart, K. M. (Ed.). (1981). *Children's understanding of mathematics: 11–16.* London: John Murray.

Hartup, W. W. (1983). Peer relations. In P. H. Mussen & E. M. Hetherington (Eds.), *Handbook of child psychology* (Vol. IV). New York: Wiley.

Hatano, G., & Inagaki, K. (1991). Sharing cognition through collective comprehension activity. In L. B. Resnick, J. M. Levine, & S. Teasley (Eds.), *Perspectives on socially shared cognition* (pp. 331–348). Washington, DC: American Psychological Association.

Hatano, G., & Inagaki, K. (1994). Young children's naive theory of biology. *Cognition, 50,* 171–188.

Heath, S. B. (1983). *Ways with words.* New York: Cambridge University Press.

Hewison, J., & Tizard, J. (1980). Parental involvement and reaching attainment. *British Journal of Educational Psychology, 50,* 209–215.

Hickling, A. K., & Gelman, S. A. (1994). How does your garden grow? Early conceptualization of seeds and their place in the plant growth cycle. *Child Development, 66,* 856–876.

Hiebert, J., & Wearne, D. (1986). Procedures over concepts: The acquisition of decimal number knowledge. In J. Hiebert (Ed.), *Conceptual and procedural knowledge: The case of mathematics* (pp. 199–223). Hillsdale, NJ: Lawrence Erlbaum Associates Inc.

Higgins, E. T. (1981). Role-taking and social judgment: Alternative developmental perspectives and processes. In J. H. Flavell & L. Ross (Eds.), *Social cognitive development: Frontiers and possible futures.* New York: Cambridge University Press.

Higgins, E. T., Feldman, N. S., & Ruble, D. N. (1980). Accuracy and differentiation in social prediction: A developmental perspective. *Journal of Personality, 48,* 520–540.

Hilton, D. J. (1990). Conversational processes and causal explanation. *Psychological Bulletin, 107,* 65–81.

Hilton, D. J. (1995). The social context of reasoning: Conversational inference and rational judgment. *Psychological Bulletin, 118,* 248–271.

Hirschfeld, L. A., & Gelman, S. A. (Eds.). (1994). *Mapping the mind: Domain specificity in cognition and culture.* New York: Cambridge University Press.

Hockett, C. F. (1963). The problem of universals in language. In J.H. Greenberg (Ed.), *Universals in language.* Cambridge, MA: MIT Press.

Hoffman, M. L. (1970). Moral development. In P. Mussen (Ed.), *Carmichael's manual of child psychology:* Vol. II (3rd edn.). New York: Wiley.

Howe, M. L. (1991). Misleading children's story recall: Forgetting and reminiscence of the facts. *Developmental Psychology, 27,* 746–762.

Hudson, T. (1983). Correspondences and numerical differences between disjoint sets. *Child Development, 54,* 84–90.

Hughes, M. (1986). *Children and number.* Oxford, UK: Blackwell.

Hughes, M., & Grieve, R. (1983). On asking children bizarre questions. In M. Donaldson, R. Grieve, & C. Pratt (Eds.), *Child development and education.* Oxford, UK: Blackwell.

Hunt, E., & Agnoli, F. (1991). The Whorfian hypothesis: A cognitive psychology perspective, *Psychological Review, 98,* 377–389.

Huston, A. C. (1983). Sex-typing. In P. H. Mussen & E. M. Hetherington (Eds.), *Handbook of child psychology:* Vol. 4 (4th edn.). New York: Wiley.

Hymel, S. (1983). Preschool children's peer relations: Issues in sociometric assessment. *Merrill-Palmer Quarterly, 29,* 237–260.

Inagaki, K., & Hatano, K. (1993). Young children's understanding of the mind–body distinction. *Child Development, 64,* 1534–1549.

Inhelder, B., & Piaget, J. (1958). *Growth of logical thinking from childhood to adolescence.* New York: Basic Books.

Izard, C. (1993). Four systems for emotion activation: Cognitive and noncognitive processes. *Psychological Review, 100,* 68–90.

Izard, C. E. (1994). Innate and universal facial expressions: Evidence from developmental and cross-cultural research. *Psychological Bulletin, 115,* 288–299.

James, W. (1960). *The principles of psychology.* New York: Dover. (Original work published 1890.)

Johnson, M. H., Dziurawiec, S., Ellis, H., & Morton, J. (1991). Newborns' preferential tracking of face-like stimuli and its subsequent decline. *Cognition, 40,* 1–19.

Johnson, M. K., & Foley, M. A. (1984). Differentiating fact from fantasy: The reliability of children's memory. *Journal of Social Issues, 40,* 33–50.

Johnson, M. K., Hashtroudi, S., & Lindsay, D. S. (1993). Source monitoring. *Psychological Bulletin, 114,* 3–28.

Johnson, M. M. (1963). Sex role learning in the nuclear family. *Child Development, 34,* 315–333.

Johnson, M. M. (1975). Fathers, mothers, and sex typing. *Sociological Inquiry, 45,* 15–26.

Johnson-Laird, P. N. (1983). Mental models. Cambridge, MA: Harvard University Press.

Johnson-Laird, P. N., Oakhill, J., & Bull, D. (1986). Children's syllogistic reasoning. *Quarterly Journal of Experimental Psychology, 38A,* 35–58.

Kalish, C. W. (1996). Preschoolers' understanding of germs as invisible mechanisms. *Cognitive Development, 11,* 83–106.

Kareev, Y. (1995). Through a narrow window: Working memory capacity and the detection of covariation. *Cognition, 56,* 263–269.

Karmiloff-Smith, A. (1977). More about the same: Children's understanding of postarticles. *Journal of Child Language, 4,* 377–394.

Karmiloff-Smith, A. (1986). From meta-processes to conscious access: Evidence from children's metalinguistic and repair data. *Cognition, 23,* 95–147.

Karniol, R., & Ross, M. (1976). The development of causal attributions in social perception. *Journal of Personality and Social Psychology, 34,* 455–464.

Kasher, A. (1991). On the pragmatic modules: A lecture. *Journal of Pragmatics, 16,* 381–397.

Kashima, Y., Siegal, M., Tanaka, K., & Kashima, E. S. (1992). Do people believe that attitudes are consistent with behaviour? Towards a cultural psychology of attribution processes. *British Journal of Social Psychology, 31,* 111–124.

Kaye, K. L., & Bower, T. G. R. (1994). Learning and intermodal transfer of information in newborns. *Psychological Science, 5,* 286–288.

Keil, F. C. (1979). *Semantic and conceptual development: An ontological perspective.* Cambridge, MA: Harvard University Press.

Keil, F. C. (1983). On the emergence of semantic and conceptual distinctions. *Journal of Experimental Psychology: General, 112,* 357–385.

Keil, F. C. (1989). *Concepts, kinds, and cognitive development.* Cambridge, MA: MIT Press.

Kelley, H. H. (1973). The process of causal attribution. *American Psychologist, 28,* 107–128.

Kellman, P. J., Spelke, E. S., & Short, K. R. (1986). Infant perception of object unity from translatory motion in depth and vertical translation. *Child Development, 57*, 72–86.

Kerig, P. K., Cowan, P. A., & Cowan, C. P. (1993). Marital quality and gender differences in parent–child interaction. *Developmental Psychology, 29*, 931–939.

Kerslake, D. (1986). *Fractions: Children's strategies and errors.* Windsor, UK: NFER-Nelson.

Kister, M. C., & Patterson, C. J. (1980). Children's conceptions of the causes of illness: Understanding of contagion and use of immanent justice. *Child Development, 51*, 839–846.

Kleinman, A. (1986). Some uses and misuses of the social sciences in medicine. In D. W. Fiske & R. A. Shweder (Eds.), *Metatheory in social science.* Chicago, IL: University of Chicago Press.

Klemchuk, H. P., Bond, L. A., & Howell, D. C. (1990). Coherence and correlates of Level 1 perspective taking in young children. *Merrill-Palmer Quarterly, 36*, 347–367.

Kobayashi, M. (1988). *New ideas of teaching mathematics in Japan.* Tokyo: Chuo University Press.

Kohlberg, L. (1966). A cognitive-developmental analysis of children's sex-role concepts and attitudes. In E. E. Maccoby (Ed.), *The development of sex differences.* Stanford, CA: Stanford University Press.

Kohlberg, L., & Ullian, D. (1974). Stages in the development of psychosexual concepts and attitudes. In R. C. Friedman, R. M. Richart, & R. L. Van de Wiele (Eds.), *Sex differences in behavior.* New York: Wiley.

Kuczaj, S. A. (1975). On the acquisition of a semantic system. *Journal of Verbal Learning and Verbal Behavior, 14*, 340–358.

Kuczynski, L., Kochanska, G., Radke-Yarrow, M., & Girnius-Brown, O. (1987). A developmental interpretation of young children's noncompliance. *Developmental Psychology, 23*, 799–806.

Kuzmak, S. D., & Gelman, R. (1986). Young children's understanding of random phenomena. *Child Development, 57*, 559–566.

Labov, W. (1972). *Language in the inner city: Studies in the black English vernacular.* Philadelphia, PA: University of Pennsylvania Press.

Ladd, G. W. (1983). Social networks of popular, average, and rejected children in school settings. *Merrill-Palmer Quarterly, 29*, 283–307

Ladd, G. W., Price, J. M., & Hart, C. H. (1988). Predicting preschoolers' peer status from their playground behaviors. *Child Development, 59*, 986–992.

Lampert, M. (1986). Knowing, doing, and teaching multiplication. *Cognition and Instruction, 3*, 305–342.

Langlois, J. H., & Downs, J. H. (1980). Mothers, fathers, and peers as socialization agents of sex-typed play behaviors in young children. *Child Development, 51*, 1217–1247.

Laupa, M. (1991). Children's reasoning about three authority attributes: Adult status, knowledge, and social position. *Developmental Psychology, 27*, 321–324.

Leahy, R. L. (1983). Development of the conception of economic inequality: II. Explanations, justifications, and concepts of social mobility and change. *Developmental Psychology, 19*, 111–125.

Lee, L. (1963). *Cider with Rosie.* London: Hogarth Press.

Leech, G. (1983). *Principles of pragmatics.* London: Longman.

Leippe, M. R., & Romanczyk, A. (1989). Reactions to child (versus adult) witnesses. *Law and Human Behavior, 13*, 103–132.

Lepper, M. R. (1983). Social-control processes and the internalization of social values: An attributional perspective. In E. T. Higgins, D. N. Ruble, & W. W. Hartup (Eds.), *Social cognition and social development: A sociocultural perspective.* New York: Cambridge University Press.

Lepper, M. R., & Gilovich, M. R. (1981). The multiple functions of reward: A social developmental perspective. In S. S. Brehm, S. M. Kassin, & F. X. Gibbons (Eds.), *Developmental social psychology.* New York: Oxford University Press.

Leslie, A. M. (1994). *Pretending and believing*: Issues in the theory of ToMM. *Cognition, 50*, 211–238.

Leslie, A. M., & Keeble, S. (1987). Do six-month-old infants perceive causality? *Cognition, 25*, 265–288.

Levin, I. (1982). The nature and development of time. In W. J. Friedman (Ed.), *The developmental psychology of time*. New York: Academic Press.

Levinson, S. C. (1989). A review of *Relevance*. *Journal of Linguistics, 25*, 455–472.

Levy, G. D., Taylor, M. G., & Gelman, S. A. (1995). Traditional and evaluative aspects of flexibility in gender roles, social conventions, moral rules, and physical laws. *Child Development, 66*, 515–531.

Lewis, C., & Mitchell, P. (Eds.). (1994). *Children's early understanding of mind: Origins and development*. Hove, UK: Lawrence Erlbaum Associates Ltd.

Lewis, C., & Osborne, A. (1990). Three-year-olds' problems with false belief: Conceptual deficit or linguistic artifact? *Child Development, 61*, 1514–1519.

Lewis, C. C. (1981). The effects of parental firm control: A reinterpretation. *Psychological Bulletin, 31*, 547–563.

Lewis, M., & Sullivan, M. W. (1985). Imitation in the first six months of life. *Merrill-Palmer Quarterly, 31*, 315–333.

Liben, L. (1978). Perspective-taking skills in young children: Seeing the world through rose-colored glasses. *Developmental Psychology, 14*, 87–92.

Liberman, K. (1981). Understanding Aborigines in Australian courts of law. *Human Organization, 40*, 247–255.

Light, P. H., Buckingham, N., & Robins, A. H. (1979). The conservation task in an interactional setting. *British Journal of Educational Psychology, 49*, 304–310.

Light, P. H., & Perret-Clermont, A. N. (1989). Social context effects in learning and testing. In A. Gellaty, D. Rogers, & J. A. Sloboda (Eds.), *Cognition and social worlds* (pp. 99–112). Oxford, U.K.: Oxford Science Publications.

Lindsay, D. S. (1990). Misleading suggestions can impair eyewitnesses' ability to remember event details. *Journal of Experimental Psychology: Learning Memory, and Cognition, 16*, 1077–1083.

List, J. A. (1986). Age and schematic differences in the reliability of eyewitness testimony. *Developmental Psychology, 22*, 56–57.

Lloyd, P., Camaioni, L., & Ercolari, P. (1995). Assessing referential communication skills in the primary school years: A comparative study. *British Journal of Developmental Psychology, 13*, 13–29.

Loftus, E. F., & Davies, G. H. (1984). Distortions in the memory of children. *Journal of Social Issues, 40*, 51–67.

Loftus, E. F., Feldman, J., & Dashiell, R. (1995). The reality of illusory memories. In D. L. Schacter (Ed.), *Memory distortion* (pp. 47–68). Cambridge, MA: Harvard University Press.

Loftus, E. F., & Hoffman, H. G. (1989). Misinformation and memory: The creation of new memories. *Journal of Experimental Psychology: General, 118*, 100–104.

Loftus, E. F., Miller, D. G., & Burns, H. J. (1978). Semantic integration of verbal information into visual memory. *Journal of Experimental Psychology: Learning Memory, and Cognition, 4*, 19–31.

Lourenço, O., & Machado, A. (1996). In defense of Piaget's theory: A reply to 10 common criticisms. *Psychological Review, 103*, 143–164.

Lynn, D. B. (1959). A note on sex differences in the development of masculine and feminine identification. *Psychological Review, 66*, 126–135.

Lynn, D. B. (1962). Sex role and parental identification. *Child Development, 33*, 555–564.

Maccoby, E. E., & Jacklin, C. N. (1974). *The psychology of sex differences*. Stanford, CA: Stanford University Press.

Macnamara, J. (1982). *Names for things*. Cambridge, MA: Bradford Books/MIT Press.

Macnamara, J. (1986). *A border dispute: The place of logic in psychology.* Cambridge, MA: MIT Press.

Main, M., Kaplan, N., & Cassidy, J. (1985). Security in infancy, childhood, and adulthood: A move to the level of representation. In I. Bretherton & E. Waters (Eds.), Growing points of attachment theory and research, *Monographs of the Society for Research in Child Development, 50* (Serial No. 209), 66–104.

Mandler, J. M. (1987). How to build a baby: On the development of an accessible representational system. *Cognitive Development, 3,* 113–136.

Mandler, J. M. (1992). How to build a baby: II. Conceptual primitives. *Psychological Review, 99,* 587–604.

Marcus, D. E., & Overton, W. F. (1978). The development of cognitive gender constancy and sex role preferences. *Child Development, 49,* 434–444.

Marin, B. V., Holmes, D. L., Guth, M., & Kovac, P. (1979). The potential of children as eyewitnesses. *Law and Human Behavior, 3,* 295–305.

Markman, E. M. (1981). Comprehension monitoring. In W. P. Dickson (Ed.), *Children's oral communication* (pp. 61–84). New York: Academic Press.

Martin, C. L., & Halverson, C. F. (1981). A schematic processing model of sex typing and stereotyping in children. *Child Development, 52,* 1119–1134.

Martin, C. L., & Halverson, C. F. (1983). Gender constancy: A methodological and theoretical analysis. *Sex Roles, 9,* 775–790.

Marzolf, M. P., & DeLoache, J. S. (1994). Transfer in young children's understanding of spatial representations. *Child Development, 65,* 1–15.

Massey, C., & Gelman, R. (1988). Preschoolers' ability to decide whether a pictured unfamiliar object can move itself. *Developmental Psychology, 24,* 307–317.

Masten, A. S. (1986). Humor and competence in school-aged children. *Child Development, 57,* 461–473.

Matsumoto, Y. (1988). Re-examination of the universality of face: Politeness phenomena in Japanese. *Journal of Pragmatics, 12,* 403–426.

McCloskey, M., & Zaragoza, M. (1985). Misleading post-event information and memory for events: Arguments and evidence against memory impairment hypothesis. *Journal of Experimental Psychology: General, 114,* 1–16.

McGarrigle, J., Grieve, R., & Hughes, M. (1978). Interpreting inclusion: A contribution to the study of the child's cognitive and linguistic development. *Journal of Experimental Child Psychology, 25,* 528–550.

McGee, R., Williams, S., Share, D. L., Anderson, J., & Silva, P. (1986). The relationship between specific reading retardation, general reading backwardness and behavioural problems in a large sample of Dunedin boys: A longitudinal study from five to eleven years. *Journal of Child Psychology and Psychiatry, 27,* 597–610.

McGhee, P. E. (1979). *Humor: Its origin and development.* San Francisco, CA: W. H. Freeman & Co.

McGhee, P. E., & Lloyd, S. (1982). Behavioral characteristics associated with the development of humor in young children. *Journal of Genetic Psychology, 141,* 253–259.

McGough, L. S. (1994). *Child witnesses: Fragile voices in the American legal system.* New Haven, CT: Yale University Press.

McGuire, K. D., & Weisz, J. R. (1982). Social cognition and behavior correlates preadolescent chumship. *Child Development, 53,* 1478–1484.

McHale, S. M., Bartko, W. T., Crouter, A. C., & Perry-Jenkins, M. (1990). Children's housework and psychosocial functioning: The mediating effects of parents' sex-role behaviors and attitudes. *Child Development, 61,* 1413–1426.

McKenzie, B., & Over, R. (1983). Young infants fail to imitate facial and manual gestures. *Infant Behavior and Development, 2,* 85–93.

Meltzoff, A. N. (1995). Understanding the intentions of others: Re-enactment of intended acts by 18-month-old children. *Developmental Psychology, 31*, 838–850.

Meltzoff, A. N., & Borton, R. W. (1979). Intermodal matching by human neonates. *Nature, 282*, 403–404.

Meltzoff, A. N., & Moore, M. K. (1977). Imitation of facial and manual gestures by human neonates. *Science, 218*, 179–181.

Mendelson, M. J., & Haith, M. M. (1976). The relation between audition and vision in the newborn. *Monographs of the Society for Research in Child Development, 41* (Serial No. 167).

Miller, K. (1984). Child as the measurer of all things: Measurement procedures and the development of quantitative concepts. In C. Sophian (Ed.), *Origins of cognitive skills*. Hillsdale, NJ: Lawrence Erlbaum Associates Inc.

Miller, K. F., Smith, C. M., Zhu, J., & Zhang, H. (1995). Preschool origins of cross-national differences in mathematical competence: The role of number-naming systems. *Psychological Science, 6*, 56–60.

Miller, S. A. (1986). Parents' beliefs about their children's cognitive abilities. *Developmental Psychology, 22*, 276–284.

Miller, S. A. (1988). Parents' beliefs about children's cognitive development. *Child Development, 59*, 259–285.

Miller, S. A., Manhal, M., & Mee, L. L. (1991). Parents beliefs, parental accuracy, and children's cognitive performance: A search for causal relations. *Developmental Psychology, 27*, 267–276.

Milton, K. (1988). Foraging behaviour and the evolution of primate intelligence. In R. W. Byrne & A. Whiten (Eds.), *Machiavellian intelligence*. Oxford: Clarendon Press.

Mischel, W., & Rodriguez, M. L. (1993). Psychological distance in self-imposed delay of gratification. In R. R. Cocking & K. A. Renninger (Eds.), *The development and meaning of psychological distance* (pp. 109–121). Hillsdale, NJ: Lawrence Erlbaum Associates Inc.

Mischel, W., Shoda, Y., & Rodriguez, M. L. (1989). Delay of gratification in children. *Science, 244*, 933–938.

Mitchell, P., & Lacohée, H. (1991). Children's early understanding of false belief. *Cognition, 39*, 107–127.

Mitchell, P., Robinson, E. J., Isaacs, J. E., & Nye, R. M. (1996). Contamination in reasoning about false belief: An instance of realistic bias in adults but not children. *Cognition, 59*, 1–21.

Morton, J. (1990). The development of event memory. *The Psychologist, 1*, 3–10.

Morton, J., Hammersley, R. H., & Bekerian, D. A. (1985). Headed records: A model for memory and its failures. *Cognition, 20*, 1–23.

Murdock, G. P. (1980). *Theories of illness: A world survey*. Pittsburgh, PA: University of Pittsburgh Press.

Neilson, I., Dockrell, J., & McKechnie, J. (1983). Does repetition of the question influence children's performance in conservation tasks? *British Journal of Developmental Psychology, 1*, 163–174.

Nelson, K. (1993a). Events, narratives, memory: What develops? *Minnesota Symposia on Child Psychology, 26*, 1–24.

Nelson, K. (1993b). The psychological and social origins of autobiographical memory. *Psychological Science, 4*, 7–14.

Nelson, K., Fivush, R., Hudson, J., & Lucariello, J. (1983). Scripts and the development of memory. In M. T. H. Chi (Ed.), *Trends in memory development research: Contributions to human development* (Vol. 9; pp. 12–20). Basel, Switzerland: Karger.

Nemeroff, C., & Rozin, P. (1994). The contagion concept in adult thinking in the United States: Transmission of germs and of interpersonal influence. *Ethos, 22*, 158–186.

Newcomb, A. F. & Bukowski, W. M. (1984). A longitudinal study of the utility of social preference and social impact sociometric classification schemes. *Child Development, 55*, 1434–1447.

Newcombe, N., & Huttenlocher, J. (1992). Children's early ability to solve perspective-taking problems. *Developmental Psychology, 28*, 635–643.

Newcombe, P. A., & Siegal, M. (1996). Where to look first for suggestibility in young children. *Cognition, 59*, 337–356.

Nisan, M. (1987). Moral norms and social conventions: A cross-cultural comparison. *Developmental Psychology, 23*, 719–725.

Nisan, M. (1988). A story of a pot, or a cross-cultural comparison of basic moral evaluations: A response to the critique by Turiel, Nucci, and Smetana (1988). *Developmental Psychology, 24*, 144–146.

Nucci, L., & Nucci, M. S. (1982). Children's social interactions in the context of moral and conventional transgressions. *Child Development, 53*, 403–412.

Nucci, L., & Turiel, E. (1978). Social interactions and the development of social concepts in preschool children. *Child Development, 49*, 400–407.

Nugent, R. (1994). *Humour and peer status in children.* Unpublished PhD thesis, University of Queensland.

Occhipinti, S., & Siegal, M. (1994). Reasoning about food and contamination. *Journal of Personality and Social Psychology, 66*, 243–253.

Ochs, E. (1983). Cultural dimensions of language acquisition. In E. Ochs & B. B. Schieffelin (Eds.), *Acquiring conversational competence* (pp. 185–191). London: Routledge & Kegan Paul.

Olson, D. R. (1980). Some social aspects of meaning in oral and written communication. In D. R. Olson (Ed.), *The social foundations of language and thought: Essays in honour of Jerome S. Bruner* (pp. 90–108). New York: Norton.

Passingham, R. E. (1982). *The human primate.* Oxford, UK: W. H. Freeman.

Peery, J. C. (1979). Popular, amiable, isolated, rejected: A reconceptualization of sociometric status in preschool children. *Child Development, 50*, 1231–1234.

Perner, J. (1991). *Understanding the representational mind.* Cambridge, MA: MIT Press.

Perner, J., Leekam, S. R., & Wimmer, H. (1986). *The insincerity of conservation questions: Children's growing insensitivity to experimenter's intentions.* Unpublished manuscript, University of Sussex.

Perner, J., Leekam, S. R., & Wimmer, H. (1987). Three year olds' difficulty with false belief: The case for a conceptual deficit. *British Journal of Developmental Psychology, 5*, 125–137.

Perry, D. G., White, A. J., & Perry, L. C. (1984). Does early sex typing result from children's attempts to match their behavior to sex role stereotypes? *Child Development, 55*, 2114–2121.

Peters, D. P. (1991). The influence of stress and arousal on the child witness. In J. L. Doris (Ed.), *The suggestibility of children's recollections* (pp. 60–76). Washington, DC: American Psychological Association.

Peterson, C. C. (1995). The role of perceived intention to deceive in children's and adults' concepts of lying. *British Journal of Developmental Psychology, 13*, 237–260.

Peterson, C. C., Peterson, J., & Seeto, D. (1983). Developmental changes in ideas about lying. *Child Development, 54*, 1529–1535.

Petitto, L. A. (1986). "Language" in the prelinguistic child. In F. Kessel (Ed.), *The development of language and language researchers.* Hillsdale, NJ: Lawrence Erlbaum Associates Inc.

Piaget, J. (1928). *Judgment and reasoning in the child.* London: Routledge & Kegan Paul.

Piaget, J. (1929). *The child's conception of the world.* London: Routledge & Kegan Paul.

Piaget, J. (1930). *The child's conception of physical causality.* London: Routledge & Kegan Paul.

Piaget, J. (1932). *The moral judgement of the child.* London: Routledge & Kegan Paul.

Piaget, J. (1952). *The child's conception of number.* London: Routledge & Kegan Paul.

Piaget, J. (1954). *The construction of reality in the child.* New York: Basic Books.

Piaget, J. (1970). Piaget's theory. In P. H. Mussen (Ed.), *Carmichael's manual of child psychology* (Vol. 1; pp. 703–731). New York: Wiley.

Piaget, J. (1972, October 19). Piaget sees science dooming psychoanalysis. *New York Times.*

Piaget. J., & Inhelder. B. (1956). *The child's conception of space.* New York: Norton.

Piaget, J., Inhelder, B., & Szeminska, A. (1964). *The child's conception of geometry.* New York: Harper Torchbook.

Politzer, G., & Nguyen-Xuan, A. (1992). Reasoning about conditional promises and warnings: Darwinian algorithms, mental models, relevance judgments or pragmatic schemes? *Quarterly Journal of Experimental Psychology, 44A,* 401–421.

Poole, D. A., & White, L. T. (1993). Two years later: Effects of question repetition and retention interval on the eyewitness testimony of children and adults. *Developmental Psychology, 29,* 844–853.

Pratt, C., & Bryant, P. (1990). Young children understand that looking leads to knowing (so long as they are looking into a single barrel). *Child Development, 61,* 946–961.

Presson, C. C., & Ihrig, L.H. (1982). Using mother as a spatial landmark: Evidence against egocentric coding in infancy. *Developmental Psychology, 18,* 699–703.

Pylyshyn, Z. W. (1984). *Computation and cognition.* Cambridge, MA: MIT Press.

Reissland, N. (1988). Neonatal imitation in the first hour of life: Observations in rural Nepal. *Developmental Psychology, 24,* 464–469.

Resnick, L. B., & Ford, W. W. (1981). *The psychology of mathematics for instruction.* Hillsdale, NJ: Lawrence Erlbaum Associates Inc.

Revusky, S. H., & Garcia, J. (1970). Learned associations over long delays. In G. H. Bower (Ed.), *The psychology of learning and motivation* (Vol. 4; pp. 1–84). New York: Academic Press.

Ricks, M. H. (1985). The social transmission of parental behavior: Attachment across generations. In I. Bretherton & E. Waters (Eds.), Growing points of attachment theory and research. *Monographs of the Society for Research in Child Development, 50* (Serial No. 209), 211–227.

Robinson, E. J., & Whittaker, S. J. (1986). Learning about verbal referential communication in the early school years. In K. Durkin (Ed.), *Language development in the preschool years* (pp. 155–171). London: Croom Helm.

Rogoff, B. (1990). *Apprenticeship in thinking: Cognitive development in context.* New York: Oxford University Press.

Rogoff, B., & Mistry, J. (1990). The social and functional context of children's remembering. In R. Fivush & J. A. Hudson (Eds.), *Knowing and remembering in young children* (pp. 197–222). New York: Cambridge University Press.

Rogoff, B., & Wertsch, J. V. (Eds.). (1984). *Children's learning in the "zone of proximal development"* (New Directions for Child Development, No. 23). San Francisco, CA: Jossey-Bass.

Rommetveit, R. (1979). On the relationship between children's mastery of Piagetian cognitive operations and their semantic competence. In R. Rommetveit & R. M. Blakar (Eds.), *Studies of language, thought, and verbal communication* (pp. 457–466). London: Academic Press.

Rose, S. A., & Blank, M. (1974). The potency of context in children's cognition: An illustration through conservation. *Child Development, 45,* 499–502.

Rosen, A. B., & Rozin, P. (1993). Now you see it . . . now you don't: The preschool child's conception of invisible particles in the context of dissolving. *Developmental Psychology, 29,* 300–311.

Rosenberg, C. E. (1962). *The cholera years: The United States in 1832 and 1866.* Chicago, IL: University of Chicago Press.

Rothbaum, F., Weisz, J. R., & Snyder, S. S. (1982). Changing the world and changing the self: A two-process model of perceived control. *Journal of Personality and Social Psychology, 42,* 5–37.

Rovee-Collier, C. (1993). The capacity for long-term memory in infants. *Current Directions in Psychological Science, 2,* 130–135.

Rovee-Collier, C., Sullivan, M. W., Enright, M., Lucas, D., & Fagen, J. W. (1980). Reactivation of infant memory. *Science, 208,* 1159–1161.

Rozin, P. (1976a). One-trial acquired likes and dislikes in humans: Disgust as a US, food predominance, and negative learning predominance. *Learning and Motivation, 17,* 180–189.

Rozin, P. (1976b). The evolution of intelligence and access to the cognitive unconscious. In J. M. Sprague & A. N. Epstein (Eds.), *Progress in psychobiology and physiological psychology* (Vol. 6; pp. 245–280). New York: Academic Press.

Rozin, P. (1990). Development in the food domain. *Developmental Psychology, 26,* 555–562.

Rozin, P., & Fallon, A. E. (1987). A perspective on disgust. *Psychological Review, 94,* 23–41.

Rozin, P., Fallon, A., & Augustoni-Ziskind, M. (1985). The child's conception of food: The development of contamination sensitivity to "disgusting" substances. *Developmental Psychology, 21,* 1075–1079.

Rozin, P., & Schull, J. (1988). The adaptive-evolutionary point of view in experimental psychology. In R. Atkinson, R. J. Herrnstein, G. Lindzey, & R. D. Luce (Eds.), *Handbook of experimental psychology* (pp. 503–546). New York: Wiley.

Rubin, K. H., & Mills, R. S. L. (1988). The many faces of social isolation in childhood. *Journal of Consulting and Clinical Psychology, 56,* 916–924.

Ruble, D. N., Balaban, T., & Cooper, J. (1981). Gender constancy and the effects of sex-typed televised toy commercials. *Child Development, 52,* 667–673.

Rudy, L., & Goodman, G. S. (1991). Effects of participation on children's reports: Implications for children's testimony. *Developmental Psychology, 27,* 527–538.

Rumain, B., Connell, J., & Braine, M. D. S. (1983). Conversational processes are responsible for reasoning fallacies in children as well as adults: *If* is not the biconditional. *Developmental Psychology, 19,* 471–481.

Samuel, J., & Bryant, P. (1984). Asking only one question in the conservation experiment. *Journal of Child Psychology and Psychiatry, 25,* 315–318.

Sanderson, J. A. (1996). *Preschoolers' understanding of friendship.* Unpublished doctoral thesis, University of Queensland.

Sanderson, J. A., & Siegal, M. (1988). Conceptions of moral and social rules in rejected and nonrejected preschoolers. *Journal of Clinical Child Psychology, 17,* 66–72.

Schegloff, E. A. (1987). Some sources of misunderstanding in talk-in-interaction. *Linguistics, 25,* 201–218.

Schieffelin, B. B. (1983). Talking like birds: Sound play in a cultural perspective. In E. Ochs & B. B. Schieffelin (Eds.), *Acquiring conversational competence* (pp. 177–184). London: Routledge & Kegan Paul.

Schieffelin, B. B. (1986). Teasing and shaming in Kaluli children's interactions. In B. B. Schieffelin & E. Ochs (Eds.), *Language socialization across cultures* (pp. 165–181). New York: Cambridge University Press.

Schieffelin, B. B. (1990). *The give and take of everyday life: Language socialization of Kaluli children.* New York: Cambridge University Press.

Schiff, W. (1983). Conservation of length redux: A perceptual-linguistic phenomenon. *Child Development, 54,* 1497–1506.

Scholnick, E. K. & Wing, C. S. (1995). Logic in conversation: Comparative studies of deduction in children and adults. *Cognitive Development, 10,* 319–345.

Scribner, S. (1977). Modes of thinking and ways of speaking: Culture and logic reconsidered. In *Thinking: Readings in cognitive science* (pp. 483–500). Cambridge, UK: Cambridge University Press.

Selman, R. L. (1980). *The growth of interpersonal understanding: Developmental and clinical analyses.* New York: Academic Press.

Shatz, M. (1994). Theory of mind and the development of social-linguistic intelligence in early childhood. In C. Lewis & P. Mitchell (Eds.), *Children's early understanding of mind: Origins and development* (pp. 311–329). Hove, UK: Lawrence Erlbaum Associates Ltd.

Shatz, M., & Gelman, R. (1973). The development of communication skills: Modifications in the speech of young children as a function of listener. *Monographs of the Society for Research in Child Development, 38*(5, Serial No. 152).

Shultz, T. R. (1982a). Causal reasoning in the social and nonsocial realms. *Canadian Journal of Behavioural Science, 14,* 307–322.

Shultz, T. R. (1982b). Rules of causal attribution. *Monographs of the Society for Research in Child Development* (Serial No. 194).

Shultz, T. R., Fisher, G. W., Pratt, C. C., & Ruff, S. (1986). Selection of causal rules. *Child Development, 57,* 143–152.

Shweder, R. A. (1977). Likeness and likelihood in everyday thought: Magical thinking in judgments about personality. *Current Anthropology, 18,* 637–658.

Shweder, R. A. (1986). Divergent rationalities. In D. W. Fiske & R. A. Shweder (Eds.), *Metatheory in social science.* Chicago, IL: University of Chicago Press.

Shweder, R. A., Mahapatra, M., & Miller, J. (1987). Culture and moral development. In J. Kagan & S. Lamb (Eds.), *The emergence of morality in young children* (pp. 1–83). Chicago, IL: University of Chicago Press.

Siegal, M. (1982). *Fairness in children.* London: Academic Press.

Siegal, M. (1985). *Children, parenthood, and social welfare.* Oxford: Oxford University Press.

Siegal, M. (1987). Are sons and daughters treated more differently by fathers than by mothers? *Developmental Review, 7,* 183–206.

Siegal, M. (1988a). Children's knowledge of contagion and contamination as causes of illness. *Child Development, 59,* 1353–1359.

Siegal, M. (1988b). Culture, social knowledge, and the determination of criminal responsibility in children: Issues in justice for Aboriginal youth. *Australian Psychologist, 23,* 171–182.

Siegal, M. (1991). A clash of conversational worlds: Interpreting cognitive development through communication. In L. B. Resnick, J. M. Levine, & S. Behrens (Eds.), *Perspectives on socially shared cognition* (pp. 23–40). Washington, DC: American Psychological Association.

Siegal, M. (1993). Making instruction relevant. *Dokkyo International Review, 6,* 173–201.

Siegal, M., & Barclay. M. S. (1985). Children's evaluations of fathers' socialization behaviors. *Developmental Psychology, 21,* 1090–1096.

Siegal, M., & Beattie, K. (1991). Where to look first for children's knowledge of false beliefs. *Cognition, 38,* 1–12.

Siegal, M., Carrington, J., & Radel, M. (1996). Theory of mind and pragmatic understanding following right hemisphere brain damage. *Brain and Language, 53,* 40–50.

Siegal, M., & Cowen, J. (1984). Appraisals of intervention: The mother's versus the culprit's behavior as determinants of children's evaluations of discipline techniques. *Child Development, 55,* 1760–1766.

Siegal, M., & Peterson, C. C. (1994). Children's theory of mind and the conversational territory of cognitive development. In C. Lewis & P. Mitchell (Eds.), *Children's early understanding of mind: Origins and development* (pp. 427–455). Hove, UK: Lawrence Erlbaum Associates Ltd.

Siegal, M., & Peterson, C. C. (1996). Breaking the mold: A fresh look at children's understanding of questions about lies and mistakes. *Developmental Psychology, 32,* 322–334.

Siegal, M., & Peterson, C. C. (in preparation). *Can preschoolers truly exonerate perpetrators for their mistakes if warranted?*

Siegal, M., & Robinson, J. (1987). Order effects in children's gender constancy responses. *Developmental Psychology, 23,* 283–286.

Siegal, M., & Share, D.L. (1990). Contamination sensitivity in young children. *Developmental Psychology, 26,* 455–458.

Siegal, M., Share, D. L., & Robinson, J. (1989). Mechanisms of development: Is the real candidate the distinction between appearance and reality? In M. A. Luczcz & T. Nettelbeck (Eds.), *Psychological development: Perspectives across the life-span* (pp. 161–171). Amsterdam: Elsevier Science.

Siegal, M., & Storey, R. M. (1985). Daycare and children's conceptions of moral and social rules. *Child Development, 56,* 1001–1008.

Siegal, M., Waters, L. J., & Dinwiddy, L. S. (1988). Misleading children: Causal attributions for inconsistency under repeated questioning. *Journal of Experimental Child Psychology*, *45*, 438–456.

Siegel, L. S. (1978). The relationship of language and thought in the preoperational child: A reconsideration of nonverbal alternatives to Piagetian tasks. In L. S. Siegel & C. J. Brainerd (Eds.), *Alternatives to Piaget: Critical essays on the theory*. New York: Academic Press.

Siegler, R. S. (1981). Developmental sequences within and between concepts. *Monographs of the Society for Research in Child Development*, *46* (Serial No. 189).

Siegler, R. S. (1986). *Children's thinking*. Englewood Cliffs, NJ: Prentice-Hall.

Siegler, R. S. (1995). How does change occur: A microgenetic study of number conservation. *Cognitive Psychology*, *28*, 225–273.

Sigel, I. E. (1974). When do we know what a child knows. *Human Development*, *17*, 201–217.

Sigel, I. E. (1981). Social experience in the development of representational thought: Distancing theory. In I. E. Sigel, D. M. Brodzinsky, & R. M. Golinkoff (Eds.), *New directions in Piagetian theory and practice*. Hillsdale, NJ: Lawrence Erlbaum Associates Inc.

Sigel, I. E. (1993). The centrality of a distancing model for the development of representational competence. In R. R. Cocking & K. A. Renninger (Eds.), *The development and meaning of psychological distance* (pp. 141–158). Hillsdale, NJ: Lawrence Erlbaum Associates Inc.

Simons, D. J., & Keil, F. C. (1995). An abstract to concrete shift in the development of biological thought: The *insides* story. *Cognition*, *46*, 129–163.

Slaby, R. G., & Frey, K. S. (1975). Development of gender constancy and selective attention to same-sex models. *Child Development*, *46*, 849–856.

Slade, A. (1987). Quality of attachment and early symbolic play. *Developmental Psychology*, *23*, 78–85.

Smetana, J. G. (1981). Preschool children's conceptions of moral and social rules. *Child Development*, *52*, 1333–1336.

Smetana, J. G. (1985). Preschool children's conceptions of transgressions: The effects of varying moral and conventional domain-related attributes. *Developmental Psychology*, *21*, 18–29.

Smetana, J. G., & Letourneau, K. J. (1984). Development of gender constancy and children's sex-typed free play behavior. *Developmental Psychology*. *20*, 691–696.

Smith, C. L. (1979). Children's understanding of natural language hierarchies. *Journal of Experimental Child Psychology*, *27*, 437–458.

Smith, L. (1985). Making educational sense of Piaget's theory. *Oxford Review of Education*, *11*, 181–191.

Snow, C. E., Pan, B. A., Imbens-Bailey, A., & Herman, J. (1996). Learning to say what one means: A longitudinal study of children's speech act use. *Social Development*, *5*, 58–84.

Sobol, M. P., & Earn, B. M. (1985). Assessment of children's attributions from social experiences: Implications for social skills training. In B. H. Schneider, K. H. Rubin, & J. E. Ledingham (Eds.), *Children's peer relations: Issues in assessment and intervention*. New York: Springer-Verlag.

Sobol, M. P., Earn, B. M., Bennett, D., & Humphries, T. (1983). A categorical analysis of social attributions of learning-disabled children. *Journal of Abnormal Child Psychology*, *11*, 217–228.

Solomon, G. E. A., Johnson, S. C., Zaitchik, D., & Carey, S. (1996). Like father, like son: Young children's understanding of how and why offspring resemble their parents. *Child Development*, *67*, 151–171.

Sophian, C. (1995). Representation and reasoning in early numerical development: Counting, conservation, and comparisons between sets. *Child Development*, *66*, 547–558.

Sophian, C., & Huber, A. (1984). Early development in children's causal judgements. *Child Development*, *55*, 512–526.

Sophian, C., Wood, A. M., & Vong, K. I. (1995). Making numbers count: The early development of numerical inferences. *Developmental Psychology*, *31*, 263–273.

Spelke, E. (1994). Initial knowledge: Six suggestions. *Cognition, 50,* 431–445.

Spelke, E. S. (1981). The infant's acquisition of bimodally specified events. *Journal of Experimental Child Psychology, 31,* 279–299.

Spencer, J. R., & Flin, R. (1990). *The evidence of children: The law and the psychology.* London: Blackstone.

Sperber, D., & Wilson, D. (1986). *Relevance.* Oxford, UK: Blackwell.

Springer, K. (1995). Acquiring a naive theory of kinship through inference. *Child Development, 66,* 547–558.

Springer, K., & Belk, A. (1994). The role of physical contact and association in early contamination sensitivity. *Developmental Psychology, 30,* 864–868.

Springer, K., Ngyuen, T., & Samaniego, R. (1996). Early understanding of age- and environment-related noxiousness in biological kinds: Evidence for a naive theory. *Cognitive Development, 11,* 65–82.

Stanovich, K. E. (1986). Matthew effects in reading: Some consequences of individual differences in the acquisition of literacy. *Reading Research Quarterly, 21,* 360–406.

Starkey, P. (1992). The early development of numerical reasoning. *Cognition, 43,* 93–126.

Starkey, P., & Cooper, R. G. (1980). Perception of numbers by human infants. *Science, 210,* 1033–1035.

Starkey, P., Spelke, E. S., & Gelman, R, (1983). Detection of intermodal number correspondences by human infants. *Science, 222,* 179–181.

Stevenson, H. W., Chen, C., & Lee, S. Y. (1993). Mathematics achievement of Chinese, Japanese, and American children: Ten years later. *Science, 259,* 53–58.

Stevenson, H. W., Lee, S. Y., & Stigler, J. W. (1986). Mathematics achievement of Chinese, Japanese, and American children. *Science, 231,* 693–699.

Strichartz, A. F., & Burton, R. V. (1990). Lies and truth: A study of the development of the concept. *Child Development, 61,* 211–220.

Sugarman, S. (1987). *Piaget's construction of the child's reality.* New York: Cambridge University Press.

Sullivan, K., & Winner, E. (1991). When 3-year-olds understand ignorance, false belief and representational change. *British Journal of Developmental Psychology, 9,* 159–171.

Sullivan, K., & Winner, E. (1993). Three-year-olds' understanding of mental states: The influence of trickery. *Journal of Experimental Child Psychology, 56,* 135–148.

Surian, L., & Leslie, A. (1995). *Competence and performance in false belief understanding.* Paper presented at the Biennial Meeting of the Society for Research in Child Development, Indianapolis.

Suzuki, H. (1994). The centrality of analogy in knowledge acquisition in instructional contexts. *Human Development, 37,* 207–219.

Tauber, M. A. (1979). Sex differences in parent-child interaction styles during a free-play situation. *Child Development, 50,* 981–988.

Tisak, M. S. (1986). Children's conceptions of parental authority. *Child Development. 57,* 166–176.

Tisak, M. S., & Tisak, J. (1990). Children's conceptions of parental authority, friendship, and sibling relations. *Merrill-Palmer Quarterly, 36,* 347–367.

Toglia, M. P., Hembrooke, H., Ceci, S. J., & Ross, D. F. (1992). *Children's resistance to misleading postevent information: When does it occur?* Paper presented at the Annual Convention of the American Psychological Society, San Diego, CA.

Tomasello, M., Kruger, A. C., & Ratner, H. H. (1993). Cultural learning. *Behavioral and Brain Sciences, 16,* 495–552.

Turiel, E. (1983). *The development of social knowledge: Morality and convention.* New York: Cambridge University Press.

Turiel, E. (1989). Domain-specific social judgment and domain ambiguities. *Merrill-Palmer Quarterly, 35,* 89–114.

Turiel, E., Nucci, L. P., & Smetana, J. G. (1988). A cross-cultural comparison about what? A critique of Nisan's (1987) study of morality and convention. *Developmental Psychology, 24*, 140–143.

Turner, P. J., & Gervai, J. (1995). A multidimensional study of gender typing in preschool children and their parents: Personality, attitudes, preferences, behavior and cultural differences. *Developmental Psychology, 31*, 759–772.

Ullian, D. (1984). "Why are girls good": A constructivist view. *Sex Roles, 11*, 241–256.

Valsiner, J., & van der Veer, R. (1993). The encoding of distance: The concept of the zone of proximal development and its implications. In R. R. Cocking & K. A. Renninger (Eds.), *The development and meaning of psychological distance* (pp. 35–62). Hillsdale, NJ: Lawrence Erlbaum Associates Inc.

Vygotsky, L. S. (1962). *Thought and language.* Cambridge, MA: MIT Press.

Vygotsky, L. S. (1978). *Mind in society.* Cambridge, MA: Harvard University Press.

Wald, M., Carlsmith, M., Leiderman, P. H., & Smith, C. (1983). Intervention to protect abused and neglected children. *Minnesota Symposia on Child Psychology, 16*, 207–231.

Walker, S. J. (1992). Supernatural beliefs, natural kinds, and conceptual structure. *Memory and Cognition, 20*, 655–662.

Warren, R. M., & Warren. R. P. (1968). *Helmholtz on perception.* New York: Wiley.

Waters, H. S., & Tinsley, V. S. (1985). Evaluating the discriminant and convergent validity of developmental constructs: Another look at egocentrism. *Psychological Bulletin, 97*, 483–496.

Weinraub, M., Clemens, L. P., Sockloft, A., Ethridge, T., Gracely, E., & Myers, B. (1984). The development of sex role stereotypes in the third year: Relationships to gender labelling, gender identity, sex-types toy preference, and family characteristics. *Child Development, 55*, 1493–1503.

Wellman, H. M., & Bartsch, K. (1988). Young children's reasoning about beliefs. *Cognition, 30*, 239–277.

Wellman, H. M., & Bartsch, K. (1994). Before belief: Children's early psychological theory. In C. Lewis & P. Mitchell (Eds.), *Children's early understanding of mind: Origins and development* (pp. 427–455). Hove, UK: Lawrence Erlbaum Associates Ltd.

Wellman, H. M., & Estes, D. (1986). Early understanding of mental entities: A reexamination of childhood realism. *Child Development, 57*, 910–923.

Wellman, H. M., & Woolley, J. D. (1990). From simple desires to ordinary beliefs: The early development of everyday beliefs. *Cognition, 35*, 245–275.

Wentzel, K. R., & Asher, S. R. (1995). The academic lives of neglected, rejected, popular, and controversial children. *Child Development, 66*, 754–763.

Werker, J., & Desjardins, R. N. (1995). Listening to speech in the 1st year of life: Experiential influences on phoneme perception. *Current Directions in Psychological Science, 4*, 76–81.

Wertsch, J. V. (1985). *Vygotsky and the social formation of mind.* Cambridge, MA: Harvard University Press.

Weston, D., & Turiel, E. (1980). Act-rule relations: Children's concepts of social rules. *Developmental Psychology, 116*, 417–424.

Wilkening, F. (1981). Integrating velocity, time, and distance information: A developmental study. *Cognitive Psychology, 13*, 231–247.

Wilkening, F. (1982). Children's knowledge about time, distance, and velocity interrelations. In W. J. Friedman (Ed.), *The developmental psychology of time.* New York: Academic Press.

Wilkening, F., Levin, I., & Druyan. S. (1987). Children's counting strategies for time quantification and integration. *Developmental Psychology, 23*, 823–831.

Willis, G. B., & Fuson, K. C. (1988). Teaching children to use schematic drawings to solve addition and subtraction word problems. *Journal of Educational Psychology, 80*, 192–201.

Wilson, D. (1994). Relevance and understanding. In G. Brown, K. Malmkjaer, A. Pollitt, & J. Williams (Eds.), *Language and understanding* (pp. 37–58). Oxford, UK: Oxford University Press.

Wimmer, H., Gruber, S., & Perner, J. (1985). Young children's conception of lying: Moral intuition and the denotation and connotation of "to lie". *Developmental Psychology, 21,* 993–995.

Wimmer, H., & Hartl, M. (1991). Against the Cartesian view on mind: Young children's difficulty with own false beliefs. *British Journal of Developmental Psychology, 9,* 125–138.

Winer, G., Hemphill, J., & Craig, R. K. (1988). The effect of misleading questions in promoting nonconservation responses in children and adults. *Developmental Psychology, 24,* 197–202.

Wooley, J. D., & Wellman, H. M. (1990). Young children's understanding of realities, nonrealities, and appearances. *Child Development, 61,* 946–961.

Wynn, K. (1992). Addition and subtraction by human infants. *Nature, 358,* 749–750.

Yarmey, A. D. (1984). Age as a factor in eyewitness testimony. In G. L. Wells & E. F. Loftus (Eds.), *Eyewitness testimony: A psychological perspective* (pp. 142–154). New York: Cambridge University Press.

Youngblade, L. M., & Belsky, J. (1992). Parent–child antecedents of 5-year-olds' close friendships: A longitudinal study. *Developmental Psychology, 28,* 700–713.

Yuill, N. (1984). Young children's coordination of motive and outcome in judgments of satisfaction and morality. *British Journal of Developmental Psychology, 2,* 73–81.

Zaragoza, M. S. (1991). Preschool children's suggestibility to memory impairment. In J. Doris (Ed.), *The suggestibility of children's recollections: Implications for eyewitness testimony* (pp. 27–39). Washington, DC: American Psychological Association.

Zelazo, P. D., & Reznick, J. S. (1991). Age-related asynchrony of knowledge and action. *Child Development, 62,* 719–735.

Zigler, E. F. (1987). Formal schooling for four-year-olds? No. *American Psychologist, 42,* 254–260.

Author Index

187

Subject Index

OCT I 7 1997

P
118
.S457
1997P

DATE DUE

DEC 08 1997			
REC'D DEC 10 1997			

Demco, Inc. 38-293